GENDER AND HEALTH

Chloe Bird and Patricia Rieker argue that to improve men's and women's health, individuals, researchers, and policymakers must understand the social and biological sources of the perplexing gender differences in illness and longevity. Although individuals are increasingly aware of what they should do to improve health, competing demands for time, money, and attention discourage or prevent healthy behavior. Drawing on research and cross-national examples of family, work, community, and government policies, the authors develop a model of constrained choice that addresses how decisions and actions at each of these levels shape men's and women's health-related opportunities. Understanding the cumulative impact of their choices can inform individuals at each of these levels how to better integrate health implications into their everyday decisions and actions. Their platform for prevention calls for a radical reorientation of health science and policy to help individuals pursue health and to lower the barriers that may discourage that pursuit.

Chloe E. Bird is a Senior Sociologist with the RAND Corporation in Santa Monica, California, and Professor of Sociology at the Frederick S. Pardee RAND Graduate School. Her research focuses on assessing the determinants of gender and racial/ethnic differences in the physical and mental health of individuals and in the health care they receive. She is particularly interested in determining how social and physical characteristics of neighborhoods contribute to health disparities.

Dr. Bird is also Associate Editor of *Women's Health Issues* and Chair of the Medical Sociology Section of the American Sociological Association. She has published extensively in a wide range of journals and has co-authored numerous book chapters and reports. Among the honors bestowed on her work is the 1995 Elliot Freidson Award from the Medical Sociology Section of the American Sociological Association.

Patricia P. Rieker is Adjunct Professor at Boston University, Associate Professor of Psychiatry at Harvard Medical School, and Emeritus Professor at Simmons College. She was also formerly the Director of Psychosocial Research at the Dana Farber Cancer Institute, where her research focused on health care outcomes for men with genitourinary cancers.

Dr. Rieker is also an evaluation research consultant to the Centers for Disease Control and Prevention and has worked with the Research Triangle Institute, the National Office of the American Cancer Society and National Women's Resource Center, and the Substance Abuse and Mental Health Services Administration. Among her diverse publications, she is the co-editor of three books: *The Gender Gap in Psychotherapy, Social Realities and Psychological Processes*, and *Mental Health: Racism and Sexism* (which was named an Outstanding Book by the Myers Center for the Study of Human Rights in North America).

Her current research interests include cross-national comparisons of gender and health, the determinants of health care outcomes, and evaluation research capacity building.

D0043607

Gender and Health

The Effects of Constrained Choices and Social Policies

CHLOE E. BIRD

RAND Corporation and Pardee RAND Graduate School

PATRICIA P. RIEKER

Boston University and Harvard Medical School

CAMBRIDGE UNIVERSITY PRESS

Cambridge, New York, Melbourne, Madrid, Cape Town, Singapore,
São Paulo, Delhi, Dubai, Tokyo, Mexico City

Cambridge University Press
32 Avenue of the Americas, New York, NY 10013-2473, USA

www.cambridge.org
Information on this title: www.cambridge.org/9780521682800

First published 2008

A catalog record for this publication is available from the British Library

Library of Congress Cataloging in Publication data
Bird, Chloe E.
Gender and health : the effects of constrained choices and social policies /
Chloe E. Bird, Patricia P. Rieker.
p. ; cm.
Includes bibliographical references and index.
ISBN 978-0-521-86415-2 (hardback) – ISBN 978-0-521-68280-0 (pbk.)
1. Sex factors in disease. 2. Health – Sex differences. 3. Medical policy.
I. Rieker, Patricia Perri. II. Title.
[DNLM: 1. Sex Factors. 2. Gender Identity. 3. Health Behavior.
4. Public Policy. QZ 53 B618g 2008]
RB212.B57 2008
362.108–dc22 2007029943

ISBN 978-0-521-86415-2 Hardback
ISBN 978-0-521-68280-0 Paperback

I dedicate this book to my friends and family who provided the inspiration for this book and kindly tolerated the years of neglect.

C.B.

To the dear friends and relatives who brought a special grace to listening interspersed with witty advice and other welcome diversions.

P.R.

Contents

Preface

The idea for *Gender and Health* began with our participation in the Society and Health Working Group of the Health Institute at New England Medical Center and the Department of Health and Social Behavior at the Harvard School of Public Health. Our colleagues in this group encouraged us to explore and explain the complex dynamics between gender and health. The task of the cross-disciplinary faculty seminar (organized by Sol Levine and Al Tarlov) was to integrate the relevant concepts and findings from various disciplines to enhance and deepen the understanding of the social determinants of population health (Amick, Levine, Tarlov, & Walsh, 1995). We chose to write this book to encourage biomedical researchers and social scientists to think and work together in new ways to explore the connections between the physiological mechanisms and social processes that make the health of men and women so different.

The gender and health paradox is well documented. Women live longer than men, yet they have higher morbidity rates. Men experience more life-threatening chronic diseases and die younger, whereas women live longer but have more nonfatal acute and chronic conditions and disability. Furthermore, although men's and women's overall rate of serious mental illness is similar, the most common mental health disorders differ by gender. These perplexing patterns raise many questions for social and biomedical scientists and clinicians. At issue is whether the origins of these health differences are physiological, social, or both.

In studies of health, a gap still exists around gender differences and around the issues this paradox raises about the multifaceted connections between social and biological processes. For the most part, studies have failed to assess gender and to explain why rational people are not effectively making health a priority in their everyday lives. A growing body of research indicates that the complexity of the gender differences extends beyond narrow concepts of the relative disadvantage or advantage of men's and women's biology or the social organization of their lives. Consequently, to understand what aspects of the broader array of differences in men's and women's lives contribute to the morbidity/mortality paradox, we need a model of men's and women's health that takes into account factors other than inequality of resources, discrimination, and other unfair treatment.

Neither biological nor social research alone can answer the complex questions regarding the antecedents of the puzzling gender differences in health. Only a synthesis of these perspectives can move forward the much-needed interdisciplinary dialogues and investigations to close the knowledge gap. Although many significant voices are calling for such a synthesis to explain a variety of other health disparities, and new multidisciplinary fields are grappling with identifying and understanding the connections among biological processes and social factors, addressing gender differences is still overlooked.

Two reports from the Institute of Medicine – *Exploring the Biological Contributions to Human Health: Does Sex Matter?* and *Health and Behavior: The Interplay of Biological, Behavioral and Societal Influences* (2001a, 2001b)[1] – begin to lay the groundwork for integrated research on gender differences in health by synthesizing diverse literatures, identifying knowledge gaps, and providing new directions for research on health. These two reports are invaluable resources because they advance a new way of thinking about human health. Together, they implicitly demand an integrative approach to fully examine the connections between the physiological mechanisms and social processes that make the health of men and women so different.

---

[1] The first report distinguishes between biological sex differences and socially acquired gender differences, reviews evidence of the contribution of biological sex to men's and women's health, and calls for the evaluation of the contribution of sex in all biological and health research. The second examines the links between health and behavior, the influence of psychosocial factors on behavior, and the benefits of intervening at different levels to improve individual and population health.

A new understanding of what causes men's and women's health differences is critical, particularly in light of the *Healthy People 2010* goal of reducing social disparities in health (U.S. Department of Health and Human Services, 2000). To that end, we have reviewed and synthesized the literature on gender differences and developed a model to explain how multiple levels of constraints on choices in everyday life contribute to differences in men's and women's health.

Our ultimate goal in writing *Gender and Health* is simple: to provide a forum that will encourage researchers from the social and biomedical sciences to collaborate on studies that examine, explain, and address gender-based health differences with the aim of advancing our understanding of both men's and women's health and creating new effective and efficient points for intervention to improve health.

References

Amick III, B. C., Levine, S., Tarlov, A. R., & Walsh, D. C. (1995). *Society and Health.* New York: Oxford University Press.

Institute of Medicine. (2001a). *Exploring the Biological Contributions to Human Health: Does Sex Matter?* Washington, DC: National Academy Press.

Institute of Medicine. (2001b). *Health and Behavior: The Interplay of Biological, Behavioral and Societal Influences.* Washington, DC: National Academy Press.

U.S. Department of Health and Human Services. (2000). *Healthy People 2010: Understanding and Improving Health.* Washington, DC: U.S. Government Printing Office.

Acknowledgments

This book grew out of our friendship and collaborative work over the past 12 years and our unwillingness to take no for an answer as we began to articulate the need for a new understanding of gender differences in health. We particularly appreciated each other's creativity, tenacity, and willingness to engage in unrestrained debate as we repeatedly confronted the growing complexity of our ambitious task. Although we have contributed equally to this endeavor, Pat, continuing in her mentoring role, generously suggested that my name (Chloe) go first, for which I am grateful.

A great deal of credit goes to the many people who have contributed to this book by listening to our ideas, challenging us to extend them, encouraging us while pointing to new and different literatures to be addressed, and giving us aid and comfort at the many points when we felt overwhelmed by the daunting scope of our project. We have benefited from the talents, knowledge, and honest critiques of our friends and colleagues. It is clear to us that we could not have done this alone, yet we are fully responsible for the book's contents.

Many scholars directly influenced and facilitated this long and fruitful process. A handful of individuals provided comments at multiple points that led us to make much-needed revisions. We are particularly indebted to Allen Fremont, Joan Tucker, Stephanie Taylor, Elaine Hagopian, Carol Weisman, John Mirowsky, Maggie Weden, and Michael Kimmel. An even longer list of colleagues from a wide range of disciplines offered thoughtful feedback on specific issues and topics. We especially thank Carol Aneshensel, William Avison, Ellen Borges, Phil Brown, Elaine Carmen,

Lorraine Davies, Adeline Delavande, Iris Fineberg, Linda George, Nazli Kibria, Valerie Leiter, Jim McQuaid, Dan Monti, Teryl Nuckols, Michelle Poulin, Teresa Seeman, and Elaine Wethington.

Along the way, we received encouragement and instrumental support from many individuals, including Michael Baizerman, Cindy Bird, William Cockerham, Donald Compton, Peter Conrad, Sue Gore, Phil Hallen, Ichiro Kawachi, Richard Lansing, Rene Lavinghouze, Warren Pearse, Marta Pelusi, Katrina Reiling, Shelley Roth, Lisa Rubenstein, Jane Ryan, Jason Schnittker, and especially John Stone, who, in addition to providing feedback on the book, encouraged us to apply to the Bellagio Research and Conference Center.

We refined our arguments through innumerable conversations with colleagues who helped us work out our ideas out loud, most notably those at Bellagio (particularly Tom Basset, Gail Boyer Hayes, and Pilar Palacia), RAND, and Boston University; also helpful were discussions with students in classes that we taught at Boston University, Pardee RAND Graduate School, and Simmons College. We also took the opportunity to present our work to diverse audiences in the United States and abroad, particularly at the Health Inequalities and the Life Course Conference in 2004 in State College, PA, and meetings of the AcademyHealth, the American Sociological Association, the British Medical Sociological Association, the Royal Institute of Public Health Conference in Lisbon, and the 37th World Congress of the International Institute for Sociology in Stockholm. The comments we received helped us evaluate the evidence from disparate disciplines and further clarify our perspective.

This book would not have been possible without the financial support provided by the National Library of Medicine (grant number G13LM07584-01); the Rockefeller Foundation, which awarded us a month's residency at its Bellagio Research and Conference Center in Italy; the Falk Medical Fund, which provided a grant for research assistance; and the National Institute of Aging, which funds the RAND MiniMedical School for Social Scientists. We also received invaluable institutional support from Simmons College, which provided a grant from the dean's development fund; the Sociology Department at Boston University; and the RAND Corporation.

We also express our appreciation to those who provided clerical and administrative support, especially Krasimir Karamfilov, Katie McNamara, Denise Oberdan, and Darla Grzybowski, who repeatedly came to our aid in the face of technical and other difficulties. We want to thank the photographer at Bellagio, Silvano Gilardoni, for allowing us to use the photograph he took of us. Finally, we are grateful to Walter Cecil for his creative contribution to our book cover.

Most importantly, we thank our friend and colleague, Elizabeth Maggio, who became a part of our team through her valuable editorial contributions. Her discerning questions and astute critiques challenged us to rethink and reorganize the chapters in ways that added immeasurably to the quality (and progress) of the book, and she made a difficult and at times thorny process fun.

Finally, we recognize the editors and staff at Cambridge University Press, specifically Scott Parris, for shepherding our book through the publication process, and Barbara Walthall and Gail Naron Chalew, of Aptara, Inc., for their meticulous copy editing, which enhanced the clarity of the book.

Introduction

Gender and Health is a book intended to improve health by informing both personal choices and policy decisions. It is designed for researchers, policymakers, and others who want to understand the ways in which both differences in women's and men's lives and in their physiology contribute to the paradoxical differences in their health.

The discrepancies are clear. Women live longer than men, yet they have higher morbidity rates. Men experience more life-threatening chronic diseases, whereas women have more nonfatal acute and chronic conditions. Furthermore, although the overall rate of serious mental illness is similar for men and women, the most common mental health disorders differ by gender. Most notably, women experience higher rates of depression and anxiety disorders, whereas men have higher rates of substance abuse and antisocial behavior disorders.

Are the factors underlying these health differences physiological, social, or both? Obviously, biological sex differences have health consequences. Yet biology is not destiny. In fact, even physiological differences in adult men and women may be socially acquired. Interactions between social and biological factors as well as those between mental and physical health further complicate the picture. For example, osteoporosis traditionally has been viewed as the product of hormonal deficiency as well as the lack of weight-bearing exercise and a poor diet, both of which are related to multiple social factors. In addition, recent research indicates that depression, which may be attributable to both social and biological factors, can also increase the risk of osteoporosis. Therefore, a combination of social and biological factors can influence gender differences in physical health both directly and indirectly.

In their landmark paper, Lois Verbrugge and Deborah Wingard (1987) argue that neither a strictly biomedical interpretation of the data nor one based on social factors adequately explains gender-based health disparities. They point to ample data documenting differentials in health and mortality, but add that "little research has been devoted to explaining those differentials" (Verbrugge & Wingard, 1987).

Two decades later, little has changed in our understanding of gender-based health disparities. Intuitively the answer lies neither in an exclusively biological nor an exclusively sociological vision of reality but in a combination of both. Many new studies have been published, but no new integrated explanations of the differences in men's and women's health have emerged. Why not?

A LACK OF COMMUNICATION AND COLLABORATION

From our perspective as sociologists, we contend that, although researchers study gender differences in health, there is generally little cross-disciplinary dialogue between the biomedical community and the social science community. We encounter scientists on both sides who ignore and often even disparage the views and work of those in other disciplines due to differences in their theories and methods. Competition for scarce research funding adds fuel to the distancing between the social and biomedical sciences.

In contrast, researchers from a wide range of disciplines within the two fields do undertake interdisciplinary studies to investigate the determinants of racial/ethnic and socioeconomic disparities in health. But for the most part, researchers remain entrenched in their own singular perspectives, however insightful, when explaining gender and health.

This level of specialization and intellectual parochialism frames existing debates about gender and health, limiting the range of questions asked, hypotheses tested, and outcomes considered (Bird & Rieker, 1999; Levine, 1995). Moreover, this situation diminishes possibilities for and interest in creatively integrating diverse theories and findings regarding men's and women's health. Consequently, no unifying framework exists that brings together the ideas of both social and biomedical scientists.

This research divide is somewhat perplexing. Perhaps the biomedical explanations of health disparities between men and women are so powerful that researchers believe social aspects of gender are not an issue that needs explaining. Sociologists, in turn, may feel that biomedical explanations will never address the fundamental social cause of gender disparities in health created by inequality. However, when we have presented our ideas regarding the gender paradox at health research conferences, we have met with two interesting reactions (Rieker & Bird, 2005). Many of our colleagues are surprised by the enduring nature of the paradoxical gender differences. Others familiar with the paradox confide that they do not pursue this line of research because they are stymied by the apparent contradictions in the patterns and the need to synthesize work from many disciplines.

Even confusion over terminology contributes to the lack of clarity regarding the relative contributions of social and biological factors to the paradoxical and perplexing differences in men's and women's health. Researchers from different fields use the terms "sex" and "gender" in different and often contradictory ways. The term "sex" is often used to refer to the chromosomal structure determined at the moment of conception and, more generally, to biological characteristics and their direct consequences. Social scientists introduced the term "gender" to refer to what society and culture make of those biological differences, and this term is frequently applied to the social characteristics and patterns distinguishing women's and men's lives. In fact, many if not most health-related differences between men and women may have both social and biological antecedents; thus, the distinction between sex and gender remains confounded.

In this book we limit our use of the term "sex" to those differences that are most clearly biological in origin. Rather than coining a third term for differences that clearly have both social and biological antecedents, we employ the term "gender" when referring to observed health differences between men and women, including those differences hypothesized to be purely social and those hypothesized to result from both social and biological factors.

Sociological work demonstrates the profound influence that gender has on an individual's life experiences and why that influence is not reducible to chromosomal structures. The meaning, status, and implications of gender result from socially structured access to resources and opportunities and associated attitudes, behaviors, and values. Adding to the confusion, the term "gender" has rapidly replaced the term "sex" in medical research in recent decades. Unfortunately, this change in terminology has not helped clarify the contributions of social factors to men's and women's health. Instead, the term "gender differences" has frequently been misapplied to describe purely biological differences in human anatomy and to animal studies where the biological basis of such differences should be evident.

Even the structure of granting agencies fosters a research divide between the biomedical and social science communities. Clearly, the structure of the National Institutes of Health (NIH), the primary funder of health research, was not designed to impede interdisciplinary research. Rather, it resulted from the way science has evolved in this country with an emphasis on biomedical research and specialization. The NIH and other funding agencies did not foresee the growth and complexity of health-related research and the eventual need to bring sociological and biomedical researchers together to understand and address a wide range of health disparities, including gender differences in health. Over the past decade, the NIH and foundations have made increasing efforts to foster and fund interdisciplinary research to explain socioeconomic and racial/ethnic differences in health. At the same time, NIH has given relatively little attention to funding such cross-disciplinary work to better understand differences in men's and women's health. However, NIH's Office for Research on Women's Health created in 1990 has recently developed, implemented, and funded a group of interdisciplinary research centers and research training programs to ensure that women's health is part of the larger biomedical research agenda.

Our goal in writing this book is to move beyond the barriers that prevent us from a clear understanding of gender health differences. We hope that our synthesis of knowledge about social and biological determinants of health from diverse fields will lay the groundwork to replace current debates, exclusionary explanations, and narrow views with much-needed interdisciplinary dialogues. Only through an interdisciplinary approach that brings together both social and biological research can we hope to shed light on how and why gender differences in health occur. Such knowledge will most certainly alter the way we think about health, which in turn will create a new realm of possibilities for intervention and change.

A NEW FRAMEWORK FOR EXAMINING GENDER DIFFERENCES

We have developed an innovative sociological perspective to examine the complex antecedents of health differences between men and women and illuminate the ways in which men's and women's opportunities, and in turn their choices, are constrained. Our approach draws on the prevailing public health understanding of health disparities, which emphasizes the role of personal choices and health behaviors in enhancing or diminishing an individual's ability to live a long and healthy life. We argue that men's and women's opportunities and choices are to a certain extent constrained by decisions and actions taken by families, employers, communities, and governmental policies. In the long run, these choices can contribute to the observed patterns of gender-based health differences by creating, maintaining, or exacerbating underlying biological differences in health.

Our framework of constrained choice takes into account that an individual's decisions and even his or her allocation of resources reflect individual choices and preferences. We also recognize that the personal decisions involved are not isolated from the social forces that continually shape our lives. For example, the readiness and willingness to adopt positive and negative health behaviors are affected by social expectations and opportunities for both men and women. For instance, most Americans are aware that our culture and media images of ideal male and female bodies encourage young women to diet in unhealthy ways and lead some to anorexia and bulimia in an attempt to achieve thinness. However, few consider that, at the same time, young men are encouraged to increase muscle mass, leading some to abuse anabolic steroids, and, in the case of wrestlers, to dehydrate themselves to reduce their weight for competition, thereby increasing their risk of brain injury.

Although many of the constraints and their consequences for individual choice are similar for men and women, the health impact will vary somewhat due to differences in both biology and life experiences. In other words, an individual's choices can influence and be influenced by biological processes (in a feedback loop). For example, constrained choices affect men's and women's stress levels as they experience competing demands on their time and other resources, which can in turn affect their psychological and physical responses to stress. Constrained choices may also have an impact on health behaviors and coping styles that affect both psychological and physical functioning. Consequently, we contend that gender differences in the constraints contribute to health disparities both directly and indirectly by affecting both men's and women's choices and their cumulative biological risk.

Some of the major pathways through which social factors affect individual physiology and health involve experiences of acute and chronic stress, which have been shown to cause wear and tear on multiple physiological regulatory systems, leading to more rapid aging, increased risk of disease, and earlier death (McEwen, 1998; Seeman, Singer, Rowe, & McEwen, 2001). Many of the factors that determine an individual's current and cumulative stress exposure are outside his or her control. These factors are the products of choices in which an individual may participate as part of a larger group (e.g., the household, the community, or society) and of social and environmental barriers to choosing health in which an individual may have little or no voice, such as air quality, the degree of demand and control in the workplace, or the nature and prevalence of discrimination. Thus, even those group-level choices in which the individual participates are based in large part on other priorities, such as balancing the budget, whether for a family or the nation.

Researchers and scholars from a wide range of disciplines have contributed to the understanding of the complex dynamics of women's and men's physical and mental health, providing insight into the social/economic and racial/ethnic differences among men and among women. Not surprisingly, as social and biomedical scientists focused their attention on health disparities, significant gaps in knowledge regarding substantial gender differences in health became apparent. For example, over recent decades it became clear that men's and women's cardiovascular disease symptoms and trajectories differ in clinically important ways. Similarly, researchers and clinicians began to recognize the need for gender comparisons to better understand disorders as far ranging as immune function, depression, and even substance use. These insights into both men's and women's health produced a new appreciation for the complexity of the paradoxical gender differences in health that challenges more singular notions of the disadvantage or advantage of either gender. Rather than focusing on the fact that women are sicker or that men die younger, our aim is to provide a balanced analysis of both men's and women's experiences and potential health consequences. We seek to further the dialogue across disciplines by acknowledging both the gender differences in health and the diversity among women and among men.

Scientific advances have created the possibility that people can live longer and healthier lives, if only they can figure out which advice to follow. This conundrum has generated public demand for change because people are frustrated both with the volume of new health information and the conflicting nature of the advice.[1] As a result of the information overload and an inability to evaluate each new piece of advice, individuals are uncertain about how to choose and combine strategies for maintaining and restoring health. These scientific and popular developments moved health to the forefront of a national debate on quality of life at the same time that the paradoxical differences in men's and women's health came to public attention. In many ways, the combination of public and scientific interest in these two topics has produced a strategic moment for a collaborative effort to examine the determinants of gender differences in health.

THE IMPACT OF HEALTH INFORMATION ON MEN'S AND WOMEN'S CHOICES

We assume that everyone is interested in having a healthy life and to varying degrees in obtaining knowledge and/or information that facilitates achieving that goal. It is commonly understood that women are

---

[1] One expression of this frustration is reflected in the widespread desire to increase control over one's own health and health care. We contend that one consequence of this desire is the growing demand for and use of complementary therapies. The coexistence of a vast self-care industry and an expanding market for high-tech preventive care and treatments represent another example.

more familiar with health recommendations than are men, perhaps in part due to traditional gender roles of caring for the family and monitoring everyone's health. Consequently, gender differences in knowledge of current health information might also contribute to health disparities.

These gender differences aside, however, three major obstacles complicate the process of obtaining useful health knowledge for all of us. The first obstacle is that accurate and comprehensive information on how to lead a healthy life is not readily available. Although ample information exists on the potential benefits of engaging in health behaviors (such as exercise and diet) and avoiding health risks (such as poor air quality or chronic stress), the information is and always will be incomplete with regard to the wide array of choices that people make and the constraints they face throughout life. In fact, individuals lack the information to calculate – for example – what the actual cumulative health costs may be of living a harried and stressful life. Moreover, the information is not necessarily accessible or available in the form needed, either because it is not specific enough, the information cannot be found at the time it is needed, or it requires a relatively high level of education or even specialized knowledge to interpret and utilize. That would be enough of a challenge to impede most of us from choosing health, at least some of the time.

The second obstacle to obtaining health information is that the cumulative body of knowledge regarding the determinants of health and longevity is expanding at an unprecedented rate and involves an increasing number of specialized studies and findings, none of which simultaneously compares all of the factors that might be relevant to a given individual or family at a particular time. In reality, it is not possible to know everything that is known about health, and much of what is known includes either gaps in the information or what at this point appears to be directly conflicting information. Take, for example, the role of Omega-3 fatty acids and whether and how much fish to eat to benefit from these fatty acids without excessive exposure to mercury and other toxins. Even the most interested and avid reader of general and specialized health information is not able to stay current, and if he or she were able to keep up, there would not be enough time left in the day for the recommended amounts of exercise, sleep, and so on. In fact, many people find it extremely time consuming and stressful as they attempt to keep up with general health information or specialized knowledge related to their own known health conditions.

The third obstacle to obtaining useful health information is that until recently, the majority of health research focused on men, and less is known about how to prevent and treat many illnesses in women or whether the effectiveness of treatments varies by gender. Moreover, health information messages have been differentially targeted to men and women (and to other groups thought to be at risk for specific health conditions). For example, based on results from cardiovascular disease (CVD) prevention trials that included only men, it was assumed for years that women were at less risk for CVD. Because of this assumption, women were not advised (by physicians or the general media) to follow the same health advice as men. Consequently, women did not benefit equally even from what was known about preventing heart disease in men. In fact, numerous studies indicate that women were unaware of their substantial CVD risk, because most health messages targeted to women focused on breast cancer screening behaviors (Bassuk & Manson, 2004). During this same period, while health information for men focused on CVD, prostate cancer was virtually ignored, and yet it is another significant cause of male mortality.

In the end, making health a priority requires good information on the health effects of a tremendous array of choices, and this information is not easy to come by. Moreover, the health information that is available is not organized or presented in a form that allows men and women to use it in a meaningful way. For example, one cannot compare the health impacts of choosing a more stressful job over a less stressful one in the way one might compare their financial tradeoffs. Without specific information and a tool to project the long-term health consequences, there is no way for people to accurately assess the relative health effects of different everyday choices in order to incorporate that information into their decision-making process. Ironically, this type of information is also missing for policymakers as they consider the consequences of implementing or changing public policies, such as welfare, tax policies, and Social Security. Although they are not directly health related, such policies can nonetheless differentially affect men's and women's health.

We contend that the interdisciplinary research we are calling for will not only improve our understanding of gender differences in health but will also provide the kind of information that individuals need to make health a priority and understand the health consequences of their everyday choices.

OVERVIEW OF *GENDER AND HEALTH*

The unique perspective of this book will give readers a new way to think about gender and health, as well as insight into a different way to conduct their lives. Therefore, *Gender and Health* begins with a review and discussion of the sex- and gender-based patterns of mental and physical health over the life course and the biological and social explanations of these patterns. We then present a model of constrained choice to illustrate both the possibility of and constraints on individual agency and to demonstrate that the social organization of men's and women's lives, as well as their biology, contributes to differences in their health. The subsequent chapters elaborate on the model of constrained choice and provide examples of the ways men's and women's lives alter their individual risk and exposure. In particular, we explore the connections among physiological mechanisms, social processes, and health. Finally, we identify opportunities for changes that could improve health and reduce disparities.

In Chapter 1, we examine gender differences and similarities in men's and women's physical and mental health and focus on four specific diseases or conditions selected because of their prevalence and substantial contribution to morbidity and mortality. For physical health, we include cardiovascular disease and the combination of immune function and immune disorders; for mental health, we consider depressive disorders and substance abuse disorders. We also synthesize recent findings from diverse literatures on the major social and biological explanations for the gender patterns in health and weigh their strength and limitations in order to shed light on the complexity of the issues at hand.

In Chapter 2, we introduce our model of constrained choice to illustrate both the possibility of and constraints on individual agency. Here we demonstrate how the social organization of men's and women's lives contributes to the paradoxical differences in their health. We explore how decisions made and actions taken at the family, work, community, and societal levels influence the myriad of everyday choices individuals make that directly or indirectly affect their health. The dynamic nature of the relationship between gender roles and human agency (in other words, the extent to which individuals can and do have control over aspects of their lives) is an integral part of our perspective. We consider how social policies, such as those that advance women's careers or allow men to use paternity leave, have shaped gender roles in various countries over time.

In Chapter 3, we examine the health impact of social policies on gender differences. Every society makes policy choices regarding the type of social and economic safety net needed to protect and maintain the well-being of individuals and families. These choices include whether and how to provide for the elderly, the unemployed, and families with children. For example, entitlements, health insurance, and family policies (including subsidized or mandated parental leave) indirectly affect health by reducing or buffering the impact of economic strains.

Social policies seldom explicitly treat men and women differently. Yet, even policies that do explicitly treat them the same can affect men and women differently due to their life circumstances and health care needs. We analyze the effects of social policies and business practices by considering their differential impact on men's and women's health over the life course. Clearly, some policies are likely to have a larger impact on the health of one gender. For example, hunter safety regulations such as those requiring education are likely to have larger effects on men's health than on women's simply because the vast majority of hunters are men. Few, if any, would argue that such public health regulations should not exist on the grounds that they differentially affect men's and women's health. We discuss a range of social policies, including child care, welfare, Medicare, Medicaid, and Social Security, and private sector business practices including the provision of health insurance and parental leave.

In Chapter 4, we explore the impact of the community on health. We use the term "community" to refer both to social networks of relationships with family, friends, and acquaintances at home and at work, and the physical environment in which one lives. Although families shape the combinations of roles that men and women pursue throughout the life course, families do not exist in a vacuum. The communities in which people live and work influence the obligations and demands of specific roles.

Because of gender differences in role activities and role expectations, men and women differ in their exposure to specific daily hassles associated with communities, and this in turn affects their stress levels. For example, both gender-role demands and community context affect the stresses associated with getting to and from work. Furthermore, those communities with more closely knit neighborhoods, more trust among neighbors, better schools, and better policing are safer and healthier places to live.

In Chapter 5, we examine the expectations attached to men's and women's social roles and how exposure to specific stresses and burdens differs by gender. We assess how gender differences in the meaning of specific work and family roles affect men's and women's psychological well-being. For example, men are more likely to experience their work and family roles as integral or complementary, whereas women are more likely to experience theirs as competing or conflicting. We also explore how the cumulative effects of stress related to gender roles contribute to substantial differences in both mental and physical health problems for men and women.

In Chapter 6, the focus is on men and women as individuals and the comparative health behaviors they engage in over the life course. Here we are concerned with how social circumstances and biological factors might contribute to the variation in particular health behaviors that men and women adopt and that contribute to the observed disparities in their health. We address why gender and health behaviors are related in complicated ways as the association among them varies by life-course stage, the specific behavior being addressed, social economic status (SES), and other social realities. Even seemingly minor individual choices, made often in adolescence, can have a large cumulative impact on later health.

As in Chapter 3 we undertake cross-national comparisons of policy regimes to determine whether there are discernible gender patterns in health behaviors across regimes and, if so, whether such differences might be associated with the gender gap in longevity. Our argument throughout this book impels us here to raise two critical questions: *Why are some individuals able to create and maintain healthy lifestyles, while others are not?* and *Whose responsibility is health?* Although these complex questions cannot be answered fully, we address how the numerous differences in men's and women's behaviors and activities offer multiple opportunities for change and interventions at various levels of decision making that would increase opportunities to pursue health.

In Chapter 7, we highlight promising new approaches to integrating biological and social research and provide examples of innovative developments that transcend the long-standing discipline-focused division of labor in the research community. Although there are many voices calling for interdisciplinary research, we draw attention to unique contributions made possible by such cross-disciplinary work. We discuss how these emerging areas of study address the current gaps in our understanding of men's and women's health. In addition, we consider several federal reports that call for interdisciplinary research to assess the contributions of individual health behaviors and social contexts to health, but overlook the implications for understanding gender differences in health. We also discuss one report that seeks to better understand differences in men's and women's health, but that focuses only on the potential biological explanations, ignoring the benefit of simultaneously examining both social and biological factors.

Finally, we introduce the framework of constrained choice as a platform for prevention. Here we identify actions that scientists and decision makers on all levels can take to reduce the constraints on men's and women's opportunities to pursue health. Because individuals' experiences are intertwined with the social contexts in which they live and work, efforts to improve health and reduce gender disparities require that we understand the ways in which individual behaviors, family and social context, and social policies interact. Ultimately, an understanding of the consequences of these choices and the pathways that produce gender differences can inform individuals, families, communities, and societies about how to better integrate health implications into their decisions and actions. We propose actions to expand options and inform choices made by individuals and families, as well as those made by policymakers at the workplace, community, and national levels.

SOME ADDITIONAL THOUGHTS

We focus primarily on the United States as a cultural context, although we draw on research and examples of social policy from other industrialized countries. Thus, although the information contained in *Gender and Health* draws extensively from data and models that are limited to the United States, we develop specific cross-national comparisons in many chapters. As with any book, there are important topics and relevant debates that we are unable to address or discuss in any depth. We recognize that, despite substantial gender differences in health, on average, men and women do not represent two homogeneous groups. Race, ethnicity, socioeconomic position, and other aspects of social status interact with gender to produce variations in gender differences in health across subgroups. Such health disparities highlight the fact that social and health advantages do not accrue to all men, nor do disadvantages accrue to all women (MacIntyre, Hunt, & Sweeting, 1996). Nevertheless, our intent is to focus on the differences between men and women. We describe the extent to which gender differences in health are consistent across socioeconomic, racial, and ethnic groups. However, a full treatment of the health issues surrounding race and ethnicity is not feasible in this book. Furthermore, the complex issues of health care delivery are beyond the scope of this book. Thus, although it is well known that access to and quality of care and treatment vary by race, income, and gender, these topics are not covered here.

Finally, in writing this book, our intent is not to argue for a particular political or ideological position or to determine what is right or fair. Rather, our goal is to examine the consequences of policies as they exist and consider hypothetical alternatives to clarify how they might affect men's and women's opportunities to choose health.

References

Bassuk, S. S., & Manson, J. E. (2004). Gender and its impact on risk factors for cardiovascular disease. In M. J. Legato (Ed.), *Principles of Gender-Specific Medicine, Vol. 1.*, 198–214. San Diego: Elsevier Academic Press.
Bird, C. E., & Rieker, P. P. (1999). Gender matters: An integrated model for understanding men's and women's health. *Soc Sci Med, 48*(6), 745–755.

Levine, S. (1995). Time for creative integration in medical sociology. *J Health Soc Behav* (Extra Issue), 1–4.

MacIntyre, S., Hunt, K., & Sweeting, H. (1996). Gender differences in health: Are things really as simple as they seem? *Soc Sci Med, 42,* 617–624.

McEwen, B. S. (1998). Protective and damaging effects of stress mediators. *N Engl J Med, 338*(3), 171–179.

Rieker, P. P., & Bird, C. E. (2005). Rethinking gender differences in health: What's needed to integrate social and biological perspectives. *J Gerontol: Soc Sci, 60B,* 40–47.

Seeman, T. E., Singer, B., Rowe, J., & McEwen, B. S. (2001). Exploring a new concept of cumulative biological risk – Allostatic load and its health consequences: MaCarthur Studies of Successful Aging. *Proc Nat Acad Sci, 98*(8), 4770–4775.

Verbrugge, L., & Wingard, D. L. (1987). Sex differentials in health and mortality. *Women Health, 12*(2), 103–145.

ONE

Gender Differences in Health

Are They Biological, Social, or Both?

A central feature of mortality trends throughout the 20th century is the obvious gender difference in life expectancy: in the United States, women live on average 5.2 years longer than men (National Center for Health Statistics [NCHS], 2006).[1] This gender difference in mortality led many researchers to question the centuries-old assumption that women were the "weaker sex." Yet, our understanding of the differences and similarities in men's and women's physical and mental health has changed dramatically over the past 20 years. A review of these similarities and differences reveals that researchers were asking the wrong question. The question "which is the weaker sex?" is framed in the language of biological advantage and disadvantage of one sex over the other and implies that biological differences can be summed up to determine which sex is the fittest. At best, this approach produces oversimplified models of the complex patterns of gender differences in health (Bird & Rieker, 1999; Rieker & Bird, 2000, 2005).

Although men and women do seem to have some unique biological advantages and disadvantages over each other, substantial variation occurs among women and among men, and these differences seem to vary with certain social conditions. Yet, much of clinical research tends to minimize or ignore the social processes that can influence health differentially and to reify biomedical models that portray men's and women's health disparities as inherently biological. In recent years, a growing number of

---

[1] Preliminary data from NCHS 2006 show that the gender gap narrowed from 7 years in 1990 to 5.2 years in 2004.

clinical researchers have come to recognize that both *social* and *biological* factors interact in complex ways and that this interaction explains not only health or illness at the individual level but also the observed patterns of men's and women's health and longevity in general. Yet, relatively few studies examine both sets of factors.

In this chapter, we briefly review some of the major sex-based and gender-based differences and similarities in men's and women's health – both physical and mental – and assess the ramifications of overly simplistic assumptions of either male or female advantage, which frequently occur in both clinical and social research. In our discussion of gender-based health differences, we focus on four specific diseases or conditions selected because of their prevalence and substantial contribution to morbidity and mortality. For physical health, we examine cardiovascular disease and the combination of immune function and disorders; for mental health, we consider depressive disorders and substance abuse disorders. With these four disease categories as our references, we review gender differences in health and weigh the strengths and limitations of biological and sociologic explanations for those differences.

THE GENDER PARADOX IN PHYSICAL HEALTH

As we note in the Introduction to the book, differences in men's and women's physical health are paradoxical. Women live longer than men, yet they have higher morbidity rates and, in later years, a diminished quality of life. In fact, women outlive men in every region and almost every country of the world. However, the size of the gender gap and the pattern of longevity vary considerably by country (United Nations, 2000, 2005). Although many reasons for the variation have been identified, biological factors alone are not considered a sufficient explanation for the cross-national gender differences.

Since 1900, American women's life expectancy has exceeded that of men, with women experiencing lower mortality rates in every age group and for most causes of death. Although life expectancy has been increasing for both men and women, the gender gap in longevity in the United States has been closing since 1980 when men's gains began to exceed women's due in large part to men's rapid decline in smoking and decreasing mortality from cardiovascular disease (CVD) and cancer (NCHS, 2003; Pampel, 2002; Preston & Wang, 2002). For example, between 1990 and 2004 men gained 3.4 years in life expectancy compared to less than 1.6 years for women, in part due to more rapid declines in smoking among men (NCHS, 2006). In addition to experiencing more rapid gains in life expectancy in recent decades, on average men have been gaining healthy years, whereas women's gains in life expectancy reflect an increase in years spent living with a functional disability (Centers for Disease Control [CDC], 2000; Crimmins, Kim, & Hagedorn, 2002; NCHS, 2003).

The paradox of men's higher mortality and lower morbidity compared to women can be explained by gender differences in the patterns of disease, including the fact that women's risk for CVD increases after menopause (Verbrugge & Wingard, 1987). Although the three leading causes of death are the same for men and women – heart disease, cancer, and stroke – men have more life-threatening chronic diseases at younger ages, including coronary heart disease, cancer, cerebrovascular disease, emphysema, cirrhosis of the liver, kidney disease, and atherosclerosis. In contrast, women face higher rates of chronic debilitating disorders such as autoimmune diseases and rheumatologic disorders, as well as the irritating but less life-threatening diseases such as anemia, thyroid conditions, gallbladder conditions, migraines, arthritis, and eczema. Women also have more acute conditions such as upper respiratory infections, gastroenteritis, and other short-term infectious diseases (NCHS, 2003).

Although the paradoxical gender differences in disease patterns that Verbrugge and Wingard described nearly two decades ago have not changed significantly, the interpretations of and responses to these data have varied over time and across disciplines. In their influential article, Verbrugge and Wingard (1987) argued that attention had for some time been focused on men's higher mortality rates, particularly from cardiovascular disease, while less attention was paid to CVD in women and their greater morbidity from aggravating and, in some cases, debilitating illness. They sought to redirect researchers and clinicians toward broader and more complex explanations of the paradoxical differences in men's and women's health that would advance understanding of the implications of gender differences in disease prevalence.

Below, we provide a closer examination of CVD and our three other reference diseases/conditions, which reveals a more complex portrait of specific patterns of gender differences in health than previously articulated. Later in this chapter we consider some of the primary social and biological explanations of these patterns.

CARDIOVASCULAR DISEASE

We begin the discussion with cardiovascular disease (CVD) because it is the leading cause of mortality and morbidity in both men and women. In this section, rather than discussing treatment patterns, we examine how the perception of men's and women's risks and rates of cardiovascular disease has changed in recent decades.[2]

Due in part to its earlier onset for men than for women, CVD also contributes substantially to gender differences in life expectancy (Crimmins et al., 2002). Although the prevalence and age-adjusted death rate of CVD are greater in men than in women, more women ultimately die of the disease because of their greater life expectancy, their older age at onset, and the range of CVD risk factors associated with aging. For example, since 1984, CVD has claimed the lives of more females than males (American Heart Association [AHA], 2003). Crimmins and colleagues (2002) provide interesting data on life expectancy by estimating years lived with and without disease by birth cohorts of men and women over the life course. Because more women survive to older ages, the gender difference in years lived with disease is even greater than in years of life expectancy. For example, a cohort of women will experience 70% more years of life after age 65 with hypertension than a similar-sized birth cohort of men. Likewise, a group of older women also will spend more years with CVD than will older men. Thus, the typical patient undergoing treatment for CVD, hypertension, and even arthritis is likely to be a woman.

Scientists and clinicians have tried for decades to explain the gender differences in the onset of CVD and more generally to identify the biological mechanisms that contribute to men's lesser and women's greater

---

[2] For an extensive discussion of the questions related to gender-specific models of medical care and treatment, see Brittle and Bird (2007).

Gender and Health

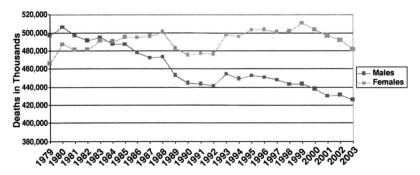

Figure 1.1. Cardiovascular Disease Mortality Trends for Males and Females United States: 1979–2003. *Source:* Centers for Disease Control and Prevention (2007a, 2007b)

longevity. Understandably, throughout most of the past two decades, clinical research focused on explaining the earlier onset of CVD in men and men's lower average life expectancy. This research emphasis, reflected in single-sex longitudinal clinical trials directed only at the prevention of CVD in men, has contributed over time to significant reductions in male mortality from CVD and has helped narrow the gender gap in longevity (Physicians' Health Study, 2006).

Although CVD in women was a less prominent health issue during this same period, in terms of total deaths since 1984, the disease has claimed the lives of more females than males. While the life-expectancy gender gap is narrowing, the CVD mortality gap continues to widen (Figure 1.1). In 2000, of the 945,836 CVD deaths, 46.5% were males and 53.5% were females (NCHS, 2002).[3]

Interestingly, over time a confluence of factors led to substantial increases in women's inclusion in research, and their greater inclusion in turn led to a dramatic shift in knowledge and understanding regarding women's risk of cardiovascular disease, in general, and of coronary heart

[3] Gender differences in the quality of diagnosis and treatment as well as in outcomes of care for cardiovascular disease also have been well documented (Rathore et al., 2000; Vaccarino, Krumholz, Yarzebski, Gore, & Goldberg, 2001). However, most research has focused on differences in treatment rates with cardiovascular procedures and subsequent outcomes, and as a result gender differences in hospital care have narrowed (Canto et al., 2000; Gan et al., 2000). But, in spite of all the substantial improvements in treatment, CVD remains a major cause of disability for both men and women.

disease (CHD) in particular. However, this shift produced little insight into the antecedents of gender differences in risk. For instance, the Nurses' Health Study, which began in 1976 and was designed to assess the long-term consequences of the use of oral contraceptives, evolved over time into a study of risk factors for major chronic diseases (Nurses' Health Study, 2007). In 1985, this prospective cohort study of 122,000 registered nurses ages 30 to 55 reported that women taking estrogen had one-third fewer heart attacks than women who had not taken the drug (Stampfer, Willett, Colditz, Rosner, Speizer, et al., 1985). For the next 17 years, the observational evidence that estrogen appeared to protect women from heart disease until menopause became the basis of standard clinical practice and was prescribed to millions of women.

Verbrugge and Wingard's 1987 work on gender-based health disparities, including their landmark article, helped inaugurate the women's health movement, which in turn helped launch the more recent men's health movement. This focus on women's health, a predominantly lay movement, was galvanized by the underrepresentation of women in clinical research, particularly in studies of CVD prevention and intervention trials, and by what activists perceived as a "female disadvantage" in the availability of and access to health information, especially relating to women's desire to gain control over their fertility. In addition to the advocacy movement, the medical community also began to recognize the deficit of data on the epidemiology, risk factors, effective interventions, and outcomes of cardiovascular disease in women and to observe and document gender differences in the age of CVD onset, presentation, disease course, and treatment (Goldberg, 2002; Legato & Coleman, 1991).

CVD and the Women's Health Initiative

As a result of pressure from both the lay and clinical communities, the Women's Health Initiative (WHI), a comprehensive NIH-funded 15-year study, was launched in 1991. One of the largest preventive studies of its kind in the United States with 16,500 women subjects, the WHI was framed in a mainly biomedical science perspective and modeled on existing longitudinal studies of men and CHD, such as the Multiple Risk

Factor Intervention Trial (aka MRFIT study)[4] and the Physicians' Health Study. The latter, a landmark randomized trial (phase 1 began in 1982 and ended in 1995), tested the benefits and risks of aspirin and beta-carotene in the primary prevention of cardiovascular disease and cancer and has generated more than 200 articles (see http://phs.bwh.harvard.edu for a complete listing). The WHI was designed to address the lack of women in clinical trial research in general and specifically the shortage of scientific data about how to prevent and treat the most common causes of death, disability, and poor quality of life in postmenopausal women: cardiovascular disease, cancer, and osteoporosis. Focusing mostly on physiological mechanisms of action, the study consists of a set of clinical trials designed to test the effects of postmenopausal hormone replacement therapy (HRT); diet modification; and calcium and vitamin D supplements on prevention of coronary heart diseases, breast and colon cancer, and osteoporotic fractures, as well as an observational study on risk factors for these diseases (Howard et al., 2006; Prentice et al., 2006).

The HRT clinical trial arm of the WHI was based on prior scientific knowledge that estrogen provides women a more flexible circulatory system that can carry a 20% higher blood volume during pregnancy. This greater flexibility in turn produces less pressure on the vessels even at higher blood pressure, resulting in less damage from

---

[4] MRFIT, a $115 million randomized primary prevention trial that began in 1973 and ended in 1982, was designed to test the effects of lowering serum cholesterol and diastolic blood pressure and of the cessation of cigarette smoking on CHD mortality in men. The trial found negligible and modest effects. References for the Multiple Risk Factor Intervention Trial Research Group, "Multiple Risk Factor Intervention Trial: Risk Factor Changes and Mortality Results," *JAMA* 248(12): 1465–1477, September 24, 1982; Lundberg, G., "MRFIT and the Goals of The Journal," *JAMA* 248(12): 1501, September 24, 1982; Kolata, G., "Heart Study Produces a Surprise Result," *Science* 218: 31–32, October 1, 1982; Oliver, M., "Does Control of Risk Factors Prevent Coronary Heart Disease?," *Br Med J* II: 1065–1066, October 16, 1982; Editorial, "Trials of Coronary Heart Disease Prevention," *Lancet* II: 803–804, October 9, 1982; Bjermann, I., et al., "Effect of Diet and Smoking Intervention on the Incidence of Coronary Heart Disease: Report from the Oslo Study Group of a Randomised Trial in Healthy Men," *Lancet* II: 1303–1310, December 12, 1981; Rose, G., et al., "A Randomised Controlled Trial of Anti- Smoking Advice: 10-Year Results," *J Epidemiol Community Health* 36: 102–108, 1982. 8 TIMN 001983

high blood pressure in premenopausal women than in men the same age. Because of the observed role of this hormone in the cardiovascular system, clinical researchers hypothesized that giving women estrogen during and after menopause would not only address the debilitating symptoms of menopause that many women experienced but perhaps more importantly, would also continue to forestall the onset of CVD. Numerous clinical observational studies appeared to support the CVD prevention hypothesis (see review in Barbour, 2000). While such studies are able to provide data that describe the impact of a specific treatment or investigational drug over time, the observational research design (unlike a randomized clinical trial) is unable to provide results that determine cause and effect in any definitive way.

Moreover, once a particular treatment has been scientifically validated and found to be beneficial, it generally becomes part of standard care, and it is considered unethical to initiate or to continue a clinical trial or study that withholds from patients what is known to be efficacious treatment. For example, the Physicians' Health Study, which began in 1982, found that low-dose aspirin reduced the risk of first myocardial infarction by 44% in men (Steering Committee of the Physicians' Health Study Research Group et al., 1989). Consequently, this arm of the Physician's Health Study clinical trial was stopped in 1988, and low-dose aspirin therapy became the standard of care for the prevention of CVD in men. Likewise, it is also unethical to continue a clinical trial or study once a treatment is shown to be harmful, as occurred in the Women's Health Initiative trial of HRT.

Interestingly, a much smaller clinical trial of hormone replacement therapy (HRT), the Heart and Estrogen-progestin Replacement Study (HERS), began in 1993 to test the hypothesis that long-term hormone replacement therapy (HRT) would reduce cardiovascular events (including heart attack and death) among postmenopausal women with CHD (Barbour, 2000; Grady, Applegate, Bush, Furberg, Riggs, et al., 1998).[5] This study was expected to confirm the prevailing understanding of the

---

[5] The HERS clinical trial enrolled a cohort of 2,700 women and followed them over an average of 4.1 years (Hulley, Grady, & Bush, 1998).

benefits of HRT. However the results raised new questions. In fact, the study found that HRT increased the risk of heart attacks among women with CHD, indicating that HRT was not useful for secondary prevention (Hulley, Grady, & Bush, 1998). This study provides a clear example of how a clinical trial can contradict observational studies.[6]

Four years later in 2002, the WHI's HRT intervention, which was based on similarly promising observational data, was halted after a mean of 5.2 years follow-up. The Data and Safety Monitoring Board recommended stopping the trial because women receiving the estrogen/progesterone combination had an increased risk of invasive breast cancer and other negative health effects (Fletcher & Colditz, 2002; Writing Group for the Women's Health Investigators, 2002).[7] After publication of the WHI report, the medical research community concluded that the combination HRT in its current form was not a viable intervention for the primary prevention of coronary heart disease in women. HRT, which had become the standard of care for postmenopausal women (used by approximately 38% of postmenopausal women in the United States) and was considered among the most benign and potentially beneficial therapies for a variety of conditions, was suddenly discredited (Fletcher & Colditz, 2002).[8] Interestingly, despite decades of mostly positive research findings

---

[6] For a brief description of the differences between observation and clinical trial studies in relation to HRT and the public confusion over such conflicting health advice, see an excellent discussion by science journalist Gary Taubes (2007a, 2007b).

[7] A much smaller study with 720 newly menopausal women testing the same hypothesis but with different ways of administering the HRT began in September 2004.

[8] One new line of research stimulated by the WHI and currently advocated by the scientific community is to examine the impact of testosterone on men's health. Just as estrogen was thought to have beneficial effects for women's health, both the popular press and some clinicians believe that testosterone may also have a similar beneficial impact for men. Although there is less scientific evidence showing the beneficial effects of testosterone replacement therapy than there was for HRT, there are unsubstantiated claims that the hormone can help restore youthful vitality, improve mood and memory, and increase sexual drive. The increased use of physician-prescribed testosterone therapy and testosterone products by middle-aged and elderly men prompted the formation of a committee at the Institute of Medicine/National Academy of Science to make recommendations for further research on the potentially beneficial or harmful effects of such treatment. With the lessons learned from the HRT study, the committee of scientists and clinicians recommended that research into testosterone treatment begin with small clinical trials (National Academy of Sciences, 2003). Yet,

advocating the benefits of HRT, multiple articles reporting research showing its negative effects followed in rapid succession.[9]

Although the WHI represents a huge step forward in gathering scientific evidence regarding women's health, it did not, for example, question
the basic assumptions underlying physiological explanations of women's
extensive CVD mortality. Although the WHI research team and the NIH
sought to address the knowledge gap in women's health, the study did
not draw on a broader interdisciplinary model. Rather, it was designed to
test prevailing biomedical explanations, based on prior findings primarily from observational studies that indicated protective effects of estrogen
and diet in preventing the development of CVD. By studying only women,
the WHI was able to replicate the previously mentioned single-sex studies of men's health and to extend them by assessing some factors not
previously included in prior studies. But without comparable data on
both women and men, neither the WHI, the Nurses' Health Study, nor
the Physicians' Health Study is able to shed light on a broader array of
potential risk factors and social determinants of differences and similarities in men's and women's health, ironically leaving an assessment of
gender out of the equation.[10] Moreover, because of the understandable
emphasis on biological factors to explain women's health, the WHI does
not represent any movement toward integrating social and biomedical
models of health and illness or advancing an understanding of the relationship between physical and mental health. The same could be said

---

many physicians have not heeded the warning to wait for evidence-based medicine
before prescribing this therapy.

[9] The new research and subsequent publications reporting negative findings may reflect
a shift in the scientific understanding of the complex role of HRT in women's health
(see, for example, Thaul & Hotra, 1993). Such a shift generally sets into motion an
intellectual process that has the potential to alter how researchers interpret their findings
and how editors of scientific journals and their reviewers evaluate the ensuing articles.
The negative findings about HRT may also reflect advances in research design and
methodology. Changes in thinking or shifts in understanding are normal in everyday
science as the accumulation of knowledge occurs when an established (or believed to
be supported finding) is effectively disproved or brought into question and, as a result,
spawns new hypotheses and lines of research.

[10] The Framingham Heart Study, which included both men and women, is an unusual
exception to the single-sex longitudinal study. However, in contrast to the HRT and the
low-dose aspirin clinical trials, the Framingham Heart Study is an observational study
and lacks any intervention.

of the longitudinal studies of men's health, including MRFIT and the Physicians' Health Study.

IMMUNE FUNCTION AND DISORDERS

The second physical health condition we focus on includes both immune function and disorders. While we recognize that immune function and disorders are very different from our other three reference conditions, we focus on them because they represent an area of substantial gender difference in physical health.[11] This focus also provides an opportunity to introduce and explore an important and emergent literature that demonstrates some of the complex relationships between the social environment and biological functions, as well as connections between physical and mental health (Cacioppo, Berntson, Taylor, & Schacter, 2002; Kiecolt-Glaser, McGuire, Robles, & Glaser, 2002b; Seeman & McEwen, 1996; Seeman, McEwen, Singer, Albert, & Rowe, 1997).

Researchers and clinicians are challenged and perplexed by the sex-linked patterns of immune function and diseases. There is even debate about what constitutes autoimmune disease. Women's different and somewhat more intense immune response provides them with higher levels of passive immunity during pregnancy and the ability to pass on a substantial level of protective antibodies to infants during breast feeding (Grossman, Rosell, & Mendenhall, 1991; Hegde, 1991).[12] But pregnancy exacerbates the course of some autoimmune diseases (e.g., lupus), whereas it improves the course of others (e.g., rheumatoid arthritis). On the downside, women experience a greater risk of autoimmune disorders and a higher risk of genetic immune-suppression disorders than

---

[11] More than 20 diseases appear to have autoimmune pathogenesis but are underrepresented in mortality data because they have not been assigned distinct codes in the classification system used to delineate causes of mortality in official health statistics.

[12] Women's immune systems require the capacity to perform several elaborate processes in order to reproduce, which are not necessary for men. Women's bodies need to be able to avoid killing sperm even as they protect against sexually transmitted diseases. They also need to be able to host an embryo or fetus, thus actually allowing it to coexist in their body. Consequently, women's immune systems need to be both able to protect them and to disable certain mechanisms (or enable certain mechanisms) during pregnancy to prevent their immune system from attacking the embryo or fetus.

men. Consider women's rates of the following immunologic diseases compared to men: autoimmune thyroid 15:1, rheumatoid arthritis 3:1, systemic lupus erythematosus 9:1, and systemic sclerosis 4:1 (Office for Research on Women's Health, 1992). In fact, much of the disability that women experience from rheumatologic and thyroid disorders, especially in middle and older ages, is attributable to autoimmune disease (American Medical Association, 2000). Crimmins and colleagues (2002) also show that, compared to men, women live substantially more years with arthritis and more years with it than with either CVD and hypertension. In other words, women's more robust immune systems put them at greater risk of suffering from disorders in which their own immune system attacks their bodies (see also Nothnick, 2001, who argues that endometriosis may be an autoimmune disease).

Females generate a more robust immune response than males after challenge with an infectious agent, and they respond to natural and vaccine exposures by producing substantially more antibodies. Sex hormones also tend to modulate the immune response. In fact, distinct immune hormonal environments contribute to some of the sex differences in the prevalence of autoimmune disorders described above. In addition, men and women tend to develop different autoimmune conditions. While the origin of these differences would appear to be primarily biological, some physicians believe that gender – and in particular, the stress process (Pearlin, 1989; Pearlin, Leiberman, Menaghan, & Mullan, 1981) – also affects autoimmune disease incidence and severity (Legato, 2002; Lockshin, Gabriel, Zakeri, & Lockshin, 1999).

Interactions between social and biological factors may also contribute to gender differences in immune function and disorders, but the picture is far from complete. One example of such interactions comes from intriguing new research on psychosocial pathways and immune function. A growing body of evidence indicates that a variety of psychosocial factors can affect physiological processes with implications for immune function. Since the publication of Selye's (1956) original work delineating physiological responses to stress (primarily through neurohormonal pathways), research from a wide range of disciplines has greatly expanded our knowledge of human physiology and the ways that it can be influenced by social psychological phenomena. In a summary of extensive research demonstrating a connection between physical health and emotional states, Kiecolt-Glaser and colleagues (2002a) conclude that "negative emotions such as depression or anxiety can directly affect the cells of the immune system and either up- or down-regulate the secretion of proinflammatory cytokines" (p. 543).[13] In addition, they note that negative emotions can contribute to prolonged or chronic infections or to delayed wound healing, which in turn indirectly increases the production of these cytokines. For example, transient psychological stress, including that caused by test taking or daily hassles, can decrease immune function (McEwen, 1998; Stone & Bovbjerg, 1994). Chronic stress, such as that arising from caring for a spouse with Alzheimer's disease, also impairs immune function and wound healing (Kiecolt-Glaser, Marucha, Malarkey, Mercado, & Glaser, 1995). Although the samples of these studies are too small for gender comparisons, they constitute a promising direction for future research.

Various possible pathways have been described through which psychological factors affect immune function (Kiecolt-Glaser et al., 2002b). For instance, positive interpersonal relationships seem to improve immune function, whereas discordant relationships seem to have a negative impact. Even though acute and chronic stressors may operate through different physiological pathways, coping resources such as social support mediate the impact of both (Baron, Cutrona, Hicklin, Russell, & Lubaroff, 1990; Cohen & Herbert, 1996). For example, adults with a greater variety of social ties have a lower incidence of and less severe colds – findings that are counterintuitive to a purely biological explanation, which presumes that increased exposure increases risk (Cohen, Doyle, Skoner, Rabin, & Gwaltney, 1997).

Although there is considerable evidence that women tend to be embedded in larger social networks than men, a more recent debate questions how to best measure the type and number of social ties to accurately capture their impact on men's and women's health. In addition, some new work on gender and stress reactivity suggests that women may actually

---

[13] Best known for the role they play in the immune system, cytokines are intercellular chemical messengers released by one cell to regulate the function of another cell. Cytokine production is an indicator of an individual's ability to fight off infection.

respond to stress by "tending and befriending," in contrast to men's tendency to "fight or flight" (Taylor et al., 2000).

WHY DID THE UNDERSTANDING OF GENDER DIFFERENCES IN PHYSICAL HEALTH CHANGE?

As noted above, our understanding of gender differences in men's and women's health has changed dramatically over the past two decades. A variety of reasons accounts for this shift. First and foremost, much of medical research and knowledge was built on an assumption that studies of men were fully generalizable to women, with the exception of issues related to reproductive health and a few other discrete areas known to be affected by hormones. In other words, with few exceptions, for decades it was believed that men's and women's bodies functioned and aged so similarly that findings from studies based exclusively on men would be almost invariably applicable to women (for a discussion of this problem see Tavris, 1992). Therefore, medical research and practice were intentionally based on studies of men to avoid the need to examine samples large enough to account for any variations related to women's menstrual cycles and to avoid inadvertently exposing pregnant women and their fetuses to experimental medical treatments or interventions – by largely excluding women of childbearing age from participation as subjects in medical studies. Ironically, whereas women's fertility was protected at all costs in drug and other clinical trials, little if any attention was ever paid to the potential negative effects on men's fertility nor was serious consideration given to the possibility that experimental treatments on men might lead to birth defects in their offspring (Mastroianni, Faden, & Federman, 1994; Rieker, 1996; Rieker, Fitzgerald, & Kalish, 1990; Rieker et al., 1989).

The women's health movement and women's increasing representation among clinicians, researchers, and policymakers led to the reassessment of these assumptions and the recognition of the need for knowledge regarding the impact of particular treatments on women, specifically when they are pregnant. For example, in the early 1990s the Women's Health Equity Act was passed, and the Food and Drug Administration issued guidelines for the study and evaluation of gender differences in the clinical evaluation of drugs. At the same time, changes in standards for medical practice brought about a new and growing demand for evidence-based guidelines for medical practice built on findings from clinical research. These parallel developments led to breakthroughs in knowledge regarding gender differences in many areas of human biology – forcing shifts across the spectrum in the understanding of the ways in which sex differences have subtle and not so subtle effects on men's and women's health (Institute of Medicine, 2001a, 2001b). The most provocative of these scientific advances led to the development of new interdisciplinary fields, notably in areas related to immunology, and to new insights into the complex interactions between different physiological systems, such as interactions between the central nervous system and the immune system. We discuss some of these scientific advances further in Chapter 7.

REEXAMINING GENDER DIFFERENCES IN MENTAL HEALTH

In contrast to the paradoxical gender differences in physical health, men's and women's overall incidence of mental health problems is similar. However, women experience substantially higher rates of depression than men, whereas men experience higher rates of substance abuse, antisocial behavior, and suicide.

We focus on the gender differences in depression and substance abuse because both their prevalence and lifelong effects create an enormous health burden (Kessler, Berglund, et al., 2003). For example, the World Health Organization (WHO) ranks major depression and substance abuse among the most burdensome diseases in the world (WHO, 2002). Moreover, a growing body of research linking depression with physical health further illustrates the complexity of assessing the antecedents of gender differences in health.

For decades, clinicians, researchers, and even women's rights advocates believed that women suffered from higher rates of mental illness than did men (Cleary, Mechanic, & Greenly, 1982; Dohrenwend & Dohrenwend, 1976, 1977; Gove & Tudor, 1973). However, findings from the 1991 Epidemiologic Catchment Area (ECA) data on the general prevalence of mental disorders revealed that there are no large differences in men's and women's overall rates of major psychological disorders, whether one compares prevalence rates for one month, 6 months, a year, or lifetime (Anthony, Warner, & Kessler, 1994; Kessler et al., 1994; Regier et al., 1993). These findings were confirmed soon after by the National Comorbidity Survey (NCS I), which interviewed members of more than 8,000 households. The first nationally representative mental health study, the NCS found no gender difference in the overall rates of psychological disorder (Kessler et al., 1994; Kessler & Walters, 2002; Narrow, Rae, Robins, & Regier, 2002). As a result, it is now well established that the overall rates of mental health disorders in the United States are similar for men and women.

The discrepancy with respect to prior findings is partly explained by the development of more rigorous research methods and the fact that previous studies focused on rates of depressive and anxiety disorders, which are higher among women, whereas the ECA and the NCS included substance abuse, which is more common among men. Although the rates of specific disorders were consistent with prior studies, the interpretation of the overall gender differences in mental health changed radically in light of new information on the full range of mental health disorders from these population-based studies. As was the case with the Women's Health Initiative HRT trial, the new insights into men's and women's mental health reflected a typical pattern of scientific progress resulting from challenges to prior findings along with the application of more rigorous methods to answer both old and new questions.

The shifts in the understanding of men's and women's risks of depression and cardiovascular disease are examples of the evolution of scientific knowledge. The women's health movement played a central role in creating a political climate in which researchers began to question long-standing assumptions about gender differences. This in turn led to refinements in research methods and a new understanding of the similarities in men's and women's overall mental health.

Depressive Disorders

In the case of depressive disorders, women's rates are between 50 and 100% greater than men's (Gove & Tudor, 1973; Kessler, Berglund, et al., 2003; Kessler & McRae, 1981; Mirowsky & Ross, 1989). These differences occur in both treated and community samples (Nolen-Hoeksema, 1987, 1990). For example, population-based psychiatric surveys in the United States and Britain have found that women are about two-thirds more likely than men to be depressed in both yearly and lifetime estimates (Kessler et al., 1994; Meltzer, Baljit, Petticrew, & Hinds, 1995). The National Comorbidity Survey Replication (NCS-R), a face-to-face interview survey conducted in 2001–2002, substantiated women's higher lifetime rates of major depressive disorder (Kessler, Barker, et al., 2003; Kessler, Berglund, et al., 2003). Kessler and colleagues also reported that less than half of those found to have major depression in the last 12 months received adequate treatment and that severity of role impairment was dependent on illness status rather than on gender. It is now well established that women's higher rates of depression reflect a real gender difference in health, rather than an artifact of help-seeking behavior or willingness to report symptoms (Mirowsky & Ross, 1995; Nazroo, Edwards, & Brown, 1998; Weissman & Klerman, 1977).

Until the recent men's health movement, women's disproportionate depression rates generated the erroneous impression that men were comparatively immune to depression (Courtenay, 2000b). The underdiagnosis of depression in men has been attributed to clinicians' failure to recognize symptoms, men's unwillingness to seek help for such feelings, and their tendency to cope with their feelings through drinking, drug use, and other private activities or actions (Chino & Funabaki, 1984; Nolen-Hoeksema, 1987, 1990). Although studies have documented that men are less likely to seek mental health treatment, when symptoms of depression are acknowledged and diagnosed, both men and women appear to seek treatment (Nazroo, Edwards, & Brown, 1998; Rhodes, Goering, To, & Williams, 2002). In fact, a study by Rhodes and colleagues (2002) of gender differences in the use of outpatient mental health services demonstrated that mood/anxiety-related disorders predicted greater use of services by both men and women.

The gender difference in the prevalence of depression occurs at all ages. The risk for depressive disorders begins to rise in mid-puberty and persists through the mid-fifties; however, the gender gap appears to be the greatest during the reproductive years (Bebbington, 1996; Piccinelli & Wilkinson, 2000). There is some controversy about the determinants of gender differences, as well as a discrepancy between cross-sectional and longitudinal findings regarding the course of depressive disorders. Although men and women do differ in the age and rates of onset (young males have higher rates until early adolescence), cross-sectional studies indicate that, once major depression develops, the course is similar for both genders. For example, some studies attribute gender differences to higher rates of first-onset depression in girls and women rather than more frequent or long episodes (Kessler, McGonagle, Swartz, Blazer, & Nelson, 1993; Wilhelm, Parker, & Hadzi-Pavlovic, 1997). This implies that although women have a higher 12-month prevalence of depression, the gender difference in the United States is largely due to women having a higher risk of first onset. However, several longitudinal studies have reported that girls and women have longer episodes and higher rates of recurrent and chronic depression (Aneshensel, 1985; Ernst & Angst, 1992; Keitner, Ryan, Miller, Kohn, & Epstein, 1991; Kornstein et al., 2000; Sargeant, Bruce, Florio, & Weissmam, 1990; Winokur, Coryell, Keller, Endicott, & Akiskal, 1993). This controversy over the course of illness does not alter the consistently higher lifetime prevalence rates for women or the fact that depressed women also are more likely than are men to have comorbid anxiety (Gregory & Endicott, 1999; Kessler, Berglund, et al., 2003), whereas men are more likely to have comorbid substance abuse or dependence (Endicott, 1998; Kessler, Berglund, et al., 2003). A recent review of research on gender differences in depression concluded that, although some psychosocial risk factors contribute to women's higher rates, the determinants of these differences remain unclear because models combining developmental physiological and psychosocial processes are lacking (Piccinelli & Wilkinson, 2000).

Substance Abuse Disorders

The prevalence of substance abuse disorders by gender is the reverse of that seen for depression. Men have significantly higher rates of alcohol and drug use, abuse, and dependence[14] as well as antisocial behavior disorders

[14] Researchers are careful about the distinction between drug use, abuse, and dependence, with abuse considered a less severe disorder than dependence. Dependence refers to the use of illicit drugs and non-medically used psychotropic drugs.

than do women (Kessler et al., 1994; Regier et al., 1993). Overall, for most substances, a higher proportion of men than women use drugs; the same is true among adolescents. Prevalence rates show that substance use, especially illegal drug use, typically starts in middle to late adolescence and early adulthood, peaks at ages 18–25, and begins to decline after age 34 (Chen & Kandel, 1995; Kandel & Yamaguchi, 1993). The gender difference in prevalence of substance use is smallest among adolescents, increases with age, and varies by type and level of drug use (Kandel, Warner, & Kessler, 1998). Although those who initiate substance use earlier in life are more likely to continue using and to become dependent, not every user in any age group becomes dependent (even with highly addictive substances).

Substance-specific analysis reveals interesting patterns in the degree to which male and female users differ in the rates of developing dependence. There are slight differences between men and women substance users in the risk of developing dependence for tobacco, heroin, and cocaine. For alcohol and marijuana, the rate of lifetime dependence among lifetime users is more than twice as high among men as among women, whereas among non-medical users of psychotropic drugs such as sedatives and tranquilizers, women are significantly more likely than men to develop dependence (Kandel et al., 1998; Substance Abuse and Mental Health Services Administration, 2006).

The National Comorbidity Study (NCS) provides information on the prevalence of lifetime drug dependence disorders (Kessler et al., 1994; Kessler, Nelson, McGonagle, Liu, et al., 1996; Kessler et al., 1997). Dependence is most prevalent with respect to tobacco, a highly addictive but legal substance, followed by alcohol and the illicit drugs. With the exception of tobacco, the dependence rates are considerably higher for men than for women. The alcohol dependence rate is more than twice as high for men as for women (20.1 v. 8.2%), and the illicit drug dependence rate is more than 50% higher (9.2 v. 5.9%). However, once a woman has experimented with an illicit drug, her risk of developing dependence appears to be about 1 in 7.5, and among female smokers, the risk of dependence is close to 1 in 3 (Anthony et al., 1994). Gender differences in dependence among users may be in part due to greater use of alcohol by men and of psychotherapeutics by women or to other biological and environmental factors that vary by drug type.

Extensive comorbidity exists between an illicit drug disorder and alcohol disorder, although it is more likely for those with a drug disorder to have an alcohol disorder than the reverse. The extent of comorbid substance abuse and other psychiatric disorders is very high among both men and women, especially in those with a major depressive disorder (Kessler, Berglund, et al., 2003; Kessler, Nelson, McGonagle, Edlund, et al., 1996). A little more than half (51.4%) of the first NCS respondents with any lifetime substance disorder also meet the lifetime criteria for at least one other psychiatric disorder, and rates are similar among men and women. But the specific disorder pairings reflect the gender-specific distribution of psychiatric disorders in the population. Among women with illicit drug dependence, the rank order of comorbid disorders is anxiety, alcohol, and affective disorders; among men, the rankings for comorbid drug-dependence disorders are alcohol, antisocial personality, and conduct or impulse control disorders (Kandel et al., 1998; Kessler, Barker, et al., 2003). The drug dependence in 79% of both men and women is secondary to at least one other psychiatric disorder. Interestingly, both substance abuse and antisocial behavior are disorders for which men are far less likely than women to use outpatient mental health services, according to Rhodes and colleagues (2002).

WHY DID THE UNDERSTANDING OF GENDER DIFFERENCES IN MENTAL HEALTH CHANGE?

Until the early 1990s, both medical researchers and clinicians assumed that women's higher rate of depression compared to men was indicative of higher overall rates of mental health problems in women, which were attributed to sex-linked biological and hormonal influences. Community and mental health utilization studies, which found higher rates of depression among women, supported the assumption that women had poorer overall mental health (McGrath, Keita, Strickland, & Russo, 1990). In addition, the widely held belief that women generally are more emotional and express their feelings and symptoms more than men was consistent with the explanation that the hormonal basis of the gender differences in depression was at least partly biological. This interpretation was reinforced by evidence that the developmental pathways to depression differed by gender, with women experiencing more preexisting anxiety and men more externalizing disorders such as alcoholism, drug misuse, and antisocial behavior. The prevailing hypotheses involved either hormonal differences or a developmental difference attributable to a combination of as-yet-to-be-identified genes interacting with environmental factors at key developmental stages.

During the same time period, social scientists offered other theoretical and empirical explanations that viewed women's apparent psychological disadvantage as a byproduct of gender inequality (Gove & Tudor, 1973; Nathanson, 1980). For example, Gove and colleagues (Gove, 1972; Gove & Hughes, 1979; Gove & Tudor, 1973) theorized that women's higher rates of depression and mild physical illness were due to restricted gender roles and predominant nurturing, caregiving tasks that negatively affected their mental health, reduced their ability to care for themselves properly, and increased their risk of illness. Because gender differences in psychological distress were found to be greatest among married people, social explanations tended to focus on the negative impact of gender roles within the family (Rieker & Bird, 2000; Rosenfield, 1989).

Consequently, social and psychological studies focused solely on psychosocial explanations of the gender variations in mental and physical health. Rather than questioning the assumption that women had more mental health problems than men overall, they simply attributed the gender difference to women's social and economic disadvantages and greater exposure to stressors associated with their work and family roles.[15] Moreover, during this period the movement calling for women's

[15] In 1977, Weissman and Klerman conducted a thorough review of the biomedical and sociological research on sex differences in depression. They were not convinced there were any creditable data supporting Gove's argument that women's restricted social roles contributed to their excess rates of depression. However, they concluded that the most convincing evidence that social roles are important concerned the data that showed marriage had a protective effect on men's mental health but a detrimental effect for women. They also found indirect support for the hypothesized disadvantage of female roles in experimental work on animals and humans. Those studies demonstrated the negative effects of boredom – a central element of the restricted housewife role.

equal rights dominated the political and social milieu, and, with few exceptions (Rieker & Carmen, 1984), questions were seldom raised by either researchers or activists challenging the prevailing view that men's social and economic advantages and other status privileges protected them from depression and other mental health disorders.

Because social scientists typically focused on the consequences of inequality and injustice, they accepted as a social fact that women's greater depression represented greater emotional disturbance overall and assumed that work and family roles did not harm men's mental health. Some social scientists did argue that men's social roles and the changing definitions of masculinity, brought into question by women's demands for equality, contributed to men's physical health problems, including their overall higher mortality rates (see, for example, Harrison, 1978; Nathanson, 1984; Pleck, 1983, 1984; Pleck & Sawyer, 1974). However, the larger body of research findings from this period were not generalizable to or useful for understanding men's excess rates of particular psychological disorders. That is because prevailing assumptions about gender differences went unchallenged as most researchers focused primarily on the question, "Why are women emotionally disturbed at higher rates than men?" when in fact, as more recent research discussed above has shown, such problems are not more prevalent among women. In other words, the prevailing understanding was based on an inaccurate premise.

Ironically, because the model of the social determinants of depression was built on assessing the impact of female social disadvantage, this model's current form may not be directly applicable to men's excess rates of alcohol and drug dependence. Applying this type of explanation to men's mental health problems would require the development of a conceptual model of men's social role disadvantage. Research in the emerging field of men's studies recognizes that gender roles advantage men in some ways, but disadvantage them in others, and that not all men are equally advantaged nor are all women equally disadvantaged (Cameron & Bernardes, 1998; Harrison, 1978; Kimmel & Messner, 1993; Pleck, 1983; Pleck & Brannon, 1978; Rieker & Bird, 2000, 2005; Sabo & Gordon, 1995). By exploring how gender expectations shape men's lives, their choices, opportunities, and health-related lifestyles, research in this area offers a basis for a social model to explain male excess rates of specific mental health disorders, such as alcohol and substance abuse and other antisocial behaviors.[16]

More recent work by Courtenay (2000a, 2000b) and others has begun to reexamine the role of masculine identities in the development of men's unhealthy and risky behaviors and subsequent mental and physical health problems. For example, Courtenay (2000a) argues that, although the precise standards of masculinity are ambiguous in our society, men's denial of depression and unwillingness to seek treatment are the means through which they demonstrate manliness and avoid being stigmatized by what is considered a predominantly female problem. Other research on men's mental health has focused on stressors to which men are either more exposed or potentially more vulnerable, such as those in the workplace and in the military (Connell, 1987; Levant & Pollack, 1995; Sabo & Gordon, 1995). For instance, combat duty and clergy sexual abuse, which continue to be more common for men and boys, put them at risk for posttraumatic stress disorder (PTSD), whereas physical and sexual abuse remains the most likely PTSD risk factor for women (Rieker & Carmen, 1984).[17] In contrast, the stress associated with unemployment can differ depending on one's options and constraints. In this case, women may frequently have access to more socially acceptable roles including caregiver and housewife, which are more highly stigmatized for men and may therefore lead to greater stress or simply deter men from considering or accepting these roles.

Men's health studies can also contribute to theories that explain both male and female psychological health and illness and the ways these gender patterns vary across race, class, and ethnicity. Thus, although men's greater use of substances is well substantiated, the reasons for their greater use are less well understood or addressed.

---

[16] See also the 1988, 1991, and 1995 publications and reports from the National Surveys of Adolescent Males available at www.socio.com/srch/summary/aids/aid09-10.htm and http://www.urban.org/url.cfm?ID=900460, downloaded September 21, 2007.

[17] Although both combat duty and exposure to sexual abuse are PTSD risk factors for both men and women, their exposure rates differ by gender. However, women's increasing presence in combat roles and a growing recognition of the prevalence of sexual abuse of boys by clergymen may be narrowing these long-standing differences.

PREVAILING EXPLANATIONS FOR THE PARADOXICAL GENDER DIFFERENCES IN HEALTH AND LONGEVITY

Due in large part to differences in paradigms that define the subject matter and theoretical frameworks for interpreting health data, the vast majority of researchers have focused on either exclusively biological or exclusively social explanations. Consequently, no adequate explanation currently exists for the paradoxical gender differences in health.

Biological Explanations

Physical Health. Biological explanations of women's greater longevity emphasize the health advantages that accrue from different hormones and physiological systems that facilitate pregnancy and childbirth. These biological advantages have long been hypothesized to contribute to women's greater longevity by lowering their risk of coronary heart disease prior to menopause. However, results from several recent clinical trials of HRT are challenging that assumption (Fletcher & Colditz, 2002; Rossouw et al., 2002). In addition, the hypothesized advantages are not consistent with women's higher morbidity compared to men. In other words, even if all the biological differences between men and women had developed to allow women to bear children, these differences would not necessarily also provide women with greater life expectancy.

Moreover from a biological perspective, women's fortuitous advantage in life expectancy seems inconsistent with their higher rates of morbidity. One could more easily imagine that evolutionary selection factors would produce strong women whose ability to bear children also provided advantages in terms of both morbidity and mortality. Such evolutionary arguments build from the premise that natural selection favors individuals who produce more offspring, as their genes are more highly represented in subsequent generations of members of a species. The theory of natural selection, and its impact on the prevalence and distribution of specific genes, is at the core of biology. Although the evidence supporting explanations of the effects of natural selection on survival through reproductive ages is strong, the evidence is much weaker when it comes to explaining differences in men's and women's longevity well beyond prime reproductive age.[18] Moreover, the strong pursuit to identify the genetic basis of disease (and for some scientists, all behavior) has influenced funding agencies, medical schools, and the general public to once again view biological factors as a primary source of disease and the basis for treatment (Link, 2003; Nelkin & Lindee, 2000; Wheaton, 2001). Still, purely biological explanations fall short of fully explaining the gender paradox of morbidity and mortality.

Mental Health. Numerous interdisciplinary biomedical studies reveal interactions among the cardiovascular system, immune functioning, and psychological processes (see, for example, Hemingway & Marmot, 1999; Kiecolt-Glaser et al., 2002b; Lovallo, 1997). For example, considerable evidence links clinically diagnosed major depression and increased mortality in general, and CVD in particular. Although these studies do not show that depression is a predictor of mortality per se, symptoms of depression are associated with poor health and functional status, as well as increased disability, health care utilization, and cost of health services. A number of well-controlled studies have linked both serious depression and depressive symptoms with the increased incidence of CVD. For example, a 13-year prospective study showed a 4.5 times greater risk of a heart attack among those with major depression (Pratt et al., 1996), and in another study mortality was 4 times higher among depressed heart attack patients (Frasure-Smith, Lesperance, & Talajic, 1995). A recent prospective study of a large cohort of white women aged 67 or older found that depressive symptoms were associated with increased rates of cardiovascular mortality (Whooley & Browner, 1998).

Depression is also associated with both immune function and disease severity by magnifying pain and disability (Staats, 1999). Pain

---

[18] Suffice it to say that human life expectancy has exceeded the age of menopause for far too few generations to provide a evolutionary biological explanation of why it occurs or why current differences in life expectancy favor women. In fact, although biological explanations can be extrapolated to provide explanations for why men can reproduce throughout the life-span whereas women's average life-span now exceeds their reproductive years by several decades, most such extensions take into account the ways that humans shape their environment and at least allow for a large role of culture in shaping differences in men's and women's lives.

and depression can amplify each other; pain increases heart rate and blood pressure, enhances secretion of stress-related hormones including catecholamines and cortisol, and deregulates a range of immunologic activities (Kiecolt-Glaser, Page, Marucha, MacCallum, & Glaser, 1998). Moreover, in light of the interesting data on gender differences in the prevalence of autoimmune disorders, the new research on negative emotional states and immune function needs to explore gender patterns as well (Kiecolt-Glaser et al., 2002a, 2002b; Seeman, Singer, Rowe, Horwitz, & McEwen, 1997). As these studies suggest, gender differences in mental health may contribute in unknown ways to gendered patterns of physical health (McDonough & Walters, 2001) and vice versa.

Social Explanations

The increasing evidence of the multiple connections between various physiological systems and biological processes begs the question of whether and how the social organization of men's and women's lives contributes to gender differences in health.

Physical and Mental Health. At the opposite extreme, purely social explanations of both physical and mental health emphasize men's and women's social position and their differential access to protective resources (including income, education, and safe parks and other areas in which to exercise), as well as their exposure to a range of environmental factors that negatively affect health (including exposure to toxins and to social and behavioral risk factors, such as domestic violence, crime, smoking, and poor diet). Social position mediates access to the positive and negative social and environmental factors that occur at the individual, household, community, and society levels. For example, gender differences in income may result from a variety of factors over the life course, including social-role-related expectations and activities, occupational choice, opportunities for employment and advancement, and work-related skills and experience, as well as access to job benefits including health insurance, pensions, and other retirement income. Moreover, women are more likely to be single parents and thus have a lower income per capita. Although the impact of income on health would be expected to be the same for men and women, the levels of income may vary by gender for a variety of reasons other than the job one currently has or pay inequity. For example, welfare and income entitlements such as Social Security are in fact tied to both one's own employment and income history and that of one's spouse.

Other risk and protective factors may differ by gender in both exposure and their impact on health. For example, toxin exposure may be related to patterns of employment and social roles (e.g., asbestos exposure leading to mesothelioma, industrial or household use of pesticides or other chemicals, or exposure to second-hand smoke). In other words, gender differences in occupations and in the division of labor in the family affect the types of toxin exposure for which men and women are most at risk. Furthermore, exposure to a specific toxin may result either in somewhat different rates of the same problems (e.g., lung cancer) or in different health problems for men and women (e.g., breast or prostate cancer). Moreover, other resources that vary on average by gender, such as education, may provide additional knowledge, opportunity, and income with which to avoid many risk factors. Clearly, the distribution and use of toxins are regulated by social policy, but so too are protective resources such as education.

Sociological theory offers insight into women's greater morbidity and the gendered patterns of psychological disorders. But for the most part, sociologists and other social scientists have not examined the biological antecedents of gender differences in either mortality or the types and prevalence of diseases.

Social Inequalities and Health. Research on social determinants has concentrated on socioeconomic position as the "fundamental social cause" and has focused on a causal chain whereby unequal distribution of social and economic resources and related variation in exposure to stress lead to health disparities (Berkman & Kawachi, 2000; House & Williams, 2000; Link & Phelan, 1995; Marmot & Wilkinson, 1999). Moreover, applying the implicit logic of disadvantage, a majority of mental health studies have concentrated on explaining women's higher levels of depression, but not men's higher levels of substance abuse and antisocial behaviors. Thus, sociological explanations of gender differences in health examine variation in gender roles and identities, the ways in which racial and socioeconomic inequality contributes to differences in men's and women's exposure to stressors, the meaning and impact of particular stressful events and coping resources, and the physical and psychological consequences of each of these factors.

Social inequality affects gender differences in health, but models of inequality and health disparities are not sufficient to address paradoxical gender differences in health (Rieker & Bird, 2005). Although these factors are critical to understanding racial/ethnic and socioeconomic variation in morbidity and mortality among men and women, they cannot fully explain women's greater longevity and men's earlier deaths, and they only partially explain women's pattern of greater morbidity relative to men. This topic is discussed more fully in Chapter 2.

THE MISSING ELEMENTS

As shown in this chapter, neither social nor biological theories alone offer substantial insight into the paradoxical complexities of gender differences in health. Indeed, there are consequences to assuming as a matter of theory or of convenience that either biology (inherent sex differences) or social factors (socially constructed gender differences) are the primary determinants of health status. While most investigators acknowledge that factors outside their research area have some effects on health, there is a tendency to consider those contributions to be relatively inconsequential. Whether one assumes or proposes an extreme view or acknowledges that the world is more complex, the consequences of oversimplification remain the same. For example, most biologists and geneticists acknowledge that the environment shapes genetic expression and that species and individuals also shape their environment, but their research rarely tests both of these assumptions simultaneously. If oversimplification leads researchers to misspecify their theoretical models of health, they may attribute observed male/female ratios in diseases to differences in vulnerability rather than to exposure and thereby delay or overlook research that could lead to advances in prevention and treatment that would benefit both men and women. A failure to explore the sources of differences in men's and women's health leaves gaps in knowledge as to where to intervene most efficiently. For example, by focusing only on the biological explanations for gender differences, most research implies that the best points for intervention are medical treatments at the individual level, overlooking the possibilities for more systematic social interventions to improve the health of the population.

Lest it seem that these are straw man arguments designed to illustrate a long-settled controversy, one has only to look to the debates within psychology and neurobiology regarding the social and biological explanations of men's and women's physiological responses to stress (see, for example, Cacioppo et al., 2002).[19] Well-researched academic books and journal articles offering competing arguments are published with great regularity, supporting one side or the other in the debates as to whether social or biological factors explain differences between men and women on a wide range of health outcomes (including cardiovascular functioning, immune response, depression, and substance abuse). Parallel debates regarding the nature of gender differences are ongoing across numerous health-related fields of research. Furthermore, many researchers study gender differences from within one perspective without acknowledging or ever participating in debates arising from competing explanations proposed by other disciplines.[20]

---

[19] In addition to having differential exposure to particular types of stressors, men and women also differ in the types of stressors that produce physiological responses such as increases in stress hormones and cardiovascular reactivity. Although men and women experience the same range of emotions, particular stressors affect them differently and appear to lead to different emotional and physiological responses. For example, although men have been found to have more pronounced cardiovascular reactivity than women in response to a variety of tasks (Lawler, Wilcox, & Anderson, 1995; Light, Turner, Hinderliter, & Sherwood, 1993; Vogele, Jarvis, & Cheeseman, 1997), one study found that men reacted to an achievement challenge (mental arithmetic) but not to social alienation (verb disagreements), whereas women exhibited the opposite pattern (Stroud, Salovey, & Epel, 2002). Experimental studies suggest that men and women may experience different physiological responses to particular situations, such as public speaking or solving math problems vs. interpersonal conflict.

[20] Specialization within disciplines is a logical consequence of the continual increase in knowledge within and across academic fields, allowing researchers to keep up with the developments within their own area of research. Although the practice of scientific discipline-based specialization was not designed either to ignore the work of researchers in other fields or to hinder cross-disciplinary work, in reality it creates substantial barriers to such work and leads to fragmented knowledge. Whereas specialization within disciplines generates many refined lines of research and knowledge much like the production of multiple threads, weaving the threads together adds to their value by creating whole cloth.

Clearly, many elements are still missing in our theories and research of gender health differences. First, there are no integrated social and biological explanations of these gender differences. Second, the interactions between physical and mental health are not well understood. Third, there is no comprehensive social framework for considering the influence of multiple levels of social factors on gender differences in health.

In the remaining chapters of this book, we propose such a social framework and explore the connections between processes at each of a variety of levels and their impact on men's and women's health. Our ultimate goal is to encourage cross-disciplinary work among social and biomedical researchers so we can arrive at an integrated social and biological explanation for gender health differences.

References

American Heart Association (AHA). (2003). *Heart Disease and Stroke Statistics – 2004 Update*. Dallas, TX: American Heart Association.

American Medical Association. (2000). *Women's health: Sex and gender-based differences in health and disease*. Paper presented at the 2000 AMA Interim Meeting. Available at http://www.ama-assn.org/ama/pub/category/13607.html, accessed September 10, 2007 (see especially p. 5).

Aneshensel, C. (1985). The natural history of depressive symptoms. *Res Comm Ment Health, 5*, 45–74.

Anthony, J. C., Warner, L. A., & Kessler, R. C. (1994). Comparative epidemiology of dependence on tobacco, alcohol, controlled substances, and inhalants: Basic findings from the National Comorbidity Survey. *Exp Clin Psychopharmacol, 2*, 244–268.

Barbour, M. (2000). Hormone replacement therapy should not be used as secondary prevention for coronary heart disease. *Pharmacotherapy, 20*(9), 1021–1027.

Baron, R. S., Cutrona, C. E., Hicklin, D., Russell, D. W., & Lubaroff, D. M. (1990). Social support and immune function among spouses of cancer patients. *J Pers Soc Psychol, 59*(2), 344–352.

Bebbington, P. (1996). The origins of sex differences in depressive disorder: Bridging the gap. *Int Rev Psychiatry, 8*, 295–322.

Berkman, L. F., & Kawachi, I. (2000). *Social Epidemiology*. Oxford: Oxford University Press.

Bird, C. E., & Rieker, P. P. (1999). Gender matters: An integrated model for understanding men's and women's health. *Soc Sci Med, 48*(6), 745–755.

Brittle, Christine, & Chloe E. Bird. (2007). *Literature Review on Effective Sex- and Gender-Based Systems/Models of Care*. Prepared for the U.S. Dept. of Health and Human Services. Offices on Women's Health. Purchase

Order # HHSP233200600978P. Available at: <http://www.4women.gov/owh/pub/ genderbased.cfm>, downloaded September 18, 2007.

Cacioppo, J. T., Berntson, G. G., Taylor, S. E., & Schacter, D. L. (2002). *Foundations in Social Neuroscience.* Cambridge, MA: MIT Press.

Cameron, E., & Bernardes, J. (1998). Gender and disadvantage in health: Men's health for a change. *Soc Health Ill, 20*(5), 673–693.

Canto, J. G., Every, N. R., Magid, D. J., Rogers, W. J., Malmgren, J. A., Frederick, P. D., et al. (2000). The volume of primary angioplasty procedures and survival after acute myocardial infarction. National Registry of Myocardial Infarction 2 Investigators. *N Engl J Med, 342*, 1573–1580.

Centers for Disease Control (CDC). (2000). Division of Vital Statistics. *National Vital Statistics Report, 48*(11).

Centers for Disease Control and Prevention, National Center for Health Statistics. (2007). Compressed Mortality File 1979–1998 Archive. CDC WONDER On-line Database, compiled from CMF 1968–1988, Series 20, No. 2A, 2000 and CMF 1989–2000, Series 20, No. 2C 2001. Accessed at http://wonder.cdc.gov/cmf-icd9-archive1998.html on September 19, 2007.

Centers for Disease Control and Prevention, National Center for Health Statistics. (2007). Compressed Mortality File 1999–2002 Archive. CDC WONDER On-line Database, compiled from CMF 1999–2003, Series 20, No. 2I 2006. Accessed at http://wonder.cdc.gov/cmf-icd10-archive2003.html on September 19, 2007.

Chen, K., & Kandel, D. B. (1995). The natural history of drug use from adolescence to the mid-thirties in a general population sample. *Am J Pub Health, 85*, 41–47.

Chino, A. F., & Funabaki, D. (1984). A cross-validation of sex differences in the expression of depression. *Sex Roles, 11*, 175–187.

Cleary, P. D., Mechanic, D., & Greenly, J. R. (1982). Sex differences in medical care utilization: An empirical investigation. *J Health Soc Behav, 23*, 106–119.

Cohen, S., Doyle, W. J., Skoner, D. P., Rabin, B. S., & Gwaltney Jr., J. M. (1997). Social ties and susceptibility to the common cold. *JAMA, 277,* 1940–1944.

Cohen, S., & Herbert, T. B. (1996). Health psychology: Psychological factors and physical disease from the perspective of human psychoneuroimmunology. *Annu Rev Psychol, 47*, 113–142.

Connell, R. W. (1987). *Gender and Power.* Stanford, CA: Stanford University Press.

Courtenay, W. H. (2000a). Behavioral factors associated with disease, injury, and death among men: Evidence and implications for prevention. *J Men's Studies, 9*(1), 81–142.

Courtenay, W. H. (2000b). Constructions of masculinity and their influence on men's well-being: A theory of gender and health. *Soc Sci Med, 50*, 1385–1401.

Crimmins, E. M., Kim, J. K., & Hagedorn, A. (2002). Life with and without disease: Women experience more of both. *J Women Aging, 14*(1/2), 47–59.

Dohrenwend, B. P., & Dohrenwend, B. S. (1976). Sex differences and psychiatric disorders. *Am J Soc, 81*, 1147–1154.

Dohrenwend, B. P., & Dohrenwend, B. S. (1977). Reply to Gove and Tudor's Comment on "Sex Differences and Psychiatric Disorders." *Am J Soc, 82*, 1336–1345.

Endicott, J. (1998). Gender similarities and differences in the course of depression. *J Gend Specif Med, 1*(3), 40–43.

Ernst, C., & Angst, J. (1992). The Zurich Study, XII: Sex differences in depression: Evidence from longitudinal epidemiological data. *Eur Arch Psychiatry Clin Neurosci, 241,* 222–230.

Fletcher, S. W., & Colditz, G. A. (2002). Failure of estrogen plus progestin therapy for prevention. *JAMA, 288*(3), 1–7.

Frasure-Smith, N., Lesperance, F., & Talajic, M. (1995). Depression and 18-month prognosis after myocardial infarction. *Circulation, 91,* 999–1005.

Gan, S. C., Beaver, S. K., Houck, P. M., MacLehose, R. F., Lawson, H. W., & Chan, L. (2000). Treatment of acute myocardial infarction and 30-day mortality among women and men. *N Engl J Med, 343*(1), 8–15.

Goldberg, N. (2002). *Women Are Not Small Men: Life-Saving Strategies for Preventing and Healing Heart Disease in Women.* New York: Ballantine Books.

Gove, W. (1972). The relationship between sex roles, mental illness, and marital status. *Soc Forces, 51*(1), 34–44.

Gove, W., & Hughes, M. (1979). Possible causes of the apparent sex differences in physical health: An empirical investigation. *Am Soc Rev, 44,* 126–146.

Gove, W., & Tudor, J. (1973). Adult sex roles and mental illness. *Am J Soc, 78,* 812–835.

Grady, D., Applegate, W., Bush, T., Furberg, C., Riggs, B., et al. (1998). Heart and estrogen/progestin replacement study (HERS): Design, methods and baseline characteristics. *Control Clin Trials, 19,* 314–335.

Gregory, T., & Endicott, J. (1999). Understanding depression in women. *Patient Care, 33*(19), 19–20.

Grossman, C. J., Rosell, G. A., & Mendenhall, C. L. (1991). Sex steroid regulation of autoimmunity. *J Steroid Biochem Mol Biol, 40*(4–6), 649–659.

Harrison, J. (1978). Warning: The male sex role may be dangerous to your health. *J Soc Issues, 34*(1), 65–86.

Hegde, U. C. (1991). Immunomodulation of the mother during pregnancy. *Med Hypotheses, 35*(2), 159–164.

Hemingway, H., & Marmot, M. (1999). Psychosocial factors in the aetiology and prognosis of coronary heart disease: Systematic review of prospective cohort studies. *Br Med J, 318,* 1460–1467.

House, J. S., & Williams, D. R. (2000). Understanding and explaining socioeconomic and racial/ethnic disparities. In B. D. Smedley & S. L. Syme (Eds.), *Promoting Health: Intervention Strategies from Social and Behavioral Health* (pp. 81–124). Washington, DC: National Academy Press.

Howard, B. V., Van Horn, L., Hsia, J., Manson, J. E., Stefanick, M. L., Wassertheil-Smoller, S., et al. (2006). Low-fat dietary pattern and risk of cardiovascular disease: The Women's Health Initiative Randomized Controlled Dietary Modification Trial. *JAMA, 295*(6), 655–666.

Hulley, S., Grady, D., & Bush, T. for the Heart and Estrogen/progestin Replacement Study (HERS) Research Group. (1998). Randomized trial of estrogen plus progestin for secondary prevention of coronary heart disease in postmenopausal women. *JAMA, 280,* 605–613.

Institute of Medicine. (2001a). *Exploring the Biological Contributions to Human Health: Does Sex Matter?* Washington, DC: National Academy Press.

Institute of Medicine. (2001b). *Health and Behavior: The Interplay of Biological, Behavioral and Societal Influences.* Washington, DC: National Academy Press.

Kandel, D. B., Warner, L. A., & Kessler, R. C. (1998). The epidemiology of substance use and dependence among women. In C. L. Wetherington & A. B. Roman (Eds.), *Drug Addiction Research and the Health of Women. NIDA Research Monograph* (pp. 105–130). Rockville, MD: National Institute of Drug Abuse.

Kandel, D. B., & Yamaguchi, K. (1993). From beer to crack: Developmental patterns of drug involvement. *Am J Pub Health, 83,* 851–855.

Keitner, G. I., Ryan, C. E., Miller, I. W., Kohn, R., & Epstein, N. B. (1991). 12-month outcome of patients with major depression and comorbid psychiatric or medical illness (compound depression). *Am J Psychiatry, 148,* 345–350.

Kessler, R. C., Barker, P. R., Colpe, L. J., Epstein, J. F., Gfroerer, J. C., Hiripi, E., et al. (2003). Screening for serious mental illness in the general population. *Arch Gen Psychiatry, 60*(2), 184–189.

Kessler, R. C., Berglund, P., Demler, O., Jin, R., Koretz, D., Merikangas, K. R., et al. (2003). The epidemiology of major depressive disorder: Results from the National Comorbidity Survey Replication (NCS-R). *JAMA, 289*(23), 3095–3105.

Kessler, R. C., Crum, R. M., Warner, L. A., Nelson, C. B., Schulenberg, J., & Anthony, J. C. (1997). Lifetime co-occurrence of DSM-III-R alcohol abuse and dependence with other psychiatric disorders in the National Comorbidity Survey. *Arch Gen Psychiatry, 54,* 313–321.

Kessler, R. C., McGonagle, K. A., Swartz, M., Blazer, D. G., & Nelson, C. B. (1993). Sex and depression in the National Comorbidity Survey 1: Lifetime prevalence, chronicity and recurrence. *Br J Psychiatry, 168,* 17–30.

Kessler, R. C., McGonagle, K. A., Zhao, S., Nelson, C. B., Hughes, M., Eshleman, S., et al. (1994). Lifetime and 12-month prevalence of DSM-III-R psychiatric disorders in the United States: Results from the National Comorbidity Survey. *Arch Gen Psychiatry, 51*(1), 8–19.

Kessler, R. C., & McRae, J. A. (1981). Trends in the relationship between sex and psychological distress: 1957–1976. *Am Soc Rev, 46,* 443–452.

Kessler, R. C., Nelson, C. B., McGonagle, K. A., Edlund, M. J., Frank, R. G., & Leaf, P. J. (1996). The epidemiology of co-occurring addictive and mental disorders: Implications for prevention and service utilization. *Am J Orthopsychiatry, 66,* 17–31.

Kessler, R. C., Nelson, C. B., McGonagle, K. A., Liu, J., Swartz, M., & Blazer, D. G. (1996). Comorbidity of DSM-III-R major depressive disorder in the general population. *Br J Psychiatry, 168,* 17–30.

Kessler, R. C., & Walters, E. E. (2002). The National Comorbidity Survey. In M. T. Tsuang & M. Tohen (Eds.), *Textbook in Psychiatric Epidemiology* (pp. 243–262). New York: John Wiley & Sons.

Kiecolt-Glaser, J. K., Marucha, P. T., Malarkey, W. B., Mercado, A. M., & Glaser, R. (1995). Slowing of wound healing by psychological stress. *Lancet, 346*(8984), 1194–1196.

Kiecolt-Glaser, J. K., McGuire, L., Robles, T. F., & Glaser, R. (2002a). Emotions, morbidity, and mortality: New perspectives from psychoneuroimmunology. *Annu Rev Psychol, 53*, 83–107.

Kiecolt-Glaser, J. K., McGuire, L., Robles, T. F., & Glaser, R. (2002b). Psychoneuro-immunology: Psychological influences on immune function and health. *J Cousult Clin Psychol, 70*(3), 537–547.

Kiecolt-Glaser, J. K., Page, G. G., Marucha, P. T., MacCallum, R. C., & Glaser, R. (1998). Psychological influences on surgical recovery. Perspectives from psychoneuroim-munology. *Am Psychol, 53*(11), 1209–1218.

Kimmel, M. S., & Messner, M. A. (1993). *Men's Lives*. New York: Macmillan.

Kornstein, S. G., Schatzberg, A. F., Thase, M. E., Yonkers, K. A., McCullough, J. P., Keitner, G. I., et al. (2000). Gender differences in chronic major and double depres-sion. *J Affect Disord, 60*(1), 1–11.

Lawler, K. A., Wilcox, Z. C., & Anderson, S. F. (1995). Gender differences in patterns of dynamic cardiovascular regulation. *Psychosom Med, 57*, 357–365.

Legato, M. (2002). *Eve's Rib: The Groundbreaking Guide to Women's Health*. New York: Three Rivers Press.

Legato, M., & Coleman, C. (1991). *The Female Heart*. New York: Simon & Schuster.

Levant, R. F., & Pollack, W. S. (1995). *A New Psychology of Men*. New York: Basic Books.

Light, K. C., Turner, J. R., Hinderliter, A. L., & Sherwood, A. (1993). Race and gender comparisons: I. Hemodynamic responses to a series of stressors. *Health Psychol, 12*(5), 354–365.

Link, B. G. (2003). The production of understanding. *J Health Soc Behav, 44*, 457–469.

Link, B. G., & Phelan, J. (1995). Social conditions as fundamental causes of disease. *J Health Soc Behav* (Extra Issue), 80–94.

Lockshin, M. D., Gabriel, S., Zakeri, Z., & Lockshin, R. A. (1999). Gender, biology and human disease: Report of a conference. *Lupus, 8*(5), 335–338.

Lovallo, W. R. (1997). *Stress and Health: Biological and Psychological Interactions*. Thousand Oaks, CA: Sage Publications.

Marmot, M., & Wilkinson, R. G. (1999). *Social Determinants of Health*. Oxford: Oxford University Press.

Mastroianni, A. C., Faden, R., & Federman, D. (1994). *Women and Health Research: Ethical and Legal Issues of Including Women in Clinical Studies*. Washington, DC: Institute of Medicine. National Academy Press.

McDonough, P., & Walters, V. (2001). Gender and health: Reassessing patterns and explanations. *Soc Sci Med, 52*, 547–559.

McEwen, B. S. (1998). Protective and damaging effects of stress mediators. *N Engl J Med, 338*(3), 171–179.

McGrath, E., Keita, G. P., Strickland, B., & Russo, N. F. (1990). *Women and Depression: Risk Factors and Treatment Issues*. Washington, DC: American Psychiatric Associ-ation.

Meltzer, H., Baljit, G., Petticrew, M., & Hinds, K. (1995). *Prevalence of Psychiatric Morbidity Among Adults Living in Private Households*. London: HMSO.

Mirowsky, J., & Ross, C. E. (1989). *Social Causes of Psychological Distress*. New York: Aldine De Gruyter.

Mirowsky, J., & Ross, C. E. (1995). Sex differences in distress: Real or artifact? *Am Soc Rev, 60*, 449–468.

Narrow, W. E., Rae, D. S., Robins, L. N., & Regier, D. A. (2002). Revised prevalence estimates of mental disorders in the United States. *Arch Gen Psychiatry, 59*, 115–123.

Nathanson, C. A. (1980). Social roles and health status among women: The significance of employment. *Soc Sci Med, 14*, 463–471.

Nathanson, C. A. (1984). "Sex Differences in Mortality." *Annual Review of Sociology, 10*, 191–213.

National Academy of Sciences. (2003). *Report from the Committee on Assessing the Need for Clinical Trials of Testosterone Replacement Therapy*. Washington, DC: Institute of Medicine.

National Center for Health Statistics (NCHS). (2002). *Health United States*. Hyattsville, MD: US Public Health Service.

National Center for Health Statistics (NCHS). (2003). *Health United States*. Hyattsville, MD: US Public Health Service.

National Center for Health Statistics (NCHS). (2006). *Health United States, 2005*. Hyattsville, MD: US Public Health Service.

Nazroo, J. Y., Edwards, A. C., & Brown, G. (1998). Gender differences in the prevalence of depression: Artefact, alternative disorders, biology or roles? *Soc Health Ill, 20*(3), 312–330.

Nelkin, D., & Lindee, S. (2000). The DNA mystique: The gene as a cultural icon. In P. Brown (Ed.), *Perspectives in Medical Sociology* (pp. 406–424). Prospect Heights, IL: Waveland Press.

Nolen-Hoeksema, S. (1987). Sex differences in unipolar depression: Evidence and theory. *Psychol Bull, 101*(2), 259–282.

Nolen-Hoeksema, S. (1990). *Sex Differences in Depression*. Stanford, CA: Stanford University Press.

Nothnick, E. B. (2001). Treating endometriosis as an autoimmune disease. *Fertil Steril, 76*(2), 223–231.

Nurses' Health Study (2007). Available from http://www.channing.harvard.edu/nhs/, downloaded September 18, 2007.

Office for Research on Women's Health. (1992). *Report of the National Institutes of Health: Opportunities for Research on Women's Health* (No. 92–3457). Hunt Valley, MD: U.S. Department of Health and Human Services.

Pampel, F. C. (2002). Cigarette use and the narrowing sex differential in mortality. *Popul Devel Rev, 28*(1), 77–104.

Pearlin, L. (1989). The sociological study of stress. *J Health Soc Behav, 30*(3), 241–256.

Pearlin, L., Leiberman, M. A., Menaghan, E. G., & Mullan, J. T. (1981). The stress process. *J Health Soc Behav, 22*(4), 337–356.

Physicians' Health Study. Available from http://phs.bwh.harvard.edu; accessed September 5, 2006.

Piccinelli, M., & Wilkinson, G. (2000). Gender differences in depression. Critical review. *Br J Psychiatry, 177*, 486–492.

Pleck, J. H. (1983). *The Myth of Masculinity*. Cambridge, MA: MIT Press.

Pleck, J. H. (1984). Men's power with women, other men, and society: A men's movement analysis. In P. P. Rieker & E. H. Carmen (Eds.), *The Gender Gap in Psychotherapy: Social Realities in Psychological Processes* (pp. 79–90). Cambridge, MA: Perseus Publishing.

Pleck, J. H., & Brannon, R. (1978). Male roles and the male experience: Introduction. *J Soc Issues, 34*, 1–4.

Pleck, J. H., & Sawyer, J. (1974). *Men and Masculinity*. Englewood Cliffs, NJ: Prentice-Hall.

Pratt, L. A., Ford, D. E., Crum, R. M., Armenian, H. K., Gallo, J. J., & Eaton, W. W. (1996). Depression, psychotropic medication, and risk of myocardial infarction. Prospective data from the Baltimore ECA follow-up. *Circulation, 94*(12), 3123–3129.

Prentice, R. L., Caan, B., Chlebowski, R. T., Patterson, R., Kuller, L. H., Ockene, J. K., et al. (2006). Low-fat dietary pattern and risk of invasive breast cancer: The Women's Health Initiative Randomized Controlled Dietary Modification Trial. *JAMA, 295*(6), 629–642.

Preston, S. H., & Wang, H. D. (2002). Sex mortality differences in the United States: The role of cohort smoking patterns. *Demography, 43*(4), 631–646.

Rathore, S. S., Berger, A. K., Weinfurt, K. P., Feinleib, M., Oetgen, W. J., Gersh, B. J., et al. (2000). Race, sex, poverty, and the medical treatment of acute myocardial infarction in the elderly. *Circulation, 102*(6), 642–648.

Regier, D. A., Narrow, W. E., Rae, D. S., Manderscheid, R. W., Locke, B. Z., & Goodwin, F. K. (1993). The de facto US mental and addictive disorders service system: Epidemiological Catchment Area 1-year prevalence rates of disorders and services. *Arch Gen Psychiatry, 50*, 85–94.

Rhodes, A. E., Goering, P. N., To, T., & Williams, J. I. (2002). Gender and outpatient mental health service use. *Soc Sci Med, 54*, 1–10.

Rieker, P. P. (1996). How should a man with testicular cancer be counseled and what information is available to him? *Semin Urol Oncol, 14*(1), 17–23.

Rieker, P. P., & Bird, C. E. (2000). Sociological explanations of gender differences in mental and physical health. In C. E. Bird, P. Conrad, & A. M. Fremont (Eds.), *The Handbook of Medical Sociology* (5th ed., pp. 98–113). Englewood Cliffs, NJ: Prentice-Hall.

Rieker, P. P., & Bird, C. E. (2005). Rethinking gender differences in health: What's needed to integrate social and biological perspectives. *J Gerontol: Soc Sci, 60B*, 40–47.

Rieker, P. P., & Carmen, E. H. (1984). *The Gender Gap in Psychotherapy: Social Realities and Psychological Processes*. New York: Plenum Press.

Rieker, P. P., Fitzgerald, E. M., & Kalish, L. A. (1990). Adaptive behavioral responses to potential infertility among survivors of testis cancer. *J Clin Oncol, 8*(2), 347–355.

Rieker, P. P., Fitzgerald, E. M., Kalish, L. A., Richie, J. P., Lederman, G. S., Edbril, S. D., et al. (1989). Psychosocial factors, curative therapies, and behavioral outcomes: A comparison of testis cancer survivors and a control group of healthy men. *Cancer, 64*(11), 2399–2407.

Rosenfield, S. (1989). The effects of women's employment: Personal control and sex differences in mental health. *J Health Soc Behav, 30*, 77–91.

Rossouw, J. E., Anderson, G. L., Prentice, R. L., LaCroix, A. Z., Kooperberg, C., Stefanick, M. L., et al. (2002). Risks and benefits of estrogen plus progestin in healthy postmenopausal women: Principal results from the Women's Health Initiative Randomized Controlled Trial. *JAMA, 288*(3), 321–333.

Sabo, D., & Gordon, D. F. (1995). Rethinking men's health and illness. In D. Sabo & D. F. Gordon (Eds.), *Men's Health and Illness: Gender, Power and the Body* (pp. 1–21). Thousand Oaks, CA: Sage Publications.

Sargeant, J. K., Bruce, M. L., Florio, L. P., & Weissmam, M. M. (1990). Factors associated with 1-year outcome of major depression in the community. *Arch Gen Psychiatry, 47*, 519–526.

Seeman, T. E., & McEwen, B. S. (1996). Impact of social environment characteristics on neuroendocrine function. *Psychosom Med, 58*(5), 459–471.

Seeman, T. E., McEwen, B. S., Singer, B. H., Albert, M. S., & Rowe, J. W. (1997). Increase in urinary cortisol excretion and memory declines: MacArthur studies of successful aging. *J Clin Endocrinol Metab, 82*(8), 2458–2465.

Seeman, T. E., Singer, B. H., Rowe, J. W., Horwitz, R. I., & McEwen, B. S. (1997). Price of adaptation – allostatic load and its health consequences. MacArthur studies of successful aging. *Arch Intern Med, 157*(19), 2259–2268.

Selye, H. (1956). *The Stress of Life*. New York: McGraw-Hill.

Staats, P. S. (1999). Pain, depression and survival. *Am Fam Physician, 60*(1), 42, 44.

Stampfer, M. J., Willett, W. C., Colditz, G. A., Rosner, B., Speizer, F. E., & Hennekens, C. H. (1985). A prospective study of postmenopausal estrogen therapy and coronary heart disease in U.S. women. *N Engl J Med, 313*, 1044–1049.

Steering Committee of the Physicians' Health Study Research Group, Belanger, C., Buring, J. E., Cook, N., Eberlein, K., Goldhaber, S. Z., et al. (1989). Final report on the aspirin component of the ongoing Physicians' Health Study. *N Engl J Med, 321*, 129–135.

Stone, A. A., & Bovbjerg, D. H. (1994). Stress and humoral immunity: A review of the human studies. *Adv Neuroimmunol, 4*(1), 49–56.

Stroud, L. R., Salovey, P., & Epel, E. S. (2002). Sex differences in stress responses: Social rejection versus achievement stress. *Biol Psychiatry, 52*(4), 318–327.

Substance Abuse and Mental Health Services Administration. (2006). *Results from the 2005 National Survey on Drug Use and Health: National Findings* (No. SMA 06–41194). Rockville, MD: Office of Applied Studies.

Taubes, G. (2007a). Do we really know what makes us healthy? *New York Times Magazine*. September 16, 52–59, 74, 78, 80.

Taubes, G. (2007b). *Good Calories, Bad Calories: Challenging the Conventional Wisdom on Diet, Weight Control and Disease*. New York: Knopf.

Tavris, C. (1992). *The Mismeasure of Women: Why Women Are Not the Better Sex, the Inferior Sex, or the Opposite Sex*. New York: Simon & Schuster.

Taylor, S. E., Klein, L. C., Lewis, B. P., Gruenewald, T. L., Gurung, R. A., & Updegraff, J. A. (2000). Biobehavioral responses to stress in females: Tend-and-befriend, not fight-or-flight. *Psychol Rev, 107*(3), 411–429.

Thaul, S., & Hotra, D. (1993). *Committee to Review the NIH Women's Health Initiative.* Washington, DC: Institute of Medicine.

United Nations. (2000). *The World's Women 2000 – Trends and Statistics.* New York: United Nations.

United Nations. (2005). *The World's Women 2005 – Trends and Statistics.* New York: United Nations.

Vaccarino, V., Krumholz, H. M., Yarzebski, J., Gore, J. M., & Goldberg, R. J. (2001). Sex differences in 2-year mortality after hospital discharge for myocardial infarction. *Ann Intern Med, 134*(3), 173–181.

Verbrugge, L., & Wingard, D. L. (1987). Sex differentials in health and mortality. *Women Health, 12*(2), 103–145.

Vogele, C., Jarvis, A., & Cheeseman, K. (1997). Anger suppression, reactivity, and hypertension risk: Gender makes a difference. *Ann Behav Med, 19*, 61–69.

Weissman, M. M., & Klerman, G. L. (1977). Sex differences in the epidemiology of depression. *Arch Gen Psychiatry, 34*(1), 98–111.

Wheaton, B. (2001). The role of sociology in the study of mental health. *Am Soc Rev, 55*, 209–223.

Whooley, M. A., & Browner, W. S. (1998). Association between depressive symptoms and mortality in older women. *Arch Int Med, 158*, 2129–2135.

Wilhelm, K., Parker, G., & Hadzi-Pavlovic, D. (1997). Fifteen years on: Evolving ideas in researching sex differences in depression. *Psychol Med, 27*, 875–883.

Winokur, G., Coryell, W., Keller, M., Endicott, J., & Akiskal, H. (1993). A prospective follow-up of patients with bipolar and primary unipolar affective disorder. *Arch Gen Psychiatry, 50*, 456–465.

World Health Organization. (2002). *The WHO Report: Reducing Risks, Promoting Healthy Life.* Geneva: World Health Organization.

Writing Group for the Women's Health Investigators. (2002). Risks and benefits of estrogen plus progestin in healthy postmenopausal women: Principal results from the Women's Health Initiative Randomized Controlled Trial. *JAMA, 288*, 321–333.

TWO

Gender and Barriers to Health

Constrained Choice in Everyday Decisions

In the previous chapter, we concluded that something was missing from
the variety of ways in which scientists have tried to make sense of the
perplexing gender differences in physical and mental health. Although
current biological and social explanations are plausible when taken separately, neither are sufficient to explain the observed gender-based health
variations. Instead, we contend that to explain these gender differences,
models of health determinants need to be modified to include the concept of constrained choice; that is, the many ways in which decisions
made and actions taken at the family, work, community, and government levels differentially shape the health-related choices of men and
women.

This chapter sets the stage for the remainder of our book. First we
explore why current models of racial/ethnic and socioeconomic inequality do not adequately explain observed gender differences in health. Then
we introduce our framework for explaining these differences from the
innovative sociological perspective of constrained choice. This framework is meant to shed light on how decisions by different social groups –
from governments to employers and families – influence the extent to
which individuals incorporate health into a broad array of everyday
choices. Last, we review sociological theories of rational action that provide insight into health behavior.

By introducing the concept of constrained choice, we aim to address
two central questions in the complex scenario of gender and health
differences: (1) *What keeps men and women from making health an*

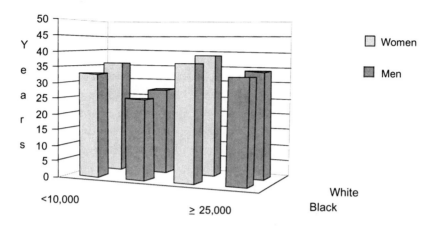

Figure 2.1. Life Expectancy at Age 45 by Gender, Race, and Family Income. *Source:* National Center for Health Statistics, *Health United States 1998*; Hyattsville, MD: U.S. Public Health Service 1998, p. 152

everyday priority? and (2) *What factors contribute to the differences in men's and women's choices?*

DOES INEQUALITY EXPLAIN THE PARADOXICAL GENDER DIFFERENCES IN HEALTH?

Some social scientists argue that models of inequality can explain many if not all observed gender differences in health. Clearly, racial/ethnic and socioeconomic health disparities contribute to, and in some cases interact with, the gender differences. However, as shown in Chapter 1, a growing body of research indicates that the complexity of gender differences in health extends beyond narrow concepts of the relative disadvantage or advantage of men's and women's biology or the social organization of their lives. Consequently, to understand what aspects of the broader array of differences in men's and women's lives and their physiology contribute to the morbidity/mortality paradox, we need a model that takes into account factors other than inequality of resources, discrimination, and other unfair treatment.

Although gender differences in morbidity and mortality vary across racial/ethnic and socioeconomic groups, they persist within these groups. For example, as shown in Figure 2.1, a gender difference in life expectancy at age 45 occurs in all groups, although women's advantage is larger for those with lower household incomes and for blacks than whites.

Explanations of racial/ethnic and socioeconomic disparities focus in large part on the multiple and cumulative consequences of poverty and discrimination (Bruner & Marmot, 1999; House & Williams, 2000; King & Williams, 1995; Link & Phelan, 1995; Smaje, 2000). Although social inequality does affect gender differences in health, models of inequality and health disparities are not sufficient to address the observed paradoxical gender differences either within or across countries. For example, such factors as poverty and discrimination, although critical to understanding racial/ethnic and socioeconomic variation in morbidity and mortality among men and women (Williams, 2002, 2003), cannot fully explain women's greater longevity and men's earlier deaths, and they only partially explain women's pattern of greater morbidity relative to men.

Furthermore, some aspects of racial/ethnic and socioeconomic explanations of health disparities do not apply to gender differences. In particular, because neighborhoods are segregated by race/ethnicity and by income, an examination of neighborhood-level segregation can provide considerable insight into related health disparities. However, this approach is inadequate for examining the contribution of race/ethnicity and socioeconomic status to gender differences in health because neighborhoods are not segregated along gender lines. Consequently, analyses of neighborhood-level and even household-level resources and characteristics do not capture a large proportion of the differences in men's and women's lives.

Unlike racial/ethnic and socioeconomic disparities in health, men's and women's social and economic needs can and do differ in part because of biological and longevity differences in their lives. For example, because women are more likely to become single parents, to be caregiver to an aging spouse, to be widowed, and to live well into their eighties and beyond, they have different social and economic needs and thus may not be served equally well by social policies designed to ignore these differences. In fact, a wide range of social and economic policies, including but not limited to those directly aimed at public health and health care, can create or exacerbate differences in health status and behaviors between gender groups, as they do with racial/ethnic and economic groups (see, for example, Graham, 2004).

In some ways, assessing the wide array of gender differences in health, rather than focusing only on those attributable to disparities, is more difficult because many of the pathways involved are comparatively opaque and have been studied less.

WHAT IS MISSING FROM CURRENT MODELS OF SOCIAL DETERMINANTS OF HEALTH?

One of the most influential sociological perspectives on health focuses on social position, including the unequal distribution of social and economic resources, and the related variation in exposure to stress as a "fundamental cause" of health disparities (see, for example, Berkman & Kawachi, 2000; House & Williams, 2000; Link & Phelan, 1995; Marmot & Wilkinson, 1999). However, viewing gender as a fundamental cause sheds little light on how social factors contribute to the gender health paradox, including whether and how they affect or interact with biological processes.

We cannot simply substitute gender for race/ethnicity or socioeconomic status (SES) in existing models because they are not constructed to capture the complex ways in which men and women are advantaged and disadvantaged in both mortality and morbidity. Such models are based on the implicit hypothesis that the health effects produced by inequality and discrimination go in the same direction for biological and social factors. Although most models of social determinants of health incorporate biological processes, only recently have researchers begun to assess these factors simultaneously. In the case of racial/ethnic and socioeconomic disparities, the issue is how to parcel out the social and biological antecedents, assuming they do not confound each other, as may well occur with gender differences in either morbidity or mortality. For example, on the face of it, men's general economic advantages would not likely explain their earlier mortality compared to women (although SES partially explains the mortality difference between white and African American men [Williams, 2003]).

If social factors contribute to gender in ways that extend beyond inequality, models of gender differences need to capture the specific processes and pathways that lead to health outcomes. Although researchers have examined some of the pathways through which social factors might differentially affect men's and women's health (including positive and negative health behaviors, exposure to stressors, and coping styles), for the most part this approach has not been used to explain gender differences in health. Notable exceptions include studies by Taylor and colleagues (2000) of how and why men and women respond differently to particular types of stressors, and assessments by Ross (2000) of the extent to which fear of crime differentially affects men's and women's exercise.

Our proposed model of constrained choice addresses these missing elements in current models of inequality and health disparities. Constrained choice provides a comprehensive social framework for considering the influence of multiple levels of social factors, including individual agency or choice, on gender differences in health. Specifically, it incorporates contextual effects at the levels of family, community, and social policy in ways that extend beyond models of gender inequality and inequity. Further, our framework also facilitates the broader integration of social and biological processes to achieve a better understanding of differences in men's and women's health.

CONSTRAINTS ON CHOICE IN EVERYDAY LIFE

Clearly, individuals make deliberate choices that affect their health, such as whether or not to smoke. However, we contend that a wide variety of decisions and actions by governments, states, communities, employers, and families can also influence health and gender differences in health, both directly and indirectly, by constraining individual choices to varying degrees. Although many of the constraints and their consequences for individual choice are similar for men and women, their health impact will vary somewhat due to gender differences in biology and life experiences.

Consider the following vignette, which illustrates some of the dynamics of constrained choice that we discuss in this chapter:

Susan and John are in their early forties. They met in graduate school. Susan works in a public health agency, and John is a manager in a Fortune 500 company. John's position was the best opportunity for him, but Susan's job was not her first choice. Married for 9 years, they are the proud parents of 6-year-old David, a first grader, and 2-year-old Katy, who attends a day care center near home. They bought a house in a middle-class neighborhood, even though the mortgage stretches their budget and safety is still a concern. Susan and John chose their neighborhood because of its good schools, but lately they have become concerned since the state has cut the budget for education 2 years in a row, and the community has stopped passing school bonds. Consequently, the schools put on numer-ous fundraising activities throughout the year, and the families are asked to make sizeable donations in addition to the periodic requests for con-tributions toward supplies for their children's classroom. The couple is also concerned that the state has cut the school health budget, and many schools now face losing their school nurse.

John drops the kids off at school and day care before his 30-minute commute to work. Susan picks them up after work. Even though this adds another 15 minutes to Susan's normal 20-minute commute, it gives her an opportunity to talk with the caregivers at Katy's preschool and at David's after-school program. Because neither Susan nor John has family in the area, they lack the backup that grandparents can often provide for school vacation days or when one of the kids is sick. Furthermore, neither employer offers on-site day care or sick-child care.

With a few exceptions, Susan and John are fairly healthy. He has border-line high blood pressure and cluster headaches. She has a family history of breast cancer that concerns her, and she often doesn't get enough sleep, in part because of son David's mild asthma that frequently keeps him up at night. Both John and Susan resolved to lose some weight this year and start making exercise a higher priority. In fact, their health care plan pro-vides a modest incentive to defray the cost of a health club membership. John works out at a club near work a couple of times a week on his lunch hour or after work, except when things get busy, as they frequently do. Susan does aerobics at the community center near their home a couple of times a month, when it doesn't conflict with school-related functions or meetings for one of the children.

Like most of their friends, Susan and John have enough income to cover expenses, but not much left over after paying for child care and so on. They share most of the housework and child care – or try to. They would like to change their diet, but neither has the time to cook, so they eat prepared foods a couple of nights a week and order pizza on Fridays.

They try to see friends once a month for a meal, which is usually take-out or delivered.

Susan and John are reconsidering where to live. They bought their current home hoping the city would soon extend a light rail line that would cut John's commute in half and make it easier for him to get to the gym before or after work. But the city government has postponed building the rail line. Susan and John are discussing moving closer to John's work, even though the schools are better where they are now. If they do move, however, they won't be able to afford a similar home in a better neighborhood.

John's parents are healthy, but Susan's mother died of breast cancer 2 years ago, and her dad is not doing well. He has a small pension, but even with Social Security and Medicare, he can't keep up with the bills. John and Susan are discussing the possibility of moving him closer to them or in with them. They hadn't planned for this and don't have an extra bedroom to easily accommodate him without giving up the dining room or one of the children's bedrooms.

On a day-to-day basis, Susan and John's main concerns are about their kids and balancing the budget, not their health or even where to live. Both Susan and John want to spend more time with their children. John would like to attend David's soccer games, but he often has to work on the weekends. Similarly, Susan's job as a health educator requires her to work more evenings than she would like. They both recognize that the demands of work and family are affecting their overall well-being. It's not that Susan and John haven't discussed ways to make their lives easier or more workable, such as the changes they would have to make to reduce their work hours. However, they are concerned about the resulting tradeoffs between their current health and family needs and the potential financial demands – including their children's education and possibly helping to pay for elder care – looming in their future.

Susan and John's situation lays out a host of questions about the multiple factors that affect their health and constrain their choices regarding health behaviors. Although many of these factors may affect Susan and John similarly, each experiences some of them differently, in part, because of differences in their gender roles. Other gender differences may also exist in their exposure to particular stressors, including what they are asked to do for others and their sense of responsibility for managing and balancing work and family.

EVERYDAY LIFE DECISIONS

To better understand the implications of constrained choice for men's and women's health, consider the range and types of decisions that Susan and John (and many other young families) are currently facing:

- *Decisions about neighborhood and housing*

Where to live; whether to relocate near better schools or closer to work; opportunities to exercise outdoors; neighborhood safety; whether to get a larger home with space for elderly or ill parents, etc.

- *Decisions about jobs*

Do one or both spouses work, how much, which jobs, and with what income and benefits; what are the tradeoff costs in terms of stress, unpredictability, demand/control, hours, occupational/industry hazards, security or lack thereof, degree of physical activity, availability of nutritious food during the workday, coworkers' health behaviors, etc.

- *Decisions about raising and caring for their children*

Which schools and day care arrangements; how to divide child care at home and household labor; will both parents work outside the home and, if so, how and to what extent are career and job choices made to accommodate family life, etc.

- *Decisions about family income*

How to use disposable income; proportion of income directed to savings (for retirement, college, etc.); whether to increase income by working more or reduce work hours and learn to live on less, etc.

- *Decisions about intergenerational support*

Whether to accept/provide help (financial or otherwise) from/to another generation; if doing so, how to transfer income or other resources, including caregiving, among generations (grandparents, parents, children); etc.

Such decisions are constrained to varying extents by a variety of factors – ranging from time and money to the options available at a particular decision point and the tradeoffs required to pursue a particular choice – each of which, in turn, may be shaped by larger social policies. Obviously for those having difficulty making ends meet, earning enough money to put food on the table and pay the rent or mortgage becomes a higher priority than exercise, stress reduction, or getting sufficient sleep.[1]

We assume that people have the opportunity and ability to make choices that affect their day-to-day lives and, in many ways, the course of their lives. Like Susan and John, individuals and couples make a myriad of choices every day that affect their health directly or indirectly, such as what occupation to pursue, what foods to eat, and whether to participate in healthy or dangerous leisure activities. Although maintaining one's health is theoretically a universal goal, making health a high priority is a luxury that comes after meeting competing goals, including earning an adequate income, finding a safe neighborhood, and having sufficient time and energy to meet the demands of being a worker, a spouse, and a parent.

A variety of factors at the societal and community levels influence individual choices. For example, a recession or a decline or an expansion in an industry or occupation may affect when and how often an individual is either pushed or drawn to reconsider his or her employment choices and options. The context may also determine the extent to which the individual considers, either in the short or long term, the health implications of making or reconsidering such an employment choice. For example, increased employment opportunities may allow a person the opportunity to make health a higher priority as part of an effort to improve his or her quality of life (for example, by changing careers or reducing work hours). In contrast, decreased employment opportunities or resources may lead an individual to make choices (for example, giving up a health

---

[1] We have deliberately chosen a middle-class family as an example to illustrate that the need to balance multiple and often conflicting demands on one's time and energy is not restricted to a particular minority of the population, such as those with low incomes or elder care responsibilities. However, the burdens and health consequences of such competing demands are likely to be greater for single parents regardless of gender. Because more women than men experience single parenthood, this can lead to the kind of gender health disparities addressed in our book.

club membership) that drop health to a lower priority, at least in the short run. In reality, priorities are often reevaluated and reordered for a number of reasons that may or may not be under an individual's control, ranging from a change in preferences or circumstances to a life-changing event such as the death of a spouse.

Typically, individuals have both implicit and explicit priorities. It is a given that individuals construct choices out of their priorities and values, some of which are acquired through their upbringing, location, customs, religion, and so on.[2] However, choices do not take place in a vacuum. Rather, both choices and priorities are shaped by the context(s) in which they are formulated and made. This is a dynamic process in which a person may have occasional or frequent opportunities to revisit a particular choice or set of priorities. Consequently, scholars, researchers, and the general public often do not recognize the many links between the choices men and women make, the constraints they face, and the cumulative impact those choices have on their mental and physical well-being.

TOWARD A SOCIOLOGY OF CONSTRAINED CHOICE

Our concept of constrained choice is illustrated in Figure 2.2, which shows three levels of organizational contexts that influence men's and women's lives, as well as how decisions at each of these levels can individually and collectively impinge on the opportunities of individuals and groups to choose health. We are not posing constrained choice as a deviation from an idealized notion of "free" choice. Rather, we are describing a process by which choices are made – choices that can differentially affect the health of men and women. Moreover, the connections between broader social contexts and individual choices on which we are focusing are rarely transparent, and their health consequences are often underestimated and frequently overlooked.

Specifically, gender differences in the constraints contribute to health disparities, directly and indirectly, by affecting both men's and women's choices and their exposure to stressors and other risk factors that affect

---

[2] In some cases, an individual's values or priorities may be so strong that he or she perceives few if any options and little opportunity for choice.

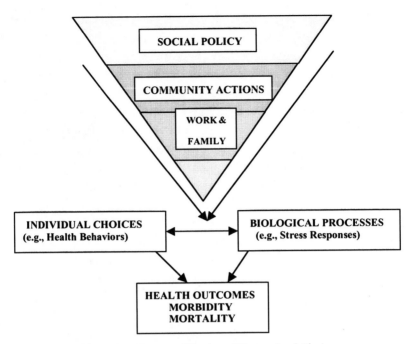

Figure 2.2. Conceptualization of Constrained Choice.

their biological processes, which in turn lead to differential health outcomes. Such effects could occur through gender differences in exposure to role-related chronic stressors; for example, caring for a chronically ill family member, which can ultimately exacerbate stress reactivity leading to dysregulation and dysfunction in both cardiovascular and immune responses. Constrained choices may also affect positive and negative health behaviors and coping styles that affect both psychological and physical functioning.

We argue that men's and women's opportunities and choices are to a certain extent constrained by decisions and actions taken by families, the organizations in which people work, communities, and governmental policies.[3] Here we briefly introduce the three levels of organizational

---

[3] The Institute of Medicine's Committee on Assuring the Health of the Public in the 21st Century produced a more elaborated model of the range of social and biological factors that affect health (Institute of Medicine, 2003). More recent work by Glass and

contexts that influence men's and women's lives and constrain choice.[4]
Each level is described more fully in the ensuing chapters.

Social Policy

Although a given social policy or decision at any level does not necessarily
aim to constrain choices in ways that affect health or men and women
differently, many do so. For example, Social Security is primarily intended
as a safety net to keep older adults out of poverty, but for those with the
least means it has a larger impact on the affordability of a good diet and a
safe place to live and the ability to meet other basic needs that have health
consequences. Social Security, like other policies, faces a double-edged
sword of whether to treat men and women the same or to address their
differential needs. Because of women's lower wages and greater longevity,
they pay less into Social Security and subsequently receive lower payments
over a substantially longer average life-span.

Just as individuals and families must create budgets, all governments,
regardless of per capita income levels, must grapple with how to set priorities and allocate resources regarding the public's health and welfare.
Clearly, as part of that agenda, societies need and want to design public
health and other policies, including but not limited to health care utilization, that positively affect health and reduce risk behaviors. In this
priority-setting process, tradeoffs are often made between the public
good and individual rights and benefits. For example, antismoking policies aimed at improving public health intentionally constrain individual
choices related to smoking behavior. We explore the health impact of
social policies in greater detail in Chapter 3.

McAtee (2006) provides a detailed theoretical discussion and offers a framework for
integrating the natural and behavioral sciences into the study of behavior and health.

[4] Our description of constrained choice in some ways is consistent with H. Simon's (1982,
1997b) discussion of "bounded rationality." Bounded rationality refers to rational
choices that take place under limitations of both knowledge and cognitive capacity and
that shape the possible alternatives one perceives. Although his mathematic models of
the factors that limit the extent to which an actor can make a fully rational decision
were applied to industrial organizations (H. Simon, 1997a) rather than the personal
behavior we are addressing, Simon recognized that an individual would be unable to
know all the alternatives or the consequences that follow each decision.

Community Actions

We use the term "communities" to refer to both social networks of relationships with family, friends, and acquaintances at home and at work
and the physical environment in which one lives. Communities differ in
the extent to which they minimize or exacerbate daily hassles. Just as we
see with John and Susan, social and physical environments affect the ease
or difficulty that men and women face in meeting the demands of specific
roles. Because of gender differences in role activities and role expectations, men and women differ in their exposure to specific daily hassles,
which in turn affects their stress levels. For instance compared to men,
women make more trips to engage in shopping and other household-
sustaining activities, and women with children are more likely to "chain"
these trips with travel to and from work (McGuckin & Murakami, 1999).
Thus, both gender role demands and community context affect the stress
associated with getting to and from work.

Just as individuals differ in their social and economic resources, so
do communities. Those with more closely knit neighborhoods, more
trust among neighbors, better schools, and better policing are safer and
healthier places to live. Such resources are referred to as social capital. In
places with less trust and fewer resources there are easier access to liquor
stores (Truong & Sturm, 2007) and higher rates of violence, including
more homicide among men and higher rates of violence against women
(Sampson, Raudenbush, & Earls, 1997). As a result, men and women
differ in the extent to which they feel comfortable and safe walking outdoors and exercising in their neighborhoods. Thus, their willingness to
engage in certain health behaviors is in part a function of the community
in which they live. We explore the health impact of community actions
in greater detail in Chapter 4.

Work and Family Level

The structure of the family and the structure of work have undergone
massive changes in recent decades. Such continual change produces what
Mirowsky and Ross (1989) refer to as a cultural lag, whereby men's and
women's social roles and expectations have not kept pace with changing

opportunities and demands. As a result, expectations for occupational and family roles create what for many, at least at times, are irreconcilable objectives. Furthermore, there are no models for how to resolve conflicting and competing demands either as individuals or as families and no framework for how to choose health in this evolving context. Consequently, every day brings about a myriad of decisions about how to balance competing and even conflicting priorities and related negotiations at home and in the workplace. This is clearly seen in the lives of Susan and John, who have innumerable decisions to make about work and family within the larger contexts of what resources and barriers exist in their communities. While adding children to the mix brings rewards, it adds considerable complexity.

We are also affected by the culture of our workplace, including relationships with coworkers. Some occupations and work environments encourage healthy behaviors such as exercising; others unintentionally promote destructive behaviors such as smoking, poor diet, or excess alcohol consumption. In addition, the culture of one's workplace sets expectations regarding the hours one will work and the possibilities of balancing work and family. A workplace that demands long hours will place greater strain on those who have more demands at home, which is more common for women than men. Such a culture also increases the costs and consequences of achieving success at work by reducing the possibility of balancing work and family. This in turn increases the costs for one's career of taking on greater responsibilities at home through entering parenthood or becoming a caregiver to another family member. These demands shape men's and women's choices regarding work and family. Thus, because gender roles differ, the effect of workplace cultures affects men's and women's experience of time pressure and their stress levels differently. We explore the health impact of work and family life in greater detail in Chapter 5.

ARE PEOPLE ACTING IRRATIONALLY WHEN THEY DON'T MAKE HEALTH A PRIORITY?

Current models of health behavior, including economic theories of rational behavior and the psychological health beliefs model, imply that people act irrationally when they make life choices that are not good for their health in the long run.

However, recognizing the constraints and the context of everyday decisions made by individuals reveals how such choices and behavior can be understood to be rational, even if they do not appear to be consistent with people's priorities. The fact that choices are constrained is not intended to suggest that individuals are not responsible for their actions. The vignette describing Susan and John's life shows how both are consciously and unconsciously making daily tradeoffs between engaging in healthy behaviors and meeting other priorities. They may behave rationally in choosing to grab a quick but not nutritious breakfast and to work through lunch, even if these choices are not consistent with their intention to make health a priority. It is well established that an individual's knowledge of the general benefits of engaging in particular health behaviors does not predict whether he or she will act on that knowledge. However, his or her choices may partially reflect how cognizant the individual is of the precise short-term and long-term health consequences of specific actions.

Under different circumstances, an individual may have more or fewer opportunities to chose health and thus to take responsibility for their own health. Some choices are more urgent and consequential than others. One can imagine several circumstances in which an individual has few degrees of freedom with regard to choosing health. In an extreme case, a person's health status – for example, having a severe chronic illness such as ulcerative colitis that necessitates an elaborate medical regimen – may require the individual to consciously choose health in almost every decision throughout every day of his or her life. In another case, a moderately healthy person's life circumstances – for example, unemployment due to downsizing – may significantly constrain his or her opportunities to chose either to reduce exposure to health risks or to engage in protective behaviors.

Sociological Theories of Rational Action

Economists have addressed the larger issues of what constitutes rational behavior or action, but recently several sociologists have questioned whether economic theory offers the only model for understanding health behavior. In his essay "Beyond Rational Choice Theory," Raymond Boudon (2003) argues that health behaviors generally depend on an individual's beliefs, which are shaped both by cognitive perceptions and social context. Social actors attempt to act in congruence with their reasons, beliefs, and attitudes. In fact, strongly held beliefs may produce rational and even altruistic choices based on valuing something above or beyond the direct costs and benefits to the individual. Therefore, he contends that sociologists need a broader notion of instrumental rationality to understand health behavior than is offered by the powerful framework of Rational Choice Theory (RCT) that underlies so many explanations of social behaviors and other phenomena (see also H. Simon, 1997a, 1997b).

As Boudon states, there are no general criteria of rationality: "Rationality is one thing; (the) expected utility (of a particular action) is another." Thus, reasons dealing with cost and benefits should not be given more attention than they deserve. Moreover, he contends that rational choices must not be confused with efficient ones, as making a series of rational choices will not necessarily win a game or leave one in a tenable position. Nor are rational actions necessarily wise or effective in achieving one's desired outcomes.

Rational Choice Theory argues that individuals choose the best option for achieving their objectives and that such "instrumental" choices and actions are rational. However, we recognize that the reasoning of an individual man, woman, family, community, or policymaking body – although rational – may not be instrumental and thus may not lead them to an effective option for achieving their objective. Yet, RCT assumes that any social phenomenon, which broadly defines all social interactions and instrumental choices, is the outcome of rational actions by one or more individuals.

As an alternative to RCT, Boudon proposes a Cognitive Theory of Action (CTA). This model assumes that an action can be explained by (1) its meaning to the actor and (2) his or her perception of the strength of the underlying system of reasoning that made the action meaningful. For example, in our vignette, being a good mother has meaning to Susan, and therefore she engages in actions that she perceives as consistent with being a good mother. If she reasoned that exercising was critical to her having the energy to be able to be a good mother, this would increase the likelihood that she would make the tradeoffs necessary to have time to exercise regularly (or even religiously). Boudon would argue that, for Susan, the meaning of being a good mother and the actions that she reasons follow from that meaning could be instinctual or normative, common or uncommon, and descriptive or prescriptive.

We recognize that choices made by families, communities, and governments are similarly constrained and value laden. In contrast, RCT equates the choices of such groups with a process of rationing resources and typically assumes that everyone makes priorities based on the same values.

Therefore, a sociological theory is needed to explain how such choices may rely on or consist of something other than rationing. Here, we draw on the theoretical work of Donald W. Light and David Hughes that distinguishes a sociology of choice from economic arguments, which portray resource allocation decisions as an inevitable form of rationing. In their essay, "A Sociological Perspective on Rationing: Power, Rhetoric and Situated Practices," Light and Hughes (2001) challenge an economic model of equating choices with rationing, and they question whether this is the only way to define the process of choosing how to allocate resources. Light and Hughes discuss whether and how policymakers (and the general public) weigh options in light of potential health consequences and whether those involved perceive this process as rationing health care. Given that not all people have the same values and priorities, Light and Hughes question why these choices are defined as rationing, arguing that it would be more fruitful to view the process as "a form of collective planning that suppresses individual choice." Thus, whether group decisions by families, communities, and governments are viewed as collective actions or specifically as a form of rationing, they do to some extent constrain individual choices (in both intended and unintended ways).

In contrast to Light and Hughes, in this book we focus on understanding how and why rational men and women make, on average, somewhat different choices, many of which can affect their health to varying degrees. Clearly, a rational individual will not necessarily always make choices that maximize his or her health. In fact, most choices we make in everyday life are probably made based on the availability of other resources – for example, time and money – against a background of priorities and competing demands.

Attaching Meaning to Circumstances, Events, and Roles

The sociology of constrained choice provides a means for understanding how individuals have agency (the ability to act on their own behalf) and are rational actors with competing demands and limited resources that shape their choices. Individuals typically make what they perceive to be the best choices they can within the constraints they face. So even if health is a high priority, acting in concordance with their priorities may not result in healthy behaviors.

Individual agency evolves out of the way in which individuals and groups assign meaning to the costs, benefits, and stresses associated with particular options and the tradeoffs involved in pursuing those options. For example, a group of parents all of whom rank education as a high priority might chose very different types of schools for their children based on what education means to them. To a particular parent, what constitutes an ideal education may include a specific peer group (elite or culturally diverse) or specific types of training or skills (such as a specialized, liberal arts, or religious curriculum).

Social scientists and philosophers have examined how people ascribe meaning to events and circumstances in their lives and especially to their social roles. For example, a growing body of work in psychology and sociology examines the ways in which meanings attributed to life events shape their impact on the individual. Although meaning derives in large part from wider cultural values, it also varies across cultural subgroups including, but not limited to, those defined by religion, race, ethnicity, sexual preferences, and citizenship status.

One source of gender differences is the meaning that men and women attach to particular events and social roles, including changes in those roles and the perceived value or anticipated long-term consequences of both the roles and the transitions. For instance, what it means to be divorced affects both one's choices and efforts to attain or avoid this event and the psychological consequences of this particular change in status. Although men and women largely share the meanings of social roles such as spouse, parent, and employee, there are important gender differences in the perceived benefits and costs of each of these roles. For example, for men, being a good breadwinner is both consistent with and part of being a good spouse and parent (R. W. Simon, 1995, 1997). In contrast for women, being a good worker in a demanding job may at times be in conflict with being a good spouse and parent, particularly when a child is ill. Thus, mothers are more likely to feel stressed and guilty both about not being able to be with a sick child and being distracted at work. Over time, experiences of stress and unremitting role conflict can affect both physical and mental health.

Research on meaning also suggests that negative events that are more normative (in some sense more common) are somewhat less stressful; events may become normative either because of timing or prevalence. For example in the industrialized world, it is normal to outlive one's parents, but neither normal nor common to do so at a young age. Likewise, in some countries with lower life expectancy it is far more common to face the death of a young child. This in no way detracts from the meaning of the experience, but may make it more likely to be anticipated, understood, and shared with others who have faced the same negative (undesirable) event.

The meaning attached to changes in circumstances or status that have the greatest impact on central components of one's identity or sense of self is most likely to lead to a reformulation of priorities. Becoming a parent and entry into or exit from other salient roles are obvious examples. For instance, researchers have shown that for cancer survivors, what matters most in recovering their pre-illness identity is the meaning they attach to the disease and associated symptoms and their ability to resume prior social roles (Rieker, Fitzgerald, & Kalish, 1990; Taylor, 1989). Achieving this equilibrium depends on whether they interpret the disease and its consequences as an assault on their sense of self and thus perceive themselves to be "damaged goods," or whether they are able to construct a narrative that makes sense of the traumatic events and to reestablish an identity that incorporates it. In resuming normal roles, cancer survivors often perceive the opportunity to reorder their priorities (i.e., to make healthy lifestyle choices a top priority) as a positive outcome arising from the negative event of the life-threatening illness (see Rieker, Fitzgerald, & Kalish, 1990; Taylor, 1989).

Priorities often change because the meaning of things changes following a personal event, such as the death of a friend, or a societal event, such as the country entering a war or the September 11, 2001, terrorist attacks that destroyed the World Trade Center. A dramatic change in economic or political conditions may lead to a demographic event, such as a wave of marriages or births, or a shift in people's perceptions of their safety or security in the world both at home and abroad. These events in turn may alter people's priorities and behavior regarding travel; for many, the events lead to an increased interest in spending more time with family or taking better care of their health, at least in the short run.

CONTEXT OF EVERYDAY CHOICES

The factors that lead to decision points and shape priorities include experiences and events that are not limited to the individual. Context can refer to many different levels, including a wide array of factors that shape individual experiences and lives. Context ranges from immediate family dynamics or circumstances to the state of the economy and international relations. In this book, we focus on three specific levels of social context – society, community, and work and family – that can influence individual health behavior. In Chapter 3, we examine the larger social, economic, and health care policies that shape and modify gender differences in quality of life. In Chapter 4, we consider the ways in which community factors (including policies enacted by state and local government regarding employment, transit, zoning, housing stock, parks, and recreation) affect men's and women's choices and their incentives and disincentives to choose health. Next, in Chapter 5, we examine how work and families contribute to differences in men's and women's health through gender roles, the allocation of resources and responsibilities, and opportunities to choose health behaviors. We consider individual choices in Chapter 6, where we assess the most proximal factors that have traditionally been examined to understand health and risk behaviors and an individual's exposure to particular risks and stressors, including individual social and economic resources, occupational hazards, and health behaviors.

References

Berkman, L. F., & Kawachi, I. (2000). *Social Epidemiology*. Oxford: Oxford University Press.

Boudon, R. (2003). Beyond rational choice theory. *Ann Rev Sociol, 29*, 1–21.

Bruner, E., & Marmot, M. G. (1999). Social organization, stress, and health. In M. G. Marmot & R. G. Wilkinson (Eds.), *Social Determinants of Health* (pp. 17–34). Oxford: Oxford University Press.

Glass, T. A., & McAtee, M. J. (2006). Behavioral science at the crossroads in public health: Extending horizons, envisioning the future. *Soc Sci Med, 62*(7), 1650–1671.

Graham, H. (2004). Social determinants and their unequal distribution: Clarifying policy understandings. *Mil Q, 82*, 101–124.

House, J. S., & Williams, D. R. (2000). Understanding and explaining socioeconomic and racial/ethnic disparities. In B. D. Smedley & S. L. Syme (Eds.), *Promoting Health: Intervention Strategies from Social and Behavioral Health* (pp. 81–124). Washington, DC: National Academy Press.

Institute of Medicine. (2003). *The Future of the Public's Health in the 21st Century*. Washington, DC: National Academy Press.

King, G., & Williams, D. R. (1995). Race and health: A multidimensional approach to African American health. In B. C. Amick III, S. Levine, A. R. Tarlov, & D. C. Walsh (Eds.), *Society and Health* (pp. 93–130). New York: Oxford University Press.

Light, D., & Hughes, D. (2001). Introduction: A sociological perspective on rationing: Power, rhetoric and situated practices. *Soc Health Ill, 23*(5), 551–569.

Link, B. G., & Phelan, J. (1995). Social conditions as fundamental causes of disease. *J Health Soc Behav* (Extra Issue), 80–94.

Marmot, M., & Wilkinson, R. G. (1999). *Social Determinants of Health*. Oxford: Oxford University Press.

McGuckin, N., & Murakami, E. (1999). Examining trip-chaining behavior: A comparison of travel by men and women. *Transp Res Rec, 1693*, 79–85.

Mirowsky, J., & Ross, C. E. (1989). *Social Causes of Psychological Distress*. New York: Aldine De Gruyter.

Rieker, P. P., Fitzgerald, E. M., & Kalish, L. A. (1990). Adaptive behavioral responses to potential infertility among survivors of testis cancer. *J Clin Oncol, 8*(2), 347–355.

Ross, C. E. (2000). Walking, exercise, and smoking: Does neighborhood matter? *Soc Sci Med, 51*(2), 265–274.

Sampson, R. J., Raudenbush, S. W., & Earls, F. (1997). Neighborhoods and violent crime: A multilevel study of collective efficacy. *Science, 277*(5328), 918–924.

Simon, H. (1982). *Models of Bounded Rationality, Vols. 1 & 2*. Cambridge, MA: MIT Press.

Simon, H. (1997a). *Administrative Behavior: A Study of Decision-Making Processes in Administrative Organizations* (4th ed.). New York: Free Press.

Simon, H. (1997b). *Models of Bounded Rationality, Vol. 3*. Cambridge, MA: MIT Press.

Simon, R. W. (1995). Gender, multiple roles, role meaning, and mental health. *J Health Soc Behav, 36*(2), 182–194.

Simon, R. W. (1997). The meanings individuals attach to role identities and their implications for mental health. *J Health Soc Behav, 38*(3), 256–274.

Smaje, C. (2000). Race, ethnicity, and health. In C. E. Bird, P. Conrad, & A. M. Fremont (Eds.), *Handbook of Medical Sociology* (pp. 114–128). Englewood Cliffs, NJ: Prentice Hall.

Taylor, S. E. (1989). *Positive Illusions: Creative Self-Deception and the Healthy Mind.* New York: Basic Books.

Taylor, S. E., Klein, L. C., Lewis, B. P., Gruenewald, T. L., Gurung, R. A., & Updegraff, J. A. (2000). Biobehavioral responses to stress in females: Tend-and-befriend, not fight-or-flight. *Psychol Rev, 107*(3), 411–429.

Truong, K., & Sturm, R. (2007). Alcohol outlets and problem drinking among adults in California. *J Studies on Alcohol and Drugs.* In Press.

Williams, D. (2002). Racial/ethnic variations in women's health: The social embeddedness of health. *Am J Pub Health, 92,* 588–597.

Williams, D. (2003). The health of men: Structured inequalities and opportunities. *Am J Pub Health, 93,* 724–731.

THREE

National Social Policies and Constrained Choice

In this chapter, we present evidence that illustrates how a country's decisions about social provisions and safety nets, as well as other governmental actions at the national level of policymaking, can contribute to differences in men's and women's opportunities and choices in ways that ultimately affect their health. To elaborate the model of constrained choice described in Chapter 2 (Figure 2.2), we consider a wide range of national policies and regulations that can, and do, directly or indirectly affect individual health either by differentially limiting or broadening men's and women's options or by affecting other aspects of their lives in ways that shape perceptions of their expectations, priorities, and needs. Such policies also affect the organization and quality of men's and women's lives by establishing universal regulations that often deliberately encourage or discourage individual and family choices. Examples include laws and regulations regarding marriage and parental rights, antidiscrimination ordinances, employment equity/workplace regulations, and reproductive rights, among others. Less obvious examples might include tax benefit policies, occupational safety regulations, land use planning, or immigration and defense policies.

Some public policies are intended to directly regulate individual behavior and protect the public's health by stipulating who, where, and how much one can consume alcohol, drive, use tobacco products, or own firearms; other policies indirectly discourage potentially deleterious behaviors by limiting access to tobacco and alcohol through hefty "sin" taxes on these products.[1] Such policies are not our primary focus nor are those that are directly related to the provision of health care. However, we employ some examples of public health and health care policy in our discussion to illustrate how they can also differentially affect men's and women's opportunities and in turn choices that affect their health.[2]

In the United States, for example, a wide range of laws and regulations regarding equal opportunity employment, parental leave, occupational safety, and the lack of national day care have affected men's and women's decisions about careers, families, and work both inside and outside the home. This effect can be seen in the lives of Susan and John in the vignette presented in Chapter 2. Susan has chosen to work as a health educator near her home so she can be more available in case her child's health or other crisis requires immediate action in the daytime. However, this was not the best job that she was offered as it often requires her to work evenings when she would rather be home with her children. In addition, she recognizes that her husband's job with its higher earnings and greater chances for career advancement is more likely to yield the additional

---

[1] Such constraints can be as simple as reducing the opportunity to engage in certain negative health behaviors by regulating the use of public spaces. For example, communities and even countries are increasingly extending the nature and scope of nonsmoking policies (e.g., from the city ordinance that bans smoking on the beach in Solana Beach (9/03) and Santa Monica, California (3/04), to the Irish Republic's ban in 2004 on workplace smoking that ended lighting up in pubs, or the State of Massachusetts's 2004 law prohibiting smoking in worksites. The Hawaii smoke-free workplace law enacted in November, 2006 makes it the 18th U.S. state to enact such a law. Although most of the bans are antipollution regulations designed to limit exposure to second-hand smoke and other toxins, they still discourage health risk behaviors (see U.S. Surgeon General Report, 2006)). In a similar action, the evolving concept of public health urban planning aims to encourage healthy behaviors by creating opportunities for exercise through the provision of safe, easily accessible green space, walking and jogging paths, playing fields, and bike lanes (see, for example, Brownson, Baker, Housemann, Brennan, & Bacak, 2001; Giles-Corti & Donovan, 2002, 2003; Powell, Martin, & Chowdbury, 2003). The fact that such decisions are also made by individual states and communities is an issue that is explored in greater detail in Chapter 4.

[2] For instance, in terms of health care policy in the United States, Medicare was originally designed to provide hospitalization for major acute health events for adults over age 65 with no intention of treating men and women differently. Although the policy has expanded over time, however, it remains less equipped to serve those with chronic illnesses, which are more common in women, resulting in greater out-of-pocket expenses for them (Sambamoorthi, Shea, & Crystal, 2003). Thus, a policy that is manifestly gender neutral can and does differentially affect men's and women's ability to create and maintain a healthy life.

income they need to buy a larger home to accommodate Susan's retired and ailing father who now lives in another city. She is aware that the compromise and tradeoff she has made between job and proximity to home may eventually exacerbate the differences in their earnings and career potential. The lack of high-quality and inexpensive public day care for her 2-year-old daughter and affordable long-term health care for her elderly father means the family cannot afford to move to a larger home that would give them the space to accommodate him. Susan and John also continue to seek ways to resolve the constant worries and tensions they have about both the lack of money and time needed to achieve their priorities. Neither Susan nor John is fully cognizant of the cumulative effects that the continuous stress-related wear and tear arising from these conflicts may have on their health nor that these conflicts have their origins in national policy. As they approach mid-life, pursuing health may require Susan and John to reconsider their priorities and the tradeoffs they are making between work, caring for others, securing their children's future, and self-care.

National policies are at the top of our conceptualized constrained choice diagram (Figure 2.2), and their impact on men's and women's opportunities and life choices is not as transparent as that of influences lower down in the diagram. Moreover, as we examine national policies, we need to underscore that a country creates a variety of policies and their impacts cannot be disentangled easily. Therefore, assessing the separate impact of a single policy on men's and women's lives, their choices, and the subsequent health consequences presents considerable challenges.

To surmount these challenges, we instead talk about the influence of *policy regimes* on gender differences in health. Policy regime, a term used widely by policy analysts, refers to the range of national policies and regulations enacted over time within a particular country that collectively reflect a broader philosophical orientation that transcends any individual administration. A country's policy regime creates priorities and establishes the guidelines for what rights and entitlements are to be covered through general social provisions, as well as the basic protections that serve as a safety net for its citizens. What constitutes general social provisions and the degree to which such provisions are implemented through public or private mechanisms vary greatly from country to country. Many social and economic forces affect the nature and scope of policy regimes, including changes in population demographics, fertility and mortality rates (overall and within particular age groups), and responses to national disasters and other crises of various forms.

The evolution of a country's policy regimes is inherently complex. The process involves philosophical and practical decisions that are influenced not only by social and economic forces but also by the political ideologies of those policymakers who over time maintain or change the direction, and in some cases the objectives, of a country's social policy and welfare agenda.[3] We are concerned here with how policy regimes influence life choices in general and men's and women's opportunities and ability to pursue health over the life course, not with how they evolve. Thus, our discussion of policy regimes and constrained choice both departs from and relies on the body of analytic work that examines the origin and economic and political impact of such entities.

As we compare and contrast the regimes of different countries, it is worth noting too that social policies often lag behind social and economic changes, and so it is not surprising that many have not kept pace with social and demographic trends, such as the significant advances in longevity and the extensive shift in the gender composition of the labor force.[4] Furthermore, even those social trends currently challenging policymakers in many developed countries, such as women's increasing labor force participation and population aging, are not occurring at the same rate in every region of the world. Thus, policy regimes are likely to be at different points both in terms of recognizing and addressing specific social trends. The fact that policy formulation is a dynamic process and not a static activity complicates the task of comparing policy regimes and examining the gender and health consequences of decisions. We also recognize

---

[3] As a result, policies can and do change, and in addition, policy objectives themselves can shift over time. For example, although Social Security was originally intended to provide supplemental retirement income, for many it has become the sole source of income, and the length of coverage has extended with increasing longevity. This shift, also known as "objective creep," frequently occurs with both policies and regulations. In fact, new or different constraints on choices will inevitably arise over time due to objective creep or other social and demographic changes.

[4] To examine these trends, see Table 3.1 in O'Connor et al., 1999; see also UN Human Development Report and Index, 2005; U.S. Bureau of Labor Statistics, 2004b).

that the cumulative effects of particular policies may play out over many decades, especially those that entail public spending for families with children or for educational opportunities that provide young adults with resources that can have health benefits throughout the life course.

If policymakers want to create the opportunity to pursue health and to remove obstacles to making health a priority, they will need to consider gender roles and biological differences that affect how men's and women's lives are organized. Such a perspective would be effective both in the formulation of new policies and in the evaluation of existing ones. For example, the dilemmas and health ramifications associated with economic disparity are well documented, as are widespread gender differences in income, and these trends should be taken into account in the design of safety nets and other policies in the United States, as they often are in other countries. Such analysis can be time consuming and initially expensive. However, it may prove to be cost effective in the long run if it can prevent or reduce damaging health effects of constrained choices from accumulating throughout the life course.

ECONOMIC RESOURCES AND GENDER DIFFERENCES

Before examining policy regimes, we need to consider gender differences in economic means because the largest group of policies are designed to affect the distribution and impact of unequal resources. As in many countries, the disparity in men's and women's economic resources in the United States is tied largely to patterns of labor force participation over the life course, to men's historically higher incomes, and to women's greater responsibility for caring for children and the elderly. As we discuss in greater detail in Chapter 5, although women's employment patterns have become more similar to men's over time (U.S. Bureau of Labor Statistics, 2004b), women continue to be more likely than men to have absences from the labor force and to reduce their work hours at some point in their careers to accommodate the competing demands of work and family. In what constitutes a major social change since World War II, the majority of mothers now work outside the home (nearly 75% with the youngest child under 18 years of age and 60% of those with the youngest child under 3 years). Among married-couple families in which both men and women work, approximately 80% of the men earn more than their wives. In addition, the combined weekly hours worked of all married-couple families are increasing (U.S. Bureau of Labor Statistics, 2004b). Moreover, although on average men have an income and labor force advantage, this gender difference is not consistent for all races and social classes. In the United States, white men in particular are more likely than women of all races and ethnic groups (and many men of color) to have higher paying jobs that provide health insurance and pensions or other retirement benefits (U.S. Census Bureau, 2005).

Although economic disparity is lessening in some ways, the gender differences in economic resources among working-age adults become amplified in old age. For example, in the United States, because women live longer than men and tend to marry men who are a few years older than themselves, women are more likely than men to be impoverished directly by the health care costs of a chronically ill spouse, or indirectly (until recently) by the requirement that they spend down certain marital assets to become eligible for Medicaid to cover their spouse's care in a nursing home, even as they face the added psychological and physical consequences of caring for their spouse.

Women's greater longevity and lower average Social Security benefits, which are funded by payroll taxes, also make them more vulnerable than men to the low cost of living adjustments made annually for Social Security payments simply because they rely on this benefit over a much longer time frame than men. Even though older women have a greater dependency on this type of inadequate social insurance, Estes (2003) argues that the present form of Social Security, which is a citizen-based social contract, is preferable to proposed privatization schemes being suggested for reforming Social Security. She further warns that under a proposed market or property-based contract the distributional outcomes will reflect the existing disparity in economic resources and therefore provide lower benefits for women, minorities, and low-income workers. Consequently, it is not much of a stretch to project the differential impact that some decisions to reform Social Security could have on elderly men's and women's opportunity to pursue health.

Thus, even policies such as Social Security that explicitly treat men and women the same can affect them differently due to their life circumstances and health care needs, as can policies that treat them differently (e.g., paid and unpaid maternity/parental leave) but ignore the exposure to social risks and pattern of their lives.[5]

A study of Medicare payments in the 1990s also found that the health insurance program spent less per female than male beneficiaries on average because of higher deductibles for the chronic diseases that plague women late in life than for those conditions that are more common in men (Miles & Parker, 1997). In addition, the types of health-related expenses covered under expansions to Medicare benefits (e.g., pharmaceuticals or home care) could have a differential gender impact, especially when disease patterns and age are taken into account. In fact, a recent study found that nearly 8% of the older Medicare population spent more than 10% of their income on prescription drugs, and the burden of out-of-pocket expenses fell unevenly on women and those with chronic health conditions (Sambamoorthi, Shea, & Crystal, 2003). The authors conclude that Medicare reform proposals need to be evaluated for the amount and content of coverage and for their differential effect on various subgroups. One of the relevant aspects to consider when examining gender and Medicare is not only the fact that women live longer with chronic diseases such as CVD and arthritis but also that in the long run because of different needs they may actually receive more total resources (Zimmerman & Hill, 2000). Although it is plausible that health insurance should work somewhat differently for men and women, how to attain

---

[5] For instance, with the increase of women in the military (17% of the total force in 2005 according to the U.S. Census Bureau) the U.S. Defense Department has had to acknowledge that policies that worked well for men are not sufficient for women. In an attempt to respond to their different needs, VA hospitals now include obstetric care and trauma units that treat not only combat-related posttraumatic stress but also the distress that results from physical and sexual assault. Thus, the Defense Department is considering establishing a high-level victim's advocate office for military women because of the worrisome increase in allegations of sexual harassment and assault in different branches of the armed services and in the military schools that train men and women (*Boston Globe*, 2005). Not unlike the civilian population, military wives and women in the military who experience abuse are not able to report it without fear of serious repercussions from those involved or their superiors so victim advocate programs have be developed to provide the needed intervention. Although there is a separate provision in the 2005 defense spending bill that sets aside $1.8 million for a victim's advocate office, the Pentagon is still studying how best to implement this initiative.

equity is far from clear. In either case facilitating a healthier life-span for both men and women would be one of the most effective ways to reduce the increasing costs to Medicare. We contend that this requires making policy and personal adjustments earlier in the life course.

The differential exposure and effects of health insurance are related to women's greater longevity and marital status late in life, as well as to differences in the retirement income for which men and women are typically eligible based on their labor force participation and salary history (U.S. Bureau of Labor Statistics, 2004a). For the most part, countries with universal health care systems and retirement entitlements less tied to labor force participation have avoided some of the particular problems related to health care for the elderly in the United States discussed above, but policymakers in these countries still encounter difficult decisions in their attempts to understand and when and how to make the safety net and other social provisions gender neutral. These examples only hint at the complex gender and health implications of various plans advanced to address rising Social Security and Medicare costs in the United States by increasing eligibility requirements and decreasing benefits, including reducing cost of living adjustments. Clearly, most industrialized countries and welfare states are struggling with how to address the impact of aging populations on the cost and equity of existing social provisions, and some are doing so by increasing the age of retirement eligibility.

POLICY REGIMES, GENDER, AND HEALTH

Every country, regardless of economic capacity or distribution of income, makes policy choices regarding the types of social and economic safety nets (in the form of welfare benefits and other social provisions) it adopts to prevent or correct inequities, minimize the income/health gradient, and protect and maintain the well-being of individuals and families including the elderly, the unemployed, and families with children. Such policy regimes include educational requirements and incentives or disincentives for work, marriage, having children, and retirement savings, as well as regulations about earned incomes that affect the allocation of resources across generations. Thus, most national governments, depending on their economic resources and political philosophy, offer social provisions and entitlements, such as Social Security, universal health insurance, welfare and unemployment insurance, and family policies, including state-subsidized or mandated paid parental leave and child care, among others.

Policy analysts have long debated the best way to categorize national systems for purposes of comparing them on the basis of many dimensions, including the orientation, funding, type, and outcomes of their social policies. To illustrate, Esping-Andersen (1990) has developed a widely used classification of state or policy regimes as liberal, conservative-corporatist, and social democratic based on the nature and scope of the policies they choose to enact (this classification is discussed in detail later in this chapter). Although the precise categorization of a state or policy regime varies depending on the dimensions an analyst emphasizes, there is a growing literature that demonstrates how these basic types of governing regimes can and do affect gender roles and relations in a variety of ways (O'Connor, Orloff, & Shaver, 1999; Orloff, 1996; Sainsbury, 1996).

Not only can policy decisions *directly* affect health by providing universal access to health care, but we contend that they also *indirectly* affect health in part by altering or reinforcing gender-based social roles and men's and women's opportunities to engage in health-related behaviors. Policies also reduce or buffer the health impact of social and economic strains or at least create options that do so, such as providing day care so women can enter or reenter the workface or incentives for men to take parental leave so they can be involved in child care.[6] Sometimes policies can have the opposite effects than they were intended to have. Fodor and colleagues (Fodor, Glass, Kawachi, & Popescu, 2002) argue that the generosity of welfare benefits in Eastern European countries with socialist regimes ironically has had the effect of impoverishing women because it provides financial incentives for women to never enter or never return

---

[6] For example, in late 2005 Spain established new measures intended to help Spaniards balance jobs and families. Civil servants now have the option to take a shorter lunch break (less than the customary $1\frac{1}{2}$ to $2\frac{1}{2}$ hours) and leave the office by 6 p.m. rather than 7:30 p.m. Male government employees can now take 10 days off with pay to help care for newborns or newly adopted children compared with the 3 days offered previously, and all civil servants can opt to work reduced hours (with a corresponding reduction in pay) if they have children under 12 years of age.

to the labor force. Particular regime policies can also lead to different labor force participation rates for both men and women. For example, the federal family policies of the Scandinavian countries (e.g., universal child care and extensive paid maternity leave) have led to a higher proportion of women being employed full-time than for instance in the United Kingdom or Switzerland, where more women tend to work part-time (Organization for Economic Co-operation and Development [OECD], 2004c, 2005). Moreover, family-friendly policies contribute to men's and women's work and family expectations, choices, and behaviors in ways that affect the gender distribution across occupations and professions. For more details, see O'Connor et al. (1999); OECD (1994, 1996); Reskin and Padovic (1994); Ritter and Skocpol (1991); Skocpol (1992); and U.S. Bureau of Labor Statistics (2004a).

GENDER-BASED POLICY ANALYSIS

Social policies provide an economic safety net through a variety of *public* and *private* mechanisms that assure at least a minimum level of income and health care access for a country's citizens. In regimes relying primarily on public mechanisms, the state is more responsible for providing economic benefits, and in those based on private mechanisms, the benefits are more tied to market forces. Socialist regimes have tended to be more generous with such welfare benefits, but the stability of those benefits is still dependent on a strong economy. Unlike in the United States, in many countries with socialist or other social democratic regimes, basic levels of retirement entitlements and paid parental leave benefits are often set independently of either individual employment history or earnings. However, citizens of these countries are still encouraged to work and save to augment their retirement pensions.

National policies can have intended and unintended effects on gender relations and on the lives of men and women, regardless of whether such policies proceed from the assumption that men and women are the same or different (O'Connor et al., 1999). Some policies are designed specifically to bring about or assure gender equity (e.g., those prohibiting sex discrimination and sexual harassment in the workplace). However, the more critical issue is how much responsibility the state assumes for family well-being and child care and how much remains the responsibility of individuals and families.

In the 1960s and 1970s, Finland and Sweden began to provide a continuum of support to parents of young children by investing in family-friendly policies, such as flexible paid parental leave periods during the first phase of childhood, subsidized child care, extensive out-of-school hours care, and reduced working hours for both single and married parents with young children (OECD, 2005). These policies entail high public spending, higher payroll taxes, and smaller take-home incomes; they are based in part on a political philosophy that recognizes the need to reconcile work and family life and reward both paid labor and unpaid social roles (e.g., caregiving to children and the elderly) for their contribution to the household and the society. In contrast, in the United States most public assistance or social provisions are tied to employment (or workfare, the new work requirement for mothers on welfare), whereas caregiving is viewed as the responsibility of individuals and families, which often serves as a barrier to labor force participation (see O'Connor et al., 1999).

Over time, and particularly in recent decades, many developed countries have grappled explicitly and consistently with how to achieve or maintain gender equity through the provision of family-friendly and other social policies. For example, in New Zealand and Canada the safety net includes social spending on families with children, especially for single parents (or sole parents, as they are referred to elsewhere). Other countries, including Norway and Portugal, use financial incentives to encourage fathers to take paid parental leave from their jobs (OECD, 2004c), and France provides universal day care and free primary, secondary, and higher education.

As one component of this effort to achieve gender equity, policymakers have developed and applied what is referred to as gender-based analysis to assess whether particular polices meet the equity objective, where they fall short, and what their differential impact may be on women's and men's opportunities (see, for example, OECD, 2004a, 2004b, 2004c, 2005). Of course, the full impact of national policies may not be fully realized until they have been enacted for an extended period of time. This is because over time individuals begin to plan their lives and make choices based in part on the established options, incentives, and barriers that are in place and expected to endure long enough to fit with their planning. Nor would an impact assessment traditionally include health, as health effects may themselves play out over time and be difficult to capture.[7] Moreover, the health effects of everyday and larger life decisions that direct us down different tracks may similarly evolve or even expand over time even if the social benefits stay relatively constant. Yet, the total social burden and economic costs of health effects associated with particular social policies may warrant greater effort involved in measuring and addressing those effects. Analyzing social policies in order to predict or determine actual effects on men and women may prove to be a particularly important government practice for sustaining gender equity, particularly in times of economic retrenchment and the resulting increase in competition for existing resources.

Ironically, although gender-based analysis was introduced as a tool to address gender differences in the development and outcome of social policies, it has been applied mainly to address women's experiences of gender inequity in social role obligations, in wages, and in sex-segregated occupations and professions.[8] With few exceptions, proponents of gender-based analysis have largely ignored the fact that men die younger than women all over the world or that in a given country men are neither universally advantaged relative to women, nor are all women equally disadvantaged. One example of a policy that has had an unequal impact on women is the Family and Medical Leave Act (FMLA) in the United States, which provides for unpaid parental leave. By providing a guaranteed right to unpaid parental leave, it offers more of a choice and thus a greater benefit to those women in the middle class who can afford to take unpaid leave (but were not necessarily provided the opportunity to do so until it became a legitimate entitlement under the Act) than to those poor

---

[7] Consider, for example, the impact of the U.S. Family and Medical Leave Act or other countries' more generous leave benefits, such as Canada's 2-year leave allowance, on women's employment decisions. The effects may not fully play out until such policies have been in place and been used by a cohort of women who anticipated their availability while making early choices regarding how much education to pursue and what occupations would fit with other plans and goals for their lives.

[8] See, for example, http://www.swc-cfc.gc.ca/pubs/gbaperformance/index/e.html, accessed September 11, 2007; http://www.cwhn.ca/network-reseau/2-4/genderlens.html, accessed September 11, 2007.

women who cannot afford to take leave without pay but who for health or other reasons have no choice but to take an unpaid leave.[9]

The unpaid family medical leave example illustrates that protections provided by a federal social policy, though not intended to exacerbate inequalities among women, in practice lead to unequal results. In general, those with more social and economic resources typically have more opportunity to take advantage of such unpaid and other types of benefits; consequently, "universal" does not always translate into equal access or impact. Forms of targeted protection such as welfare programs or antidiscrimination policies, which are designed to protect specific disadvantaged minority groups, may not address the needs or experiences of all subgroups. Welfare policies, for instance, that target low-income people are mostly geared to families rather than individuals or more to single mothers[10] than fathers, and until recently, antidiscrimination policies were interpreted to apply to African Americans more so, for example, than to Asians or Arabic persons.

To date, gender-based analyses of social policies and provisions have provided some understanding of both the similar and differential effects that those policies have on the lives and options of men and women. However, to our knowledge, except for reproductive issues, no one has raised the question explicitly of the impact of these policies on men's and women's opportunities to pursue health, although that impact might have been the unstated intention of a specific policy. In addition, as we discuss further below, no single classification system fully captures the complexity of policy regime types in part because a given country is not necessarily consistent across the range of policies it implements.[11] Moreover, not all

[9] The FMLA did pave the way for several states to offer paid maternity leave through mandatory disability coverage for workers (in Rhode Island) or unemployment-related coverage (in California).

[10] Specifically, some have argued that welfare policies are best suited to the temporarily poor, such as middle-class women impoverished by divorce but with the education and job skills to successfully reenter or return to the labor force.

[11] It is worth noting again that countries are not static in their policies, and thus it is necessary to recognize that regimes change over time and a given country may shift considerably in the nature of its social policies. In fact, there is some debate even about the term "welfare state" as it is commonly used to describe modern state social provision because it assumes that countries promote the welfare of their citizens through social policy. Nor is it appropriate to assume that once a regime establishes a consistent set of

analysts focus on the policies' consequences for subgroups; even fewer compare the impacts on both men and women, and those analysts who do tend to ignore the effects on general health status (e.g., O'Connor et al., 1999; Sainsbury, 1993, 1994, 1996).

Policy analysts have produced an influential body of comparative research that examines the origins and effects of social provisions (most notably economic effects), but much of this mainstream work initially neglected gender. In response to this gap, a body of feminist and other gender-focused work has developed to extend the comparative research. For example, the aim of work by Orloff (1996) and others (O'Connor et al., 1999; Sainsbury, 1993, 1994, 1996) is to categorize welfare states as a way of predicting what social provision policies states might enact and their potential effects on gender roles and relations. But currently there is little dialogue between the field of policy analysis and health, a situation we hope will improve with publication of this book and particularly the discussion in the rest of this chapter.

CROSS-NATIONAL COMPARISON OF POLICY REGIMES AND HEALTH

We are specifically interested in whether and how social policies and their impacts may contribute to gender differences in opportunities and constraints that affect men and women's capacity to pursue health or to make it a priority. At issue is whether a country's social provision policies could be one pathway to reducing gender differences in morbidity and mortality and improving both men's and women's health. We also explore whether overlooking the differential gender impact of policies could undermine other efforts to improve population health and reduce gender disparities. To illustrate the possible connection between

social provision policies that together create a safety net of a certain dimension (e.g., describing the scope of the benefits provided), they cannot be reversed. For example, according to Ruggie (1984), "the welfare state is conceptualized as a state committed to modifying the play of social or market forces to achieve greater equality." However, Orloff (1993) defines the welfare state, or state social provision, simply "as interventions by the state in civil society to alter social and market forces." She does not assume that all social provisions are aimed at or actually produce greater equality among its citizens.

health status and social provision policies, we first consider how men's and women's life expectancy vary across countries by introducing and discussing the data in Tables 3.1 and 3.2. As part of that discussion we address the connection among national wealth, life expectancy, and the gender gap and consider the various explanations for cross-national differences. In the last section of the chapter we use Table 3.1 to suggest how policy regimes might contribute to gender differences in health.

Life Expectancy, National Wealth, and the Gender Gap Across Nations

Table 3.1 presents data on men's and women's life expectancy at birth arrayed by women's life expectancy at birth. In this table we have only included countries ranked high on the United Nations Human Development Index (HDI)[12] because this indicates the degree to which they invest in human capital and the comparison is less confounded by large socioeconomic disparities. Japanese women and men have the highest life expectancy (at 85.2 and 78.3 years), whereas women and men in the United States have a life expectancy that is lower by about 4 years (at 79.8 and 74.2 years). As this table shows, U.S. life expectancy is comparable to and slightly lower than that of Costa Rica, Greece, and New Zealand, among other countries. Among industrialized countries, the United States seldom ranks higher than 20th on women's life expectancy or total life expectancy. The gender gap in life expectancy ranges from 10 or more years in countries such as Lithuania, Estonia, and Latvia to 3 or more years in countries such as Israel, Bahrain and Cuba, with a mean difference of 6.1 years.

Researchers have offered numerous social and biological explanations for the variation in life-span among developed countries, and as a result this issue is a topic of much debate among analysts. Because of the paradoxical gender differences in mortality and morbidity, researchers and policymakers have also used other measures of longevity to assess years

---

[12] The Human Development Index (HDI) represents a "summary measure of human development" (United Nations 2002, p. 265). The HDI is a composite of a country's overall life expectancy, its level of "knowledge" (literacy and enrollment rates), and its gross domestic product.

Table 3.1. *Life Expectancy of Women and Men at Birth** and the Differences by Countries Rated as High on the United Nations Human Development Index**

Country	Women	Men	Difference	Country	Women	Men	Difference
Japan	85.2	78.3	6.9	Slovenia	79.7	72.5	7.2
France	82.7	75.1	7.6	Ireland	79.5	74.3	5.2
Spain	82.7	75.8	6.9	Portugal	79.5	72.5	7.0
China, Hong Kong SAR	82.7	77.2	5.5	Barbados	79.4	74.4	5.0
Sweden	82.5	77.5	5.0	Republic Of Korea	79.2	71.7	7.5
Switzerland	82.3	75.9	6.4	Denmark	79.0	74.1	4.9
Australia	82.0	76.4	5.6	Chile	78.9	72.9	6.0
Canada	81.9	76.6	5.3	Kuwait	78.9	74.8	4.1
Iceland	81.9	77.6	4.3	Brunei Darussalam	78.8	74.1	4.7
Italy	81.9	75.5	6.4	Uruguay	78.8	71.5	7.3
Norway	81.8	75.9	5.9	Czech Republic	78.6	72.0	6.6
Belgium	81.8	75.6	6.2	Cuba	78.6	74.7	3.9
Finland	81.4	74.3	7.1	Croatia	78	70.2	7.8
Austria	81.4	75.3	6.1	Poland	77.9	69.7	8.2
Luxembourg	81.3	75.0	6.3	Argentina	77.6	70.5	7.1
Germany	81.1	75.1	6.0	Lithuania	77.5	67.4	10.1
Netherlands	81.0	75.6	5.4	Slovakia	77.5	69.6	7.9
Israel	80.9	77.0	3.9	United Arab Emirates	77.3	73.2	4.1
Greece	80.9	75.7	5.2	Estonia	76.7	66.3	10.4
New Zealand	80.7	75.7	5.0	Mexico	76.3	70.3	6.0
United Kingdom	80.6	75.6	5.0	Latvia	76.1	65.4	10.7
Malta	80.6	75.8	4.8	Hungary	75.9	67.6	8.3
Cyprus	80.5	75.9	4.6	Bahrain	75.8	72.4	3.4
Costa Rica	80.5	75.7	4.8	Qatar	75.3	70.4	4.9
Singapore	80.2	75.8	4.4	Trinidad and Tobago	74.5	68.5	6.0
United States	79.8	74.2	5.6	Bahamas	70.4	63.9	6.5

** (as sorted by women's life expectancy).

* The United Nations Human Development Report (2004) does not have sex-specific life expectancy data for the following countries: Seychelles, Saint Kitts and Nevis, and Antigua and Barbuda.

Table 3.2. Comparison of 30 Countries with the Highest Life Expectancy and 30 Countries with the Lowest Life Expectancy*

Country	Life Exp. at Birth	Women	Men	Difference	GPD per capita	Life Exp. at Birth	Women	Men	Difference	Country	GPD per capita
Japan	81.5	85	78	7	31,407	49.1	50	48	2	Equatorial Guinea	4,394
Sweden	80.0	83	78	5	26,929	48.9	49	49	0	Guinea	415
China, Hong Kong SAR	79.9	83	77	6	23,800	48.8	51	45	6	South Africa	2,299
Iceland	79.7	82	78	4	29,749	48.5	49	48	1	Mali	296
Canada	79.3	82	77	5	22,777	48.3	50	47	3	Congo	825
Spain	79.2	83	76	7	15,961	46.8	47	45	2	Cameroon	575
Australia	79.1	82	76	6	20,822	46.0	46	46	0	Niger	190
Switzerland	79.1	82	76	6	36,687	45.8	47	45	2	Djibouti	869
Israel	79.1	81	77	4	15,792	45.8	46	45	1	Burkina Faso	264
Norway	78.9	82	76	6	41,974	45.7	47	45	2	Uganda	236
France	78.9	83	75	8	24,061	45.5	46	45	1	Ethiopia	90
Belgium	78.7	82	76	6	23,749	45.3	46	43	3	Namibia	1,463
Italy	78.7	82	76	6	20,528	45.2	46	44	2	Kenya	393
Austria	78.5	81	75	6	25,356	45.2	47	44	3	Guinea-Bissau	141
Netherlands	78.3	81	76	5	25,886	44.7	46	44	2	Chad	240
Luxembourg	78.3	81	75	6	47,354	43.5	44	42	2	Un. Rep. of Tanzania	267
Malta	78.3	81	76	5	9,748	41.4	40	39	1	Botswana	3,080
New Zealand	78.2	81	76	5	14,872	41.4	43	41	2	Dem. Rep. of Congo	111
Germany	78.2	81	75	6	24,051	41.2	41	41	0	Cote d'Ivoire	707

Greece	78.2	81	76	5	12,494
Cyprus	78.2	81	76	5	13,210
United Kingdom	78.1	81	76	5	26,444
Singapore	78.0	80	76	4	20,886
Costa Rica	78.0	81	76	5	4,271
Finland	77.9	82	74	8	25,295
Barbados	77.1	79	74	5	9,423
United States	77.0	80	74	6	36,006
Ireland	76.9	80	74	6	30,982
Cuba	76.7	79	75	4	
Denmark	76.6	79	74	5	32,179

Burundi	40.8	41	40	1	102
Angola	40.1	41	39	2	857
Central African Rep.	39.8	41	38	3	274
Rwanda	38.9	40	39	1	212
Mozambique	38.5	40	37	3	195
Malawi	37.8	38	37	1	177
Lesotho	36.3	38	32	6	402
Swaziland	35.7	35	33	2	1,091
Sierra Leone	34.3	35	33	2	150
Zimbabwe	33.9	33	34	−1	639
Zambia	32.7	32	33	−1	361

* All data from United Nations, 2004.

living with and without disability or chronic illness. Thus, men and women are often compared on the basis of the average number of years in good health (healthy life expectancy) expected over their predicted life-span. When the OECD measure of healthy life expectancy (not shown) is examined, the gender gap tends to narrow somewhat, but does not disappear (OECD, 2005).

National Wealth and Health Status

Many social scientists argue more broadly that the determinants of health status, and especially disparities in that status, are due either to inequalities in individual income within a country or to differences in wealth across countries (Kawachi & Kennedy, 2006). Table 3.2 highlights just how great the discrepancy in life expectancy is between very poor and wealthier countries and shows that life expectancy varies with a country's wealth in both predictable and unpredictable ways. It displays the 30 countries with the highest life expectancy (left side) and the 30 countries with the lowest life expectancy (right side) along with the gross domestic product (GDP) per capita, a measure of a country's wealth and economic well-being. The comparative rankings for total life expectancy and women's life expectancy are similar but not the same in all countries. However, the gap in life expectancy at birth between the two groups of 30 countries is dramatic. For example, total life expectancy ranges from 81.5 years in Japan to 32.7 years in Zambia.

With a few exceptions, the countries with the lowest life expectancy are mainly poor countries in Southeast Asia and sub-Saharan Africa. These countries are characterized frequently by a weak, unstable economy, inadequate infrastructure, and insufficient health care systems.

But is it simply wealth per se that confers longevity? A partial answer to this question is obtained by examining additional data. Table 3.2 also shows the discordance between rankings in life expectancy and GDP per capita. Japan ranks first in overall life expectancy but fifth in its GDP per capita of $31,407. Luxembourg ranks first in GDP per capita ($47,354), but places a distant 16th when it comes to overall life expectancy (78.3 years; 3.2 years less than Japan). In fact, none of the top five wealthiest countries ranks among the top five countries in terms of overall life expectancy. Particularly surprising are the GDPs of the United States ($36,006) and Ireland ($30,882). These countries rank 2nd and 3rd in GDP per capita, but 27th and 30th in overall life expectancy (77.0 and 76.9 years), suggesting that GDP alone cannot explain the cross-national variation in life expectancy. Both of these countries have a lower life expectancy than Costa Rica (78 years), which has a GDP of $4,271 – about one-eighth the GDP of the United States and Ireland. The same pattern is apparent when the United States and Barbados are compared; these countries have the same life expectancy, but the latter has about 26% of the U.S. GDP (UN Human Development Report and Index, 2005).

Another important aspect of Table 3.2 is that the gender life expectancy gap is greater in the 30 countries with higher life expectancy than in the 30 countries with the lowest life expectancy. In the former countries, the gap ranges from 4 years to 7 years, whereas the range in the latter countries is 1 year to 3 years, with some exceptions. In several of the 30 lowest ranked countries the gender differences are reversed (e.g., Zambia and Zimbabwe). In contrast to the worldwide pattern, in these countries women outlive men by at most 1 year, if at all. The low overall life expectancy and the reversed gender difference highlight the extent to which extreme poverty and disease-specific mortality patterns (such as AIDS) diminish the life-span for both men and women. In the case of women, the harsh social conditions attenuate any biological advantage they may have had in life expectancy. Thus, although a country's wealth (as measured by GDP) clearly contributes to population health, it is by no means the main factor determining the *gender gap in life expectancy*, especially among relatively wealthy countries.

Although socioeconomic status (SES) disparities have been shown to be a powerful predictor of life-span within a country, the cross-national data discussed above indicate that the GDP index of absolute wealth cannot fully explain life expectancy differences across countries or between the sexes. As noted above, Costa Rica is an interesting example with a GDP per capita of just over $4,000 a year, but a life expectancy of 78 years. The poorest countries, such as Ethiopia and Burundi, rank very low on the life expectancy list but are not at the very bottom of the GDP index. Whether one examines the top 30 countries by HDI, total life expectancy, or women's life expectancy, the Nordic and Western European countries are always included in the top ranking, as are the United States and Costa

Rica. One way to understand the life-span and gender gap variation in these cross-national data is to examine the distribution of wealth, consider what policy choices are made within the constraints of GDP, and analyze how these factors might differentially affect the lives of men and women. Another facet of the gender gap explanation might include the complex interaction among biology, behavior, and particular aspects of the social environment.

The variation in life expectancy, especially across wealthier countries and between men and women, highlights several issues. Women live longer than men all over the world except in those countries where extreme poverty and social instability diminish the life expectancy and health status of both men and women. But GDP per capita (admittedly a gross measure) does not predict in any consistent way either overall life expectancy or the gender gap. The life expectancy of men and women in countries at the lower end of the ranking can be explained in large part by economic capacity, the social disadvantages associated with poverty, and the disease-specific contributions to adult mortality. But that explanation is not compelling when applied to the variation in life-span or the gender gap range in the 30 countries with higher life expectancy. The three main causes of mortality (heart disease, cancer, and stroke) are the same across most developed countries and especially in those countries with higher life expectancy. However, the patterns of disease and age-related mortality rates are somewhat different in those countries with the lowest life expectancy, especially where life-threatening diseases such as AIDS or conditions such as malnutrition are widespread. *The gender gap in life expectancy across most developed countries varies in ways that up to now have not been easily or fully explained.* Biological and social processes both may be implicated, but the terms "advantage" and "disadvantage" are too limited in their ability to capture the paradoxical gender and health patterns.

If Not Wealth, What Else Determines Life-Span Differences Across Nations?

There are three prevalent approaches to explaining differences in health status and particularly life expectancy within and between countries. The first explanation focuses on the role of individual SES as generally measured by a combination of education and income, the second approach focuses on the health benefits of social status per se, and the third examines the distribution of a country's wealth.

Most health policy analysts recognize that the opportunity for individual social and economic achievement varies by race and class within and across societies and that one's social position has a persistent association with health status. In fact, the strong relationship between SES and health status is one of the most well-established associations in health research (Adler & Newman, 2002; Beckfield, 2004; Kawachi, Kennedy, & Wilkinson, 1999; Krieger, Chen, Waterman, Rehkopf, & Subramanian, 2005; Phelan, Link, Diez-Roux, Kawachi, & Levin, 2004; Schnittker, 2004; Williams, 2002, 2003). For example, Phelan and colleagues (2004) argue that income and education affect the degree to which a particular individual or family has an abundance or scarcity of opportunities for effectively using resources for reducing risk and promoting health; for example, the option to make health a priority, rather than simply an issue of survival, or in a less extreme case for families to make their long-term health and that of their children a priority rather than just focusing on meeting and managing their day-to-day needs.

Studies documenting the relationship between SES and health disparities have examined the effect of income and education on both individual well-being and population health. However, recent work examining the interaction among income, education, and health suggests that the persistent positive relationship between higher income and better health varies significantly within the 'United States in both its strength and shape by level of education (Schnittker, 2004). Schnittker's research shows not only that education improves health but also that its effects are larger at lower income levels: "Those with more education have better health for all levels of income, and fewer income-based disparities exist among the well educated than among the less well educated" (p. 286). Moreover, education is a means to attaining a higher income and status, which combine to produce greater opportunities and better health (House, Lantz, & Wray, 2005; Marmot, 2004, 2005; Mirowsky & Ross, 2003). From a research standpoint the extent of the beneficial health effects of education may be hidden, especially over the long term, when combined with income to form a measure of SES. In terms of our argument, constrained choices that affect the opportunity to obtain advanced education in earlier life stages can over time have health and other quality of life effects at later stages.

To advance the discussion of how income and education are linked to national policies and the impact on men's and women's opportunities and choices, we briefly explain the primary pathways through which individual SES and a factor known as the SES gradient affect health.

Each country and its policy regime define the extent to which education is a private or public good, thus affecting access to opportunities and the cost of early childhood education or pursuing higher education. Countries differ greatly in the extent to which they provide free access and entitlements to a university education. However, even where there is free access, there is still a question of the differential capacity of groups with varying SES to take advantage of such access. For example, wealthier families have the funds to allow their children to postpone working full time until they have obtained the education required for their career goals. Even when education is universal and "free," children from low-income families cannot always postpone working when they are young adults so they can attend school full time for an extended period. Many factors other than career goals can affect the choices of families regarding educational plans for their children, but this is especially true for low-income families with children. Seldom do those making such decisions recognize the potential downstream connection to health.

Taken together, a country's social policies establish an opportunity structure that creates both a minimum level of SES and the range of socioeconomic circumstances within which most of its citizens live, perceive options, and make choices, however constrained. Goldman (2001) and others argue that health consistently improves as one moves up the social ladder, and most research supports this conclusion. Clearly, the wealthiest are healthier than those in the middle classes who are healthier than the poor. Even small SES differences between social groups can lead to varying levels of health. This continuum has been labeled the "social gradient" of health (Goldman, 2001; Hertzman, Frank, & Evans, 1994).[13] There is also some evidence that the largest health improvements

---

[13] Various explanations have been provided for the association between SES and health. Link and Phelan (2000) suggest that this association may be reflective of the types

are found with upward mobility brought about by a rise in income to those at the lower end of the distribution, with smaller gains associated with increasing income in the highest brackets.

Goldman (2001) explores several other pathways through which SES may affect health. SES can limit or facilitate one's access to medical care and to information regarding behaviors that damage or safeguard one's health. Consequently, those individuals with more social and economic resources are more likely to obtain current information regarding health effects and become early adopters of practices shown to protect health. SES also influences the environment in which people live. Wealthier individuals can afford to live in areas that are in many ways safer than those inhabited by poorer persons (due, for example, to lower crime rates, better air quality, or greater distance from known environmental hazards). SES may govern one's ability to respond effectively and quickly to potentially damaging health problems. Higher SES individuals typically have more control over the demands on their time and greater resources for engaging in leisure-time activities. This also allows them greater freedom to engage in positive health behaviors, such as exercise, and to seek medical care when needed.[14] Finally, governments take into account income inequalities and play a large role in providing opportunities to redress disparities or inequities through social policies and

---

of work that individuals at each level of the social ladder engage in. Work-related stress explanations include the demand-control model and the effort-reward imbalance model (Siegrist, 2002; Siegrist & Marmot, 2004). In these models, sustained exposure to adverse psychosocial environments produces chronic stress reactions with long-term health consequences. According to Siegrist and Marmot (2004), such adverse working conditions occur more frequently among lower socioeconomic groups, and their already existing vulnerability increases that effect. Lower SES individuals may also be exposed to higher levels of health-damaging stress associated with poverty per se.

[14] Goldman (2001) also explores several alternative explanations for the ever-present association between SES and health. She states that scholars have argued that this association may result from a person's health leading to socioeconomic success or failure, rather than the other way around. Those individuals who are healthy are more likely to succeed financially than those with consistent health problems or disability. Goldman argues that although this association can occur (especially with regard to potentially debilitating conditions such as schizophrenia and epilepsy), these "selection" mechanisms do not provide an adequate explanation for the link. Goldman also raises the possibility that this link may be the result of nothing more than statistical manipulation.

provisions that redistribute resources, including welfare and health care as well as education and child care.

Epidemiologists and other social scientists have offered the range of income inequality as another determinant of the health disparities of populations.[15] Rather than focusing on the absolute income of individuals, these scholars have argued that the distribution of wealth across a society has its own independent impact on health. Those societies that are highly unequal in terms of the range or distribution of income generally have greater disparities in health and a relatively lower life expectancy. This would be one explanation for the higher life expectancy of the Nordic countries, which have a more even distribution of wealth compared to the United States, which has a steeper distribution of income (Kawachi & Kennedy, 2006).

These researchers offer two primary explanations for the health effects of the distribution of wealth. One concerns the threshold effect, in which those with lower incomes experience particularly worse health and lower life expectancy. In the other explanation all are affected to some extent by the unequal income distribution, leading to the health gradient observed in industrialized countries. One of the clearest examples may be the extent to which having a poor segment of the population without access to health care increases the risk of exposure to infectious disease or possibly an epidemic. Subramanian, Kawachi, and Kennedy (2001) argue that income inequality accomplishes this health gradient through a variety of mechanisms, including those already discussed above. Inequality can also be a sign of a lack of social cohesion, the existence of social exclusion, and high levels of conflict among groups, which are assumed to negatively affect health. Finally, the negative psychological reactions of citizens in unequal societies may lead to poor health. Individuals who are poor relative to the larger population frequently experience a lack of control, lack of respect, and a general sense of hopelessness that damage their

---

[15] Beckfield (2004) critically examines the body of research that has led social epidemiologists to accept the link between poor health and inequality. Beckfield argues that much of the work "uses limited samples, employs simple bivariate methods without relevant controls, fails to account for unobserved heterogeneity, and uses internationally incomparable data" (p. 231). Beckfield conducts his own test of the hypothesis and finds no statistically significant relationship between poor health and income inequality.

health (Marmot, 2004). Other researchers have argued that societies with greater inequities may make fewer investments in human capital and infrastructure (Beckfield, 2004). Such societies, it is argued, are unable to provide adequate education, health services, and other basics to those on the lower end of the income scale.[16]

SES and Social Status Do Not Explain All Gender Health Differences

The question remains: *If SES and social status per se are the main determinants of life-span and other measures of health status, then how can that be reconciled with the fact that historically men have had both greater wealth and social status but consistently higher mortality rates than women?* Few social scientists dispute the fact that individual SES and other social factors explain health status disparities among men and among women as suggested in Chapter 2, but women's income and status disadvantage do not explain their greater longevity compared to men, although these measures might in some way help explain their greater morbidity. For example, Read and Gorman (2006) show that the magnitude of the gender difference varies not only by race and ethnic group but also by the health status category used for comparison.[17] It could be the

[16] But the association between income inequality and life expectancy is not simply the result either of the health risks of those with the lowest income at the bottom of the pyramid, as some researchers contend, or of downward mobility among those who become chronically ill or disabled. A population's health is also linked to the range in distribution of income and the status differentials that result (Marmot, Boback, & Smith, 1995). Marmot (2005) argues that the health effects of status differences are so basic that they can also be found in other species, as established, for example, in the social hierarchy of baboons. Studies of both humans (and animals) demonstrate how status differential produces a biological impact through the stress created by unequal access to health-promoting resources. Those individuals in the lowest income brackets face much higher mortality rates than those at the top. Life at the top is not just better: it is also longer (*New York Times*, May 16, 2005). This health gradient was also observed among British civil servants at different hierarchical levels in the occupational structure after controlling for known health risks (see Marmot et al., 1995).

[17] Using data from the 1997–2001 waves of the National Health Interview Survey, Read and Gorman (2006) examined gender differences in self-rated health, functional limitations, and life-threatening conditions among whites, blacks, Mexicans, Puerto Ricans, and Cubans. After adjusting for SES and other background factors, the authors found consistently higher levels of functional limitations for all women compared to men in their same race and ethnic group. Comparisons of other health measures were more variable.

case that these puzzling gender differences result in part from biological processes or disease patterns yet to be identified. One pathway, for example, might be that men experience some type of chronic stress that triggers a physiological immune response different from that in women and that puts them at greater risk of early and fatal CVD. Alternatively, it is also plausible that the policy choices being made by countries contribute to gender role constraints and options that differentially affect men's and women's health. *In terms of longevity, gender-based analysis may have encouraged policy choices that have affected the social organization of women's lives more effectively than men's lives.* But then there is the issue of women's greater range of disabling, non-life-threatening illnesses.

Examining the circumstances of John and Susan, the middle-class couple discussed earlier in the chapter and in Chapter 2, provides a way to link the discussion of individual SES and health to national social policies and choice. Recalling their dilemma it is to easy to understand the stress and strain produced by the conflicts between their priorities and economic status and the tradeoffs made necessary by competing demands on their available money, time, and energy. One set of stress-producing conflicts derives from competing priorities and constraints on their choices: wanting to live in a safe neighborhood with good schools, wanting to provide the children with educational advantages and other healthy starts, and, not having the income to afford the cost of housing in a safe and stable neighborhood with good schools unless one or both of them work more hours or change jobs/careers. However, choosing the last option could compromise both Susan and John's health and possibly their access to the desirable health insurance that is a benefit of John's employment. In addition, Susan and John are both aware that providing their children with a good education will likely provide them long-term health benefits, due in part to the acquisition of problem-solving skills and the increased economic opportunities that create additional options and strategies for pursuing a healthy life. Clearly, Susan and John are working hard to optimize their children's futures, but both are experiencing significant social and economic strains in their own lives in part as a result of their efforts to prioritize and achieve this goal. Education is one key means for conveying a family's SES to its children in the United States, as in many other developed countries. But this family's time and money choices are constrained because it is difficult to maximize both their own opportunities and those of their children at the same time, much less while caring for other relatives (such as Susan's retired and ailing father). In addition, the high-quality day care they selected for their 2-year-old daughter is very expensive. The existence of policies providing universal access to all levels of education, child care, and health care regardless of income would both ease the stress and worry associated with limited resources and the need to choose among competing priorities. It would also enhance the opportunities for Susan and John, depending on career demands and worksite policies (discussed further in Chapter 5), to make their own health a priority.

However, it is essential in this discussion of national policy effects not to lose sight of the fact that in many countries married couples have some advantages that single working adults do not. With two incomes (which is now the norm among married couples in the United States) one spouse can work and put the other through school or they can take turns doing that. Many benefits are tied to employment, and married couples who both work have access to tax reductions and greater opportunities for health insurance. The latter is particularly critical for women who are less likely to have jobs that provide health insurance. It is also important for men in lower status occupations, but unlike most women these men are not likely to get benefits from a spouse's employment. The differences between married couples and single adults in opportunities and constraints are likely to be greater in those developed countries, such as the United States, that do not provide entitlements for universal health care and access to free higher education.

Another complex question to consider in this context is the extent to which social policies provide incentives intended to promote marriage and whether and how this varies across countries (Moffitt & Ploeg, 2001; O'Connor et al., 1999). Yet, in the United States the proportion of unmarried and single Americans (over the age of 15 years including those who are widowed and divorced) has been increasing for several decades; single Americans now comprise 43 percent of the adult population. The proportion of married men and women dropped from 65% and 60% in 1970 to 56% and 52%, respectively, in the year 2000. In 2003, 57% of the 29,431,000 adult persons living alone were female, and 25% of these women were 65 years or older (compared to 9% of males). Young single adults ages 30–34 are also much more common than a generation ago. For example, the proportion of single women in this age group increased from 6% in 1970 to 22% in 2000 and of single men from 9% to 30% (U.S. Census Bureau, 2005). Although most of the focus in this book is on married couples with children, single adults are discussed more fully in Chapters 5 and 6.

Clearly, socioeconomic status alone does not explain the gender difference in life-span.[18] The differences in life expectancy between men and women exist within and between social classes. Women outlive men in the same social class, and lower class women have as long a life expectancy as men in better financial positions (House, 2002; Moen, 2001; Rieker & Bird, 2005). *The discrepant pattern in these comparisons suggests that there is no simple explanation for the cross-national differences in women's and men's life expectancy.* Clearly, there must be another factor or process at work at the regime or social policy level that affects the social organization of men's and women's lives and that could be related to the gender and health status differentials across SES in these cross-national comparisons. We contend that the decisions and social policies enacted by each country shape gender roles and expectations, which in turn can enhance and constrain men's and women's ability to make health a priority. Rather than focusing on mechanisms such as SES or the unequal distribution of income that have been shown to be linked to health status, we prefer to draw attention to the structure of social provisions in policy regimes and assess their contribution to gender differences.

HOW POLICY REGIMES CONTRIBUTE TO GENDER DIFFERENCES IN HEALTH

We use Esping-Anderson's (1990) policy regime classification schema to select and group the countries presented in Table 3.3 for the purpose of comparing life expectancy and other factors, describing the nature of the social policies within each policy regime category, and identifying

---

[18] See, for example, the special issue of *The Journals of Gerontology: Series B Psychological Sciences and Social Sciences*, "Health Inequalities Across the Life Course" edited by Zarit and Pearlin (2005) and Elo and Drevenstedt (2005).

the ways in which the existence or lack of specific policies might promote or constrain men's and women's choices and well-being. Esping-Anderson's schema categorizes regimes on the basis of the policies and social provisions they have enacted, the social welfare principles underlying those provisions including citizenship entitlements, and the mechanism through which they are funded.

The cross-national comparisons of social policies and life-span described above provide a basis for assessing whether the particular social provisions that countries have enacted are associated with general health status and, specifically, with the gender gap in health. We contend that policy regimes can establish, reinforce, and transform social roles and gender relations (see Orloff, 1996). This macro-level structure of decisions affects the daily lives of individual men and women in both different and similar ways, but especially in employment patterns, career options, and child care responsibilities. We draw on the Esping-Andersen framework (based on his observations from 18 countries) because it provides a reasonable way to categorize state regimes. We recognize that there are numerous ways to label policy regimes, but debates about this issue, although interesting, are beyond the scope of this work.

As discussed earlier, Esping-Andersen argues that policy regimes fall into one of three broad categories: liberal, conservative-corporatist, and social democratic.[19] The liberal policy regime is the most successful in

---

[19] Although there is considerable debate about these categories and no single pure case, Esping-Andersen (1990) classified the United States, Canada, Australia, and probably Great Britain as liberal regimes; identified the Nordic countries as social-democratic regimes; and categorized Austria, France, Germany, Italy, and the Netherlands as conservative-corporatist regimes. The main dimension that varies across these state governments is whether and to what degree human needs are interlocked with the market's and the family's role in social provisions. "In countries with a liberal social policy, the market, rather than the state is responsible for most welfare needs. For example, in Canada, Britain and the US public pension benefits make up a smaller proportion of the incomes of the elderly than they do in Scandinavian countries or in Europe. . . . Programs in liberal regimes avoid undercutting the market by offering only stigmatizing subsistence-level grants to those unable to participate in the market" (Orloff, 1993, p. 310). Social democratic and conservative regimes provide a larger range of welfare activities, crowding out the market. Systems of social provision have stratifying effects. According to Orloff (1993, p. 304), "Not enough is known about how and to what extent systems of social provision actually do vary in the gender content, how social provision and other state institutions affect gender relations, and how the state's impact on gender relations is related to its effects on other social relations."

making individuals dependent on market forces (generally referred to as commodifying).[20]

Liberal regimes generally provide some limited cash transfers or social insurance programs to low-income individuals and families as, for example, the United States does with welfare programs, such as Aid to Dependent Children, Social Security, or aid for the physically disabled. Such policies as the welfare system in the United States or the Canadian Social Transfer and Child Care Tax Benefit are explicitly designed to encourage individuals to seek to improve their lot by entering the market as benefits are modest and are associated with a social stigma. Esping-Andersen contends that the United States, Canada, and Australia are liberal regimes.

Neither the conservative-corporatist nor the social democratic regimes depend as much on the market to fulfill basic human needs. Both of these models rely heavily on the state to take responsibility for filling this role. Esping-Andersen contends that the conservative-corporatist model establishes policies intended to maintain class differences and traditional family arrangements; the state is careful not to disrupt such social arrangements by creating incentives for individuals to adopt alternative lifestyles, such as single parenthood. And indeed there are some data to support this claim. For example, in 1991 conservative-corporatist countries such as Italy and the Netherlands had lower rates of single mothers and fathers than liberal welfare regimes such as the United States and Canada (see Table 4.2 in O'Connor et al., 1999).

In contrast, the benefits provided by social democratic regimes tend to be relatively more universalistic, thus decommodifying their citizens by reducing the degree of individual burden and dependence on market forces for their health and well-being. In this type of regime, the state takes on more responsibility and seeks to provide a similar quality of life

---

[20] Esping-Andersen (1990) describes the welfare state as a mechanism for ameliorating the destructive effects of capitalism. He argues that capitalism "commodifies" individuals. People are dependent on the market and are forced to sell themselves as one would sell any product. The welfare state can function to reduce the degree to which an individual is dependent on the capitalist market system. From his perspective, social assistance decommodifies the individual and defines the ability to survive as a right, rather than something contingent on one's ability to function in the market. However, not all welfare states use the same methods or are supported by the same ideologies. Also, the level to which individuals are successfully decommodified varies significantly from state to state.

for all of its citizens, thus allowing individuals and families to have more protection from social risks and market forces and perhaps more latitude to make choices about how they live. Where conservative-corporatist regimes can serve to discourage women with children from working, social democratic regimes provide mothers with the means and supportive child services, so they can work outside the home. Thus, social democratic regimes give women options for combining work and family. For instance, parents with young children in Helsinki, Finland, receive 520 EUR per month for full-time parental care, which is about 35% of an average income (OECD, 2005). As a result, two-thirds of mothers of very young children have the option to stay home until the child reaches 3 years old. Such policies can serve either to reduce or to increase the overall female employment rate as well as cumulative earnings for women (see also Mason & Jensen, 1995). For example, in Finland, employment declines for women as family size increases. In this complex policy scenario of benefits and effects, however, it should also be noted that the gender wage gap is smaller in Finland and Sweden than in the United States and the United Kingdom (OECD, 2005).

Unfortunately, the literature on policy regime analysis does not consider simultaneously the impact of social provisions on gender relations and health. To illustrate the type of analysis that would complement our argument, we next compare countries representative of liberal policy regimes such as the United States, Canada, Australia, and the United Kingdom and those representative of social democratic states such as Sweden, Norway, Denmark, and Finland with conservative-corporatist countries such as France, Austria, Germany, Italy, and the Netherlands. The objective here is to further examine the relationship among social provision policies, gender, and health status (for a description of this classification system see Footnote 19).

Table 3.3 provides a comparison of regime type, GDP, Gini score[21] (a measure of income inequality), and gender differences in life expectancy

---

[21] The Gini index "[m]easures the extent to which the distribution of income (or consumption) among individuals or households within a country deviates from a perfectly equal distribution. A Lorenz curve plots the cumulative percentages of total income received against the cumulative number of recipients, starting with the poorest individual or household. The Gini index measures the area between the Lorenz curve and a hypothetical line of absolute equality, expressed as a percentage of maximum area

Gender and Health

Table 3.3. *Type of Regime, Life Expectancy,* Gini, Healthy Life Expectancy, and* GDP***

Regime Type	GDP	Life Expectancy (Healthy LE)		Difference	Gini
		Women	Men		
Liberal					
United States	$36,006	80.1 (71.3)	74.6 (67.2)	5.5 (4.1)	40.8
Canada	22,777	82.1 (74.0)	77.2 (70.1)	4.9 (3.9)	33.1
Australia	20,822	82.8 (74.3)	77.8 (70.9)	5 (3.4)	35.2
United Kingdom	26,444	80.7 (72.1)	76.2 (69.1)	4.5 (3.0)	36.0
Social Democratic					
Sweden	$26,929	82.4 (74.8)	77.9 (71.9)	4.5. (2.9)	25.0
Denmark	32,179	79.5 (71.1)	74.9 (68.6)	4.6 (2.5)	24.7
Norway	41,974	81.9 (73.6)	77 (70.4)	4.9 (3.2)	25.8
Finland	25,295	81.8 (73.5)	75.1 (68.7)	6.7 (4.8)	26.9
Conservative Corporatist					
France	$24,061	82.9 (74.7)	75.8 (69.3)	7.1 (5.4)	32.7
Austria	25,356	81 (73.5)	75 (69.3)	6 (4.2)	30.0
Germany	24,051	81.3 (74.0)	75.5 (69.6)	5.8 (4.4)	28.3
Italy	20,528	82.9 (74.7)	76.9 (70.7)	6 (4.0)	36.0
Netherlands	25,866	80.9 (72.6)	76.2 (69.7)	4.7 (2.9)	32.6

* LE and HLE figures from OECD Health Data, 2005.
** GDP and Gini scores from United Nations, 2004.

along with healthy life expectancy. Except for Denmark, every country regardless of regime type has a higher life expectancy for both men and women than the United States. Moreover, every country but the United States has some form of a universal health care system as well. All of these countries, with the exception of Norway, also have a considerably lower GDP per capita than the United States. Table 3.3 shows that men's and women's life expectancy do not vary greatly across the three regime types. In addition, the gender gap in life-span ranges between 4 and 6 years with two exceptions; in Finland and France the gender gap is between 6.7 and 7.1 years. However, there is somewhat more variation in life expectancy among the liberal and social democratic regimes than among the conservative-corporatist countries. The social democratic countries (Sweden, Denmark, Norway, and Finland) have lower Gini scores than

under the line. A value of 0 represents perfect equality, a value of 100 perfect inequality" (United Nations Human Development Report and Index, 2005, p. 271).

the other two types of regimes, suggesting that there is greater income equality in these countries. The United States has the highest Gini score (40.8), indicating greater income inequality across the population. Except for Italy, the liberal regimes have higher Gini scores followed by the conservative-corporatist regimes. On the face of it, there does not seem to be a strong relationship between Gini scores and men's and women's life expectancy as Beckfield (2004) has argued. These data provide only a superficial glimpse as to how the kind of policy comparisons that we propose could become the basis for further research and a more in-depth analysis.

It makes sense to examine the policies of the countries with the largest gender gap, Finland and France, to suggest what factors might contribute to these differences. They both have similar GDP per capita, a 1-year difference in life expectancy rates and expected healthy life-span in France's favor, and a large difference in Gini scores, indicating that France has greater income inequality. The citizens in both countries have universal entitlements to health care and higher education. *But what then accounts for the relatively large gender gap in life expectancy?* Perhaps differences in individual health behaviors, such as alcohol consumption, drug abuse, smoking rates, exercise, nutrition, or variation in employment patterns, may contribute to the gender gap (these issues are discussed in detail in Chapter 6). Men in Sweden live 3 years longer than men in France and 4 years longer than men in Finland, although women live to similar ages in all three countries. The distribution and types of disease – for example, drug and alcohol dependence versus rates of depression – might differentiate men and women in these countries. There could be some underlying biological or genetic process at work that interacts with the social environment at different life-course stages and that might explain the differences between these two countries and Sweden. Immigration is far greater in France and Finland than in Sweden, and the health status of either different SES groups or minority populations might contribute to the gender gap, but this would seem to affect men more than women. Finally, there may be policies, gender norms, or work-related patterns that affect men's and women's lifestyle choices and opportunities to pursue health in dissimilar ways. Clearly, further research is required to address some of the issues we have raised with this comparison of policy regimes and life-span.

FINAL THOUGHTS AND FURTHER QUESTIONS TO BE ADDRESSED

We found great variation across nations in life-span rates and gender gaps in life expectancy that cannot be attributed solely to aggregate measures of wealth or to individual income inequality, except in the very poorest of nations. Although every country that ranked higher on life expectancy than the United States has some form of universal health care, it is not simply a matter of access to health care either, as a gender gap favoring women still exists even in those countries with universal access. Moreover, most of the countries with higher life expectancy than the United States have a lower GDP per capita. Obviously, the benefits of universal health care are economic as well as health related. It is our contention that gender differences in life expectancy are connected in complex ways to national-level policies, such as universal health care and education, retirement benefits that are not solely tied to employment, and family-friendly policies including day care and elder care, among others. The social provisions alter work and family life and affect health by increasing or constraining men's and women's opportunities and options to pursue health. Constrained choice affects individual and family stress levels and exposure to risks not in some direct, linear cause-and-effect way but by creating incentives and disincentives for engaging in particular health behaviors. Gender-based analysis of potential health impacts of policies would provide valuable information for guiding further decisions.

Social policies provide a safety net for vulnerable groups, such as children, the elderly, the unemployed, the less well educated, and sole-parent families, who might need additional support to live productive and healthy lives. With such policies the state shares the responsibility for protecting the well-being of its citizens. The degree of responsibility for health and well-being assumed by the state and that left to individuals varies considerably across policy regimes and contributes to the social organization of men's and women's lives, the opportunities and constraints on their choices, and subsequently their life-span.

Although national social provision policies provide benefits to men and women that alleviate some of their exposure to health risks, they do not completely govern "personal agency"– the choices that individuals make or the gender role division of labor in families or in the organizations where people work. Thus, according to most policy analysts men spend the majority of their time in work and work-related activities in almost all developed countries, whereas women divide their time between work and family. Men's work and family life are just as stressful as women's, but most social policies have been focused on women and children. From our perspective the question to be asked about men's shorter life-span is, *What keeps men from choosing health?* The answer may have less to do with SES and more to do with the constraints they face amidst the myriad of social demands and how they fulfill or enact their gender roles as husbands or employees.

Countries and policy regimes have grappled with whether to treat men and women the same or differently and how to affect gender roles and gender relations, but improving health is generally not the goal in these discussions. Efforts have been made to bring about gender equity in wages, to provide support for women's greater child care responsibilities, and through incentives to involve men more in child care, household labor, and caregiving. In the United States, the dominant approach to men's and women's health has focused on the modification of individual risk factors (e.g., through information and interventions to reduce smoking, improve diet, reduce stress, and increase other preventive health behaviors). There is a strong belief that if individuals are given the right information, they will make informed choices. The variation in life-spans and the gender gap challenge that belief, particularly in the United States.

Except for some more recent policies to restrict smoking, the main public health approach in the United States has been to rely on providing extensive information and confusing advice about which individual choices regarding health behaviors would promote health, rather than altering the structure of work life or making available more opportunities to pursue health. In contrast, countries where men have a higher life expectancy, for example, Sweden and Norway, have altered both men's work lives and the availability of opportunities to pursue health. Ironically, the United States emphasizes individual choice without ever altering the larger constraints that make more options and opportunities available. The structure and expectations about the centrality of work have so constrained the options as to almost make choice negligible.

Policy decisions have helped level the playing field for women, especially in those countries that have enacted social provisions based to some extent on gender-based analysis. Because most men have proportionately higher earnings and status than women, policymakers have assumed perhaps that men did not need or would not benefit from targeted social provisions. At this point, we do not have the type of research needed to examine how national policies affect behavioral and biological processes. So we have to assume that the social patterns associated with illness and health interact with biological processes and health behaviors in complex ways.

Despite our contention that national policy choices affect women's and men's health differently, the question to be addressed through further research remains: *How do particular policies increase opportunities or barriers and provide incentives and disincentives for pursuing health?* That question has not been addressed before and is therefore not a simple one to answer. Because the connections between national policy and gender health disparities are generally not transparent, at this time there are no compelling data. In our discussion we relied on examples of the everyday decisions that confront Susan and John about where to live, what jobs to pursue, how to provide for their children's day care and education, and how to find time to engage in health behaviors that reduce the probability of illness and a shorter life-span. By inference we compared their options to those of people in countries with more extensive family policies and better life expectancy.

We argue that recognizing differential gender constraints is essential to understanding how to change individual behaviors in ways that affect health. There are many opportunities to design research and do analysis that will provide a better understanding of policy impacts on men's and women's health. The pathways discussed in this chapter and gender-based analysis that addresses both men and women provide a promising direction for the cross-disciplinary research we advocate.

In this chapter we have looked at how national policies affect gender differences in health. In the next chapter we address how men's and women's choices may be constrained by policies and decisions at the community and neighborhood level.

References

Adler, N. E., & Newman, K. (2002). Socioeconomic disparities in health: Pathways and policies. *Health Affairs, 34*(1), 6–14.

Beckfield, J. (2004). Does inequality harm health? New cross-national evidence. *J Health Soc Behav, 45*, 231–248.

Boston Globe, 2005. Wellesley College advised Pentagon on victim office. P. A1, December 10.

Brownson, R. C., Baker, E. A., Housemann, R. A., Brennan, L. K., & Bacak, S. J. (2001). Environmental and policy determinants of physical activity in the United States. *Am J Pub Health, 91*, 1995–2003.

Elo, I. T., & Drevenstedt, G. L. (2005). Cause-specific contributions to sex differences in adult mortality among whites and African Americans between 1960 and 1995. *Demogr Res, 13*(19), 485–519.

Esping-Andersen, G. (1990). *The Three Worlds of Welfare Capitalism.* Princeton, NJ: Princeton University Press.

Estes, C. (2003). Social Security privatization and older women: A feminist political economy perspective. *J Aging Stud, 18*, 9–26.

Fodor, E., Glass, C., Kawachi, J., & Popescu, L. (2002). Family policies and gender in Hungary, Poland and Romania. *Comm Post-Comm Stud, 35*, 475–490.

Giles-Corti, B., & Donovan, R. J. (2002). The relative influence of individual, social and physical environment determinants of physical activity. *Soc Sci Med, 54*, 1793–1812.

Giles-Corti, B., & Donovan, R. J. (2003). Relative influences of individual, social environmental, and physical environmental correlates of walking. *Am J Pub Health, 93*(9), 1583–1590.

Goldman, N. (2001). Social inequalities in health: Disentangling the underlying mechanisms. *Ann NY Acad Sci, 954*, 118–139.

Hertzman, C., Frank, J., & Evans, E. G. (1994). Heterogeneities in health status and the determinants of population health. In M. L. Barer & T. R. Marmor (Eds.), *Why Are Some People Healthy and Other Not?: The Determinants of Health of Populations* (pp. 67–92). New York: Aldine De Gruyter.

House, J. S. (2002). Understanding social factors and inequalities in health: 20th century progress and 21st century prospects. *J Health Soc Behav, 43*, 125–142.

House, J. S., Lantz, P. M., & Wray, L. A. (2005). Continuity and change in the social stratification of aging and health over the life course: Evidence from a nationally representative longitudinal study from 1086 to 2001/2002 (Americans Changing Lives Study). *J Gerontol Ser B, 60B*(Special Issue II), 15–26.

Kawachi, I., & Kennedy, B. (2006). *The Health of Nations: Why Inequality Is Harmful to Your Health.* New York: New Press.

Kawachi, I., Kennedy, B., & Wilkinson, R. J. (1999). *Income Inequality and Health: A Reader.* New York: New Press.

Krieger, N., Chen, J. T., Waterman, P. D., Rehkopf, D. H., & Subramanian, S. V. (2005). Painting a truer picture of US socioeconomic and racial/ethnic health inequalities: The Public Health Disparities Geocoding Project. *Am J Pub Health, 95*, 312–323.

Link, B. G., & Phelan, J. (2000). Evaluating the fundamental cause explanation for social disparities in health. In C. E. Bird, P. Conrad, & A. M. Fremont (Eds.), *The Handbook of Medical Sociology* (5th ed., pp. 33–46). Upper Saddle River, NJ: Prentice-Hall.

Marmot, M. (2004). *The Status Syndrome: How Social Standing Affects Our Health and Longevity.* New York: Henry Holt & Co.

Marmot, M. (2005). Social determinants of health inequalities. *Lancet, 365,* 1099–1104.

Marmot, M., Boback, M., & Smith, G. D. (1995). Explanations for social inequalities in health. In B. C. Amick, S. Levine, A. R. Tarlov, & D. C. Walsh (Eds.), *Society and Health* (pp. 172–210). New York: Oxford University Press.

Mason, K. A., & Jensen, A. M. (1995). *Gender and Family Change in Industrialized Countries: International Studies in Demography.* Oxford: Oxford University Press.

Miles, S., & Parker, K. (1997). Men, women, and health insurance. *N Engl J Med, 336,* 218–221.

Mirowsky, J., & Ross, K. (2003). *Education, Social Status, and Health.* Hawthorne, NY: Aldine De Gruyter.

Moen, P. (2001). The gendered life course. In R. H. Binstock & L. K. George (Eds.), *Handbook of Aging and the Social Sciences* (5th ed., pp. 179–196). New York: Academic Press.

Moffitt, R. A., & Ploeg, M. V. (2001). *Evaluating Welfare Reform in an Era of Transition.* Washington, DC: National Academy Press.

O'Connor, J. S., Orloff, A. S., & Shaver, S. (1999). *States, Markets, Families: Gender Liberalism and Social Policy in Australia, Canada, Great Britain and the United States.* London: Cambridge University Press.

Organization for Economic Co-operation and Development (OECD). (1994). *Women and Structural Change: New Perspectives.* Paris: OECD.

Organization for Economic Co-operation and Development (OECD). (1996). *Earnings Inequality, Low Paid Employment and Earnings Mobility.* Paris: OECD.

Organization for Economic Co-operation and Development (OECD). (2004a). *Babies and Bosses – Reconciling Work and Family Life: Australia, Denmark and the Netherlands* (Vol. 1). Paris: OECD.

Organization for Economic Co-operation and Development (OECD). (2004b). *Babies and Bosses – Reconciling Work and Family Life: Austria, Ireland and Japan* (Vol. 2). Paris: OECD.

Organization for Economic Co-operation and Development (OECD). (2004c). *Babies and Bosses – Reconciling Work and Family Life: New Zealand, Portugal and Switzerland* (Vol. 3). Paris: OECD.

Organization for Economic Co-operation and Development (OECD). (2005). *Babies and Bosses – Reconciling Work and Family Life: Canada, Finland, Sweden and United Kingdom* (Vol. 4). Paris: OECD.

Orloff, A. S. (1993). Gender and the social rights of citizenship: The comparative analysis of gender relations and welfare states. *Am Sociol Rev, 58,* 303–328.

Orloff, A. S. (1996). Gender in the welfare state. *Annu Rev Sociol, 22,* 57–78.

Phelan, J., Link, B. G., Diez-Roux, A., Kawachi, I., & Levin, B. (2004). "Fundamental causes" of social inequalities in mortality: A test of the theory. *J Health Soc Behav, 45*(3), 265–285.

Powell, K. E., Martin, L. M., & Chowdbury, P. P. (2003). Places to walk: Convenience and regular physical activity. *Am J Pub Health, 93*(9), 1519–1521.

Read, J. G., & Gorman, B. K. (2006). Gender inequalities in US adult health: The interplay of race and ethnicity. *Soc Sci Med, 65*(5), 1045–1065.

Reskin, B. F., & Padovic, I. (1994). *Women and Men at Work.* Thousand Oaks, CA: Pine Forge Press.

Rieker, P. P., & Bird, C. E. (2005). Rethinking gender differences in health: What's needed to integrate social and biological perspectives. *J Gerontol: Soc Sci, 60B,* 40–47.

Ritter, G., & Skocpol, T. (1991). Gender and the origins of modern social policies in Britain and the United States. *Stud Am Pol Devel, 5,* 36–93.

Ruggie, M. (1984). *The State and Working Women.* Princeton, NJ: Princeton University Press.

Sainsbury, D. (1993). Dual welfare and sex segregation of access to social benefits: Income maintenance policies in the UK, the US, the Netherlands and Sweden. *J Soc Pol, 22,* 69–98.

Sainsbury, D. (1994). *Gendering Welfare States.* London: Sage Publications.

Sainsbury, D. (1996). *Gender, Equality and Welfare States.* Cambridge: Cambridge University Press.

Sambamoorthi, U., Shea, D., & Crystal, S. (2003). Total and out-of-pocket expenditures for prescription drugs among older persons. *Gerontologist, 43*(3), 345–359.

Schnittker, J. (2004). Education and the changing shape of the income gradient in health. *J Health Soc Behav, 45*(3), 286–305.

Siegrist, J. (2002). Reducing social inequalities in health: Work-related strategies. *Scand J Public Health Suppl, 59,* 49–53.

Siegrist, J., & Marmot, M. (2004). Health inequalities and the psychosocial environment-two scientific challenges. *Soc Sci Med, 58*(8), 1463–1473.

Skocpol, T. (1992). *Protecting Soldiers and Mothers: The Political Origin of Social Policy in the United States.* Cambridge, MA: Harvard University Press.

Subramanian, S. V., Kawachi, I., & Kennedy, B. P. (2001). Does the state you live in make a difference? Multilevel analysis of self-rated health in the US. *Soc Sci Med, 53*(1), 9–19.

United Nations. (2002). *Human Development Report: Deepening Democracy in a Fragmented World.* New York: United Nations Development Program. New York: Oxford University Press.

United Nations. (2004). *Human Development Report: International Cooperation at a Crossroads. AIDs, Trade, and Security in an Unequal World.* New York: United Nations Development Program.

United Nations. (2005). *Human Development Report and Index: The State of Human Development.* New York: United Nations Development Program.

U.S. Bureau of Labor Statistics. (2004a). Income, poverty, and health insurance coverage in the United States: 2004. Retrieved September 6, 2006, from http://www.census.gov/prod/2005pubs/p60-229.pdf.

U.S. Bureau of Labor Statistics. (2004b). *Working in the 21st Century.* Washington, DC: U.S. Bureau of Labor.

U.S. Census Bureau. (2005). *Current Population Reports.* Washington, DC: Census Bureau.

U.S. Surgeon General Report. (2006). The health consequences of involuntary exposure to tobacco smoke. Retrieved June 27, 2006, from http://www.surgeongeneral.gov/library/secondhandsmoke/.

Williams, D. (2002). Racial/ethnic variations in women's health: The social embeddedness of health. *Am J Pub Health, 92,* 588–597.

Williams, D. (2003). The health of men: Structured inequalities and opportunities. *Am J Pub Health, 93,* 724–731.

Zarit, S. H., & Pearlin, K. I. (2005). Health inequalities across the life course. *J Gerontol Ser B, 60*(Special Issue II).

Zimmerman, M. K., & Hill, S. A. (2000). Reforming gendered health care: An assessment of change. *Int J Health Serv, 30*(4), 771–795.

FOUR

The Impact of Community on Health

In the previous chapter, we examined how national policies can shape and constrain men's and women's choices in a myriad of ways, many of which can affect their health. Here we narrow the context to focus on state and community polices and characteristics that can also affect men's and women's choices and in turn their health. This level of influence over people's lives is one level lower on our conceptualized constrained choice diagram (Figure 2.2), and hence the impact of state and local policies on individual choice may in many respects be more apparent than that of national policies.

Although this chapter focuses on the health effects of state and local policies, these policies are neither created nor function in a vacuum. In most but not all areas, local, state, and national governments each control some dimension of policy, including funding. The extent to which local resources and problems are a function of multiple levels of governmental decision making varies across countries, and it is generally greater in those with a decentralized federal system that gives more control to states or provinces. In the United States at least, there is considerable variation in both state and local policies ranging from those regarding air quality and land use to those on aspects of the social safety net, policing, and transportation.[1] Together these policies shape the social and

---

[1] For example, national policies such as environmental policy can affect land use in a variety of ways such as protecting wetlands, prohibiting development, or limiting the construction of new housing in areas that have been found to be too vulnerable to flooding. On the local level, many cities have numerous additional requirements regarding where specifically housing and particular types of businesses may be built,

built environments of the states and communities in which we live and work.

THE IDEAL COMMUNITY

The idea that community characteristics and the policies that affect them contribute to residents' quality of life is certainly not new. Although the attributes considered most desirable may have changed over time, the concept of an ideal living environment goes back at least to the Greeks and Romans. Moreover, in the past century in America and England as well as other countries, city planners have advocated planning new communities – based on the notion that it is known what constitutes a desirable space and what characteristics of the place where you live most contribute to a good quality of life. A few planned communities have been built, such as Reston, Virginia; Columbia, Maryland; and Celebration, Florida, in the United States; a variety of communities in Scandinavia; and at least one in England. Urban planners designed these communities based in part on the assumption that by providing a good quality of life, these communities would contribute to the health and well-being of their residents. To encourage social interaction and spending time outdoors, these communities typically provide open green space, playgrounds, public space for events, natural or man-made lakes, housing with porches or verandas so residents could greet and see their neighbors, as well as layouts that facilitate or even encourage walking, such as those with easy access to basic services, good quality schools, and small businesses. In addition, planned communities also seek to create some racial/ethnic and socioeconomic diversity and offer a mix of housing.[2]

the amount of space that must be provided for parking, accessibility to the disabled in public spaces, private homes, and green space, as well as building codes intended to produce safer buildings. States themselves also establish land use policies such as those requiring a certain volume of housing construction on the part of communities to allow for population growth or those regulating the use of land near the ocean or other scenic assets.

[2] Using a combination of interviews and archival research, Forsyth (2005) examines the social, ecological, and economic successes and shortcomings in the 1960s and 1970s for three prominent planned new communities: Columbia, Irvine, and the Woodlands. In so doing, she considers how issues of race and gender evolved. Forsyth and other

The amount of green space in communities has effects that go beyond the social sphere; it even affects the weather. Expanses of concrete in urban areas retain heat, contributing to an increase in temperature sufficient to increase the incidence of thunderstorms, as has occurred in Atlanta over time (Bornstein & Lin, 2000).[3] The effects on pollution in cities that experience temperature inversions can be equally dramatic. In contrast, green spaces reduce summer temperatures, cooling costs, and the risks of power outages. Many communities now recognize the need for more green space and therefore encourage or require property owners to plant trees and reduce expanses of pavement, such as found in surface parking lots. Clearly, even on this one dimension, characteristics of the built environment and community policies can affect individuals' chances of health and well-being as well as their opportunities to improve those chances through positive health behaviors and other strategic choices. Other policy relevant environmental characteristics affect health both directly (for example, by exposure to lead paint, poor air quality, or the availability of parks) and indirectly (such as by encouraging or discouraging particular health behaviors or by contributing to the level of stress that local residents experience in their day-to-day lives).

Although it is obvious that some neighborhoods present physical hazards, such as pollution, crime, or unsafe buildings and other structures, additional aspects of place of residence are potentially of concern if living in a high-stress area, in and of itself, leads to poorer health over time. A wide range of studies suggest that exposure to daily hassles and chronic stressors can over time lead to heightened physiological reactivity, such that one becomes increasingly vulnerable to subsequent stress (Adler et al., 2002; S. Cohen et al., 2002; Fremont & Bird, 2000; Kiecolt-Glaser, McGuire, Robles, & Glaser, 2002; McEwen, 2002; McEwen & Stellar, 1993;

---

scholars (see, for example, Reeves, 2002, and Hendler, 2005) have considered whether and how policy and planning have addressed issues of gender inequality.

[3] Urban heat islands, as they are referred to by meteorologists and geographers, experience temperatures 2 to 10 degrees higher than the surrounding areas (see EPA and NASA websites [http://science.nasa.gov and http://www.epa.gov, respectively]). For a review of literature on the impact of urban areas on weather see Collier (2006). Recent research by Stone and Norman (2006) suggests that the contribution of individual land parcels to regional surface heat island formation could be reduced by approximately 40% through the adoption of land use planning policies.

Singer & Ryff, 1999).[4] Thus, Taylor, Repetti, and Seeman (1997) argue, "High stress neighborhoods, characterized by high density, high crime, and high mobility, may also lead to the development of health compromising behaviors that act as efforts to cope with stress, such as smoking, alcohol consumption and drug abuse" (p. 422). Moreover, high crime, disorder, and deteriorated housing stock, which are likely to become chronic stressors, are also more prevalent in neighborhoods lacking resources that can buffer stress, such as a high level of social integration and trust among the residents. In contrast, neighborhoods with better social and physical infrastructure also tend to have more of the resources such as safe accessible parks that encourage positive health behaviors.

HOW ARE SUSAN AND JOHN AFFECTED?

To illustrate some of the other community and neighborhood characteristics that are affected by state and local policies and that also influence health, we revisit the vignette about Susan and John introduced in Chapter 2.

Perhaps most obviously, Susan and John's stress levels, financial demands, and lack of time are related to their need for day care and quality schools for their children. Specifically, they are directly affected by the availability and cost of day care and after-school care for their two children. Consider, for example, how community characteristics such as the availability of suitable employment and child care likely affect John and Susan. In many cases, the extent to which a particular community characteristic affects men and women differently has to do with gender roles, an issue we discuss in greater detail in Chapter 5.

Problems with inadequate school funding at the state and local level have increased the pressure on Susan and John to support the schools

---

[4] To further this perspective, Teresa Seeman and colleagues proposed a model of allostatic load to show how cumulative stress affects an individual's physiological functioning and thereby increases the risk of a wide range of diseases and mortality (Seeman, Singer, Rowe, Horwitz, & McEwen, 1997). The particular disease outcomes for an individual depend in part on his or her inherent biological risk. Consequently, the model can be applied to examine the impact of stress differences for groups that also differ on average in their genetic (or other) physiological health risks.

financially and by volunteering in multiple fundraising and other efforts by the school and the Parent Teacher Association. Susan and John also have concerns about and may have even experienced problems with safety in their neighborhood, which relate both to municipal decisions about policing as well as neighborhood residential turnover and the degree of social integration and trust in the neighborhood (Earls & Carlson, 2001; Sampson, Morenoff, & Earls, 1999; Sampson, Raudenbush, & Earls, 1997). Even their commute times and related daily hassles are affected by the community decisions that contribute to the availability of mass transit, the degree of congestion on the roads, and, in John's case, the delay in the light rail system that was scheduled to be extended to their neighborhood. Other community characteristics also affect Susan and John's ability to choose health, including the availability of places to exercise and options for elder care for Susan's father.

A variety of community policies and resources shape the work and family options and constraints highlighted in the vignette. For example, states and communities have taken on such issues as the provision of child care and early childhood education. Some communities require large employers to provide space for and/or subsidize child care, which may make it more accessible and affordable for families. States and school districts also establish not only the starting ages for kindergarten and whether it is provided for a full or half-day, but some also offer half- or full-day universal preschool for 4- or even 3-year-olds. Currently California is pursuing the provision of universal preschool based on a range of studies demonstrating that every dollar spent on effective early childhood intervention and education programs can return $1.26 to $17.07, depending on the population targeted and the length of time the children were followed to assess the benefits (Karoly, Kilburn, & Cannon, 2005). The financial benefits of the preschool programs accrue as the participating children go on to perform better in school (e.g., higher academic achievement, reduced need for special education services or to repeat grades in school, and ultimately better occupational attainment). Obviously there are larger returns per dollar invested in programs serving high-risk populations rather than children at lower risk of adverse social and educational outcomes. The largest benefit-to-cost ratios were found in studies with the longest follow-up period because they captured outcomes at older ages, such as improvements in educational attainment, declines in delinquency and crime, increased earnings, and other outcomes that are most readily translated into dollar benefits. Moreover, as Karoly and her colleagues (2005) point out, these studies have not captured other social and economic benefits of interest here, including possible improved labor market performance for the parents of children participating in the programs, or stronger national economic competitiveness as a result of improvements in educational attainment of a future workforce. Policies at the local level also affect the availability, cost, and quality of elder care services for older family members (e.g., the Medicare Program of All-Inclusive Care for the Elderly [PACE] originally established in San Francisco).[5]

Because the policies and resources mentioned above overlay gender differences in earnings and division of labor, they can and do differentially affect men's and women's lives across states and communities. For example, paid maternity leave is available statewide in a comprehensive plan in California and through statewide temporary disability insurance that includes maternity leave in California, Hawaii, New Jersey, New York, and Rhode Island. Welfare, which is almost exclusively available to single mothers, also differs substantially across states and in practice across counties or communities. An even broader range of policies relate to the availability of early childhood education in the form of universal public preschool, full-day public kindergarten, as well as after-school and summer school programs. Whereas many countries address some or all of these policy issues at the national level, the United States lacks central control and funding over these areas of early child care and education so policy solutions are left in large part to the states and to local school systems.

---

[5] Introduced in San Francisco in the 1970s in response to a demand for community-based care for frail elders, PACE provides an alterative to nursing home care. This innovative managed long-term care program integrates day care for the elderly with on-site acute medical care and long-term care services, all provided by a single service organization. The program has dual goals of enabling continued community residence for the participant and providing quality care at a lower cost than Medicare, Medicaid, and the traditional fee-for-service system. Mui (2001) and Eng and colleagues (C. Eng, Pedulla, Eleazer, McCann, & Fox, 1997) offer excellent descriptions of the PACE program and its history (for additional information on the program, see http://www.medicare.gov/Nursing/Alternatives/Pace.asp, downloaded September 17, 2007).

Because women are more likely than men to be a primary caregiver to a sick or frail friend or family member, neighborhood or community characteristics that make it easier to provide such care, including services to the care recipient and those directed at supporting caregivers, may have larger effects on women's health than men's on average simply because of women's greater need for and exposure to such resources (or lack thereof). Similarly, among both married and single parents, women typically have greater responsibility for children and thus may have greater need for and exposure to community resources, as well as exposure to problems related to their children's needs and activities. Women may also perceive a greater or different kind of responsibility for their children and for these child-related community resources and draw differently on local resources and social networks. Of course, as we see with Susan and John, the gender differences in community effects are not limited to policies and resources related to parenting.

HOW DO COMMUNITIES AND NEIGHBORHOODS AFFECT HEALTH?

Despite substantial evidence that stress affects health, scientists have only begun to explore the pathways through which neighborhoods "get under the skin" as well as whether and how the health effects and pathways differ for men and women. In the discussion below, we consider whether and how policies at the state and local level, which shape the social and physical environments in which we live, may also contribute directly or indirectly to gender differences in health. In reviewing the evidence, we present examples that may reflect biological and social pathways (or, more likely, an interaction between the two). In most cases, we would expect differential effects of both state and local policies and the associated community characteristics that relate to various differences in men's and women's lives; in turn, these differences are due in large part to the social roles individuals fulfill and/or those for which they feel most responsible, either based on their own expectations or on those of others (including but not limited to their peers, coworkers, and parents).

As we noted in the Introduction to this book, we do not discuss the contribution of health care access, availability, and quality to men's and

women's health.[6] However, these issues are clearly critical components
for one's ability to create and maintain a healthy life. We take the need for
access to quality health care as a given and instead focus here on issues
above and beyond health care delivery in shaping men's and women's
opportunities to pursue healthy lives.

Because we are interested in identifying state and local policy levers
and the ways in which decisions at different governmental levels can
affect individual choices, behavior, and health outcomes, this chapter
builds on a long history of research examining effects of place on health.
We consider a large body of research on neighborhood effects on health
that has identified a wide range of links between social and geographic
area characteristics and both individual health behaviors and outcomes.
A substantial body of evidence indicates that the locales we live in can
affect our health in a variety of ways (Kirby & Kaneda, 2006; Morenoff
& Lynch, 2002; Robert, 1999; Yen & Syme, 1999); see also the review by
Patrick and Wizicker (1995).

Most of the work in this area has started from the health outcome and
looked at a range of community characteristics that might explain the patterns in the outcome. In fact, the earliest research on place effects on health
were community studies that examined differences in the rates of particular health outcomes to identify the proximal causes of excess morbidity
and mortality in a community or neighborhood (sometimes referred to
as epidemiological hot spots) or to learn what attributes contributed to
unusually low rates of a particular illness or disorder.[7] Understanding

---

[6] An extensive literature examines issues of gender differences in utilization, access, and
quality of care. The nature and complexities of the issues surrounding health care
delivery warrant a separate book.
[7] See, for example, the longitudinal Stirling County Studies of mental health effects of
social integration/cohesion (Leighton, 1959; Leighton, Hardings, Maclin, Macmillan, &
Leighton, 1963). See also the Roseto, Pennsylvania, study that found health-protective
effects of social equality and traditional values among Italian Americans (Bruhn & Wolf,
1979; Wolf et al., 1988). Follow-up studies of Roseto found that over time the adoption of modern lifestyles and weakening of social ties led to higher rates of myocardial
infarction and mortality (Lasker, Egolf, & Wolf, 1994). Subsequent research has focused
on examining the social and physical environmental characteristics and processes that
might explain why particular populations experience excess morbidity or mortality.
For example, Egolf and colleagues (Egolf, Lasker, Wolf, & Potvin, 1992) studied the
correlation between mortality from heart attack and differences in culture and social

differential mortality rates remains a primary focus of researchers, but interest in assessing the contribution of neighborhood characteristics to health status disparities and differences has increased significantly (see, for example, Winkleby & Cubbin, 2003).

More recent work examines the extent to which neighborhood effects are related to the concentration of poverty or wealth, rather than other aspects of the neighborhood (Bond-Huie, Hummer, & Rogers, 2002; Diez Roux et al., 2001; LeClere, Rogers, & Peters, 1997; Waitzman & Smith, 1998). These studies assess whether ill health is more common in poor neighborhoods because living in a high-poverty neighborhood has negative health consequences above and beyond being poor oneself. Another group of studies examine the health effects of neighborhood characteristics that are associated with the poverty rate, such as the quality of the housing stock, availability and cost of food, crime level, degree of social integration, and cohesion of the inhabitants (Browning & Cagney, 2003; Krause, 1996; MacIntyre, Ellaway, & Cummins, 2002; Sampson, Morenoff, & Gannon-Rowley, 2002). Some researchers choose to focus on the physical environment primarily because many physical features of neighborhoods are considered more amenable to change through public policy than is income inequality (Ewing, Schmid, Killingsworth, Zlot, & Raudenbush, 2003; Fisher, Li, Michael, & Cleveland, 2004; Frank, Engelke, & Schmid, 2003; King et al., 2003; Shaw, Gordon, Dorling, Mitchell, & Smith, 2000; Sturm & Cohen, 2004). Others focus on the role of community empowerment and leadership, such as examining the roles that religious institutions and leaders can play in promoting positive health behaviors.

cohesion within five towns in Pennsylvania. The Stanford Five-City Project, which studied residents in five California cities, evaluated the effects of a community health education program for the prevention of cardiovascular disease (Farquhar et al., 1985), and El-Shaarawi and colleagues (El-Shaarawi, Cherry, Forbes, & Prentice, 1976) examined county differences in mortality by cause of death across 54 counties in Ontario, Canada. During the same period, researchers in Europe examined a range of health effects including mortality (Fox, Goldblatt, & Jones, 1985; Hume & Womersley, 1985; Lloyd, Smith, Lloyd, Holland, & Gailey, 1985; Mackenbach, Looman, Kunst, Habbeman, & vander Maas, 1988), coronary heart disease (Marmot & McDowall, 1986), cardiovascular disease (Puska, Nissinen, & Tuomilehto, 1985), and life expectancy (van Poppel, 1981; Wnuk-Lipinski, 1990).

DO COMMUNITY AND NEIGHBORHOOD CHARACTERISTICS AFFECT MEN AND WOMEN DIFFERENTLY?

Although some studies have examined whether neighborhood characteristics affect men and women differently, most have either not considered or reported such analyses. However, a small but growing body of research that we discuss below indicates that residential social and built environments can and do affect men and women differently (Bird et al., 2006; Cubbin, Hadden, & Winkleby, 2000; Do et al., 2007; Ellaway & Macintyre, 2001; MacIntyre, 2001; Molinari, Ahern, & Hendryx, 1998; Raleigh & Kiri, 1997; Stafford, Cummins, Macintyre, Ellaway, & Marmot, 2005). For example, in an examination of four aspects of context (neighborhood economic and education disadvantage, as well as the degree of black and Hispanic segregation), Do and her colleagues (2007) found the effects of neighborhood disadvantage on body mass (as measured by the body mass index [BMI])[8] to be on average twice as large for women compared to men. However, black and Hispanic racial/ethnic segregation were significantly associated with men's BMI, but not with women's.[9] The findings indicate that gender differences in contextual effects exist and warrant greater attention from both researchers and policymakers.

The gendered physiological responses to stress discussed in Chapter 1 suggest that men and women may react to characteristics of the residential environment in ways that contribute to differences in their opportunities to pursue a healthy lifestyle. In the simplest case, the stressors and the constraints that men and women face in their environment (such as the availability or lack of a safe place to exercise and the time to do so) may lead them to adopt different coping styles that may either improve or damage health (see Ross, 2000). Social roles, which are discussed in Chapter 5, do influence how men and women react to community-level factors. One issue is whether men and women experience different degrees of time pressure and conflict within or across their social roles. If so, do the

---

[8] BMI is calculated by dividing an individual's weight (in kilograms) by his or her height (in meters) squared.

[9] Do and colleagues speculate that the gender differences observed may be related to the impact of neighborhood features on men's and women's physical activity (for example, the amount of walking and in their different use of parks) and to possible gender differences in the amount of time spent in one's residential neighborhood.

stresses they experience have the same or different health consequences, and are any differences related to men's and women's biology, their social and economic circumstances, or a combination of the two?

Moreover, to what extent do community factors contribute to or exacerbate such an experience? Returning to the example of women's lower rates of exercise compared to men, to what extent is this difference a function of time pressure due to multiple role-related obligations, which may be exacerbated by the lack of key resources in the community; of a sense of safety out of doors, which relates to levels of crime and social cohesion in the neighborhood; and of access to indoor exercise facilities?[10]

The questions we pose above, as well as many others, need answers if we are to understand the ways in which neighborhood characteristics shape men's and women's health-related choices. Clearly, this insight is necessary to intervene effectively to improve their health behavior and in turn their health. Moreover, to the extent that community factors affect health, only the most advantaged individuals can readily move to obtain a better environment for themselves and their families. Thus, intervention at the community level will be necessary to improve the health of the majority of those who are adversely affected by their neighborhood environment.

CHARACTERISTICS OF PLACE THAT AFFECT HEALTH

A broad range of social and physical characteristics of communities and neighborhoods that are amenable to state and local policies have been linked to health. Unfortunately for our purposes, studies have examined overlapping sets of neighborhood factors, and the emerging literature is not easily separated into distinct categories. However, a variety of studies have examined the social and physical infrastructure of neighborhoods. In the sections below, we discuss the community and neighborhood characteristics for which there is evidence indicating health effects and either evidence or a theoretical argument indicating that those health effects

---

[10] Examples of possible constraints include the presence and number of gyms and other facilities such as exercise and dance studios, the cost to use these facilities, and the cost of housing and other basic living expenses in the neighborhood as a proportion of income. Thus, the opportunities to use such facilities are a function of neighborhood characteristics as well as individual time and income.

are differentially related to gender. For the purposes of this discussion, our primary interests are those neighborhood or community character- istics or resources that can be changed by policy interventions designed to redirect resources or otherwise effect change to improve residents' health and well-being.

Disorder and Disintegration

A large body of work has assessed the impact of various aspects of neigh- borhood disorder and disintegration on health. Studies have examined physical decay (such as graffiti, litter, and boarded-up buildings), signs of disorder (such as drug dealing and other types of crime), and other social aspects (such as high turnover in occupancy and low levels of social trust and neighborhood cohesion). Research has linked these and other aspects of disorder and neighborhood disintegration to a range of health outcomes, including low self-rated health and high blood pressure, rates of cardiovascular disease, and psychological distress and depres- sion (Macintyre & Ellaway, 2000; Morenoff & Lynch, 2002; Sampson, Morenoff, & Gannon-Rowley, 2002).

We hypothesize that the health effects of neighborhood disorder and disintegration differ for men and women. In particular, aspects of disorder are related to exposure to crime and to fear of crime, which in turn affect opportunities to exercise outdoors and to move freely about one's neighborhood. We expect that such effects constrain women more than men in part because women are likely to feel (and possibly be) more vulnerable to crime. Also, many argue that in our society, women tend to be held socially responsible for being raped more than men are for either being victimized in a crime or injured in self-defense. In addition, because of their greater responsibility as caregivers to children and the elderly, women may be more sensitive to and aware of issues related to their physical safety, all of which are likely at best to be psychologically distressing. This inequity can have far-reaching results as young women are taught to protect themselves, whereas young men are taught to defend themselves.

Ironically, although both women and men in high-crime areas expe- rience high rates of victimization that can result in injury or death, men

Table 4.1. *Death Rates for Homicide by Gender, Race/Ethnicity, and Age, 2003*

	Male		Female	
	Age 15–24	Age 25–44	Age 15–24	Age 25–44
White, non-Hispanic, or Latino	5.0	5.1	1.9	2.6
Black or African American	84.6	61.0	10.1	9.8
Hispanic or Latino	30.3	17.6	4.5	3.6
American Indian or Alaskan Native	19.7	14.8	7.2	*
Asian or Pacific Islander	9.8	4.5	1.9	5.4

* Rates based on fewer than 20 deaths are considered not reliable and are not shown.
Source: U.S. Department of Health and Human Services, 2005: *Health United States*, Table 45, pages 218–220; updated online March 2006.

in these neighborhoods are also more often involved in crime as perpetrators. The health consequences of this dual exposure to violence for young African American and Hispanic males are particularly visible in their high death rates due to violence. Table 4.1 shows 2003 death rates per 100,000 for persons ages 15–24 and for those ages 25–44, by gender and race/ethnicity. Within age and racial/ethnic group categories, men's rates of death by homicide range from two to eight times that of women. Moreover, although the rates for black or African American women are 3.5 times those of non-Hispanic white women ages 25–44 (and 5.3 times those of women ages 15–24), the ratios among men are 12.0 and 16.9, respectively.

There is some evidence that the effects of aspects of neighborhood disorder extend beyond those experienced directly by victims of violence and that they can differ for men and women. For example, in a multilevel study of neighborhood violent crime, unemployment, and coronary heart disease in Stockholm, Sundquist and colleagues (2006) found that in neighborhoods with the highest rates of violent crime (quintile 5), the odds of coronary heart disease (CHD) were 1.75 and 1.39 for women and men, respectively. Similarly, in neighborhoods with the highest unemployment rates, the corresponding odds ratios were 2.05 and 1.50, respectively. Moreover, these effects were almost unaltered by the inclusion of individual-level variables. Although the trend is toward larger effects for women, there was some overlap between the confidence intervals for men's and women's outcomes.

Thus, gender differences in the effects of crime and other aspects of disorder and disintegration may vary with the level and type of disorder and the degree of neighborhood disadvantage or, as considered below, racial and socioeconomic segregation. Moreover, it is clear that the health consequences include increasing stress and risk of victimization, which in turn, shape health behaviors and coping mechanisms in ways that create and exacerbate poor health outcomes.

Neighborhood Socioeconomic Disadvantage and Segregation

Clearly, the socioeconomic aspects of place of residence, such as the prevalence of wealthy or impoverished residents and of college graduates or high-school dropouts, can represent resources or barriers to creating a healthy life with effects above and beyond an individual's income, education, or other assets. Neighborhood socioeconomic factors (as well as the resources of the larger community) may also amplify the health benefits of individual social and economic resources and the health risks of individual poverty. For example, advantaged neighborhoods may have better libraries and more collective social and economic resources, such as strong social networks, trust, and political representation and efficacy – resources that are collectively referred to as social capital. In contrast, disadvantaged neighborhoods have higher turnover, less social cohesion, and more disorder, including litter and dilapidated or abandoned buildings.

Some hypothesize that the neighborhood environment may be more important for women than for men because women traditionally spend more time in the home and are thus exposed to the neighborhood for a greater amount of time (Robert, 1999). Yet, other studies have found stronger associations between composite measures of neighborhood disadvantage and mortality among men than among women (MacIntyre, 2001; Raleigh & Kiri, 1997). LeClere and colleagues (LeClere, Rogers, & Peters, 1997) found that community median income is associated with all-cause mortality for men but not for women. A subsequent study found that census-tract-level variables – percent black, median family income, percent receiving public assistance, percent in deep poverty, and percent unemployed – are linked to the risk of CHD death for women, although all of these characteristics appear to be proxies for the percent of female-headed households in the community (LeClere, Rogers, & Peters, 1998). For example, in a British study, Stafford and colleagues (2005) found that neighborhood-level trust, integration into the wider society, left-wing political climate, physical quality of the residential environment, and unemployment rate were all linked more strongly to women's self-reported health than to men's. In contrast for men, between-neighborhood differences in health were fully explained by socioeconomic position and family type.[11] These studies suggest that neighborhood characteristics may have a stronger association to women's health than to men's (with the possible exception of young black men, particularly in the United States).

Employment Opportunities. A key aspect of the socioeconomic status of a neighborhood or community is the availability of jobs that provide the income necessary to support families. There are numerous studies on socioeconomic issues that are directly connected to employment opportunities. Although some studies find that neighborhood characteristics are less important (Browning & Cagney, 2002; Duncan, Jones, & Moon, 1995; Veugelers, Yip, & Kephart, 2001), most report strong evidence that individuals who live in lower SES neighborhoods are at greater risk for health problems, such as poor self-reported health (Malmstrom, Sundquist, & Johannson, 1999); depression (Levanthal & Brooks-Gunn, 2001; Silver, Mulvey, & Swanson, 2002); lower physical functioning (Feldman & Steptoe, 2004); chronic conditions, such as hypertension and diabetes (Jones & Duncan, 1995; Robert, 1998); and mortality (Haan, Kaplan, & Camacho, 1987; Waitzman & Smith, 1998; Yen & Kaplan, 1999). Studies of the effects of specific socioeconomic neighborhood attributes on general health outcomes for men and women tend to find that environmental factors are important for both genders, but they are inconsistent as to which factors matter the most.

---

[11] In other words for men, taking into account their social class, whether they were employed, and whether they lived alone, with one or more adults, or in a household that included children explained all of the variation in self-rated health across neighborhood. For women there was more health variation between neighborhoods, only 59% of which was explained by these individual-level characteristics.

Educational Provisions. Over time in neighborhoods with low turnover, the majority of adults in a neighborhood will have obtained their education in the local schools, particularly in areas with fewer opportunities for upward mobility. To our knowledge, local educational opportunities, particularly those for children, have not been linked directly to the health of adults in the community. However, they have been linked to child well-being, including school performance, rates of deviant behavior, and the acquisition of education, which are subsequently related to better health status in adulthood.

We argue that the quality and availability of education for children, including after-school care, and enrichment and day care when school is out of session, all contribute to the parents' well-being due in part to the strains that parents face in filling the gaps and creating individual solutions to shortfalls in availability and quality – these social and economic costs drain both their time and money. Moreover, we expect that, to the extent that these factors affect parents, mothers are in many cases likely to experience both the brunt of the time demands and, particularly in the case of single mothers, much of the economic costs as well. Here a key issue is that educational and other factors that demand a great deal of parents' time are likely to contribute to the gender division of labor mentioned above and discussed in Chapter 5.

Racial/Ethnic and Socioeconomic Segregation. Recent studies have focused largely on explaining social disparities in health mainly in relation to racial/ethnic and socioeconomic status across the life course. However, relatively little attention has been paid to possible differences in the effects of neighborhoods on men's and women's health, in part because men and women typically live in the same neighborhoods so place effects are not related to gender segregation in the way that racial differences may be related to residential segregation. Gender differences in neighborhood effects also vary by race. For example, in an examination of gender and racial differences, Jackson, Anderson, and Johnson (2000) found that black men living in an area with the highest levels of segregation are exposed to three times the mortality risk compared to those living in areas in the lowest quartile on segregation. By comparison, the increase in mortality risk for black women living in the most segregated neighborhoods is twice that of black women in the least segregated areas. In contrast, for those who are not black, the gender pattern was reversed, with larger negative effects of living in a segregated neighborhood for women than for men (1.6 times vs. 1.3 times larger). This work suggests the need for closer attention to the interactions between race and gender as researchers begin to examine neighborhood effects in greater detail.

CHALLENGES FOR RESEARCHERS

In the sections above we noted a range of neighborhood characteristics that appear to affect men and women differently; however, these effects vary considerably across studies, making them hard to group into easily described patterns. Clearly, the sheer diversity of studies in this area leads to some of these complexities. Moreover, part of the complexity arises from the fact that we seek to build on the work that has been done by bringing new questions to bear regarding the impact of contextual or place effects on men's and women's health.

Many of the problems in summarizing the literature reflect both the range of disciplines involved, each of which brings somewhat different measures, methods, and language, and the range of both characteristics of place and health outcomes examined. For example, in the case of measurement, Molinari, Ahern, and Hendryx (1998) and Ellaway and Macintyre (2001) found that perceptions of neighborhood social cohesion are important predictors of health status in women, whereas perceptions of the built environment are better predictors of health among men. In contrast, Stafford and colleagues (2005) found that a poor quality physical environment – measured using public sector housing vacancy rates and vacant land – is a stronger predictor of poor self-reported health for women than it is for men. However, the discrepancies may be an artifact of measurement, since the first two studies used individual perceptions of physical environment, whereas Stafford et al. (2005) used objective data.

Not surprisingly, research methods have varied considerably across studies and over time. This variation is in part attributable to disciplinary differences and to the questions being addressed. However, analytic techniques have also advanced rapidly over time, particularly as computational ability has improved with technological advances. As a result, researchers now employ hierarchical modeling techniques to better distinguish between the compositional effects of communities (or neighborhoods) and the contextual effects of the social and physical environment of those communities.[12]

Results also vary based in part on how a particular neighborhood characteristic is measured. For example, many studies have employed respondents' reports of neighborhood characteristics, resources, and problems. Objective data have been difficult to obtain for national studies in part because some social aspects of neighborhoods are not easily measured objectively. In many cases the respondents' reports are also indicative of the extent to which they experience particular problems, such as neighborhood disorder or fear of crime. If, for example, men and women have different expectations or concerns regarding crime, they may describe the same neighborhood differently or experience different impacts of neighborhoods that they describe similarly. For example, some studies have reported that women perceive more local problems (e.g., a lack of facilities). This gender difference in reporting has been linked in part to the presence of children in the home (Ellaway & Macintyre, 2001); a finding they attribute to women's social roles, which may be more dependent on features of the local area.

Moreover, a standard approach to categorizing neighborhood characteristics has yet to develop. One difficulty in describing the findings across studies is that even something as basic as the classification of neighborhood characteristics into social and physical is not clear cut.[13] Thus, even studies that have examined similar characteristics are likely to have

---

[12] For example, because of the socioeconomic segregation and stratification that occur across residential neighborhoods, researchers sought to differentiate between the composition of the neighborhood (e.g., a higher proportion of people living in poverty) and the possible independent effects of one's own income and that of one's neighbors on health outcomes. The basic question is, To what extent do the higher rates of poor health or mortality in a given community reflect the increased risks to individuals of having a low income and the concentration of those with low incomes in particular neighborhoods, as compared to possible additive or multiplicative effects of the combination of having a low income and living in a neighborhood with a high poverty rate?

[13] For example, air pollution might be seen as an aspect of the built environment or of commuting patterns; similarly one study might classify activity programming in parks as a social aspect of community whereas a researcher from another discipline would

categorized or measured them differently. As a consequence of the differential inclusion and grouping of community characteristics across studies and the relatively small proportion of the literature published since the advent of hierarchical modeling techniques, it is difficult to determine exactly why findings vary across studies. Additional research is needed to determine the extent to which men and women are affected by the same characteristics of place but simply experience different consequences.

Related challenges to summarizing the existing literature are that most studies have focused on a wide range of health-related outcomes, only a few have examined multiple outcomes, and the findings differ across outcomes. For example, whereas a number of studies described below indicate larger contextual effects on morbidity for women than men (Morenoff, Diez Roux, Osypuk, & Hansen, 2006; Stafford et al., 2005), others find larger contextual effects on blood pressure and mortality risk for men than for women (Cubbin et al., 2000; MacIntyre, 2001; Raleigh & Kiri, 1997).

Possible underlying biological differences in vulnerability and disease processes further complicate attempts to summarize epidemiological studies of neighborhood differences in the risk of particular diseases and disorders. For example, even when comparing studies of increased risk of cardiovascular mortality over a particular follow-up period, questions arise as to whether cumulative effects on women were fully captured, since men's and women's cardiovascular risk plays out over different time frames. Thus, to the extent that women experience later onset of cardiovascular disease compared to men, following a cohort of same-aged men and women for a specified period of time to assess the effects of exposure to a particular residential environment may capture more of the related health events that occur for men than for women simply due to biological differences in the way those effects play out.[14] Consequently,

link both air pollution and programming at parks with land use, which in and of itself could be considered either a physical or social characteristic.

[14] In addition, once women develop overt coronary heart disease, their prognosis is markedly worse than for men, a difference that is not entirely accounted for by age and disease stage at diagnosis (American Heart Association [AHA]. 2005). Researchers and clinicians now know that ascertainment bias has long plagued the ability to recognize early (and late) signs of cardiovascular disease in women due in part to their higher

even when analyses are conducted by gender, a study with 5 or even 10 years of follow-up on a cohort of men and women at midlife would not equally capture the effects on men's and women's health and mortality. Therefore, to capture the cumulative effects alternative approaches may be needed that examine changes in biological indicators of increased cardiovascular risk or extended follow-up periods to determine whether women simply experience adverse outcomes later than men.

Despite our caveats about the literature, it is clear that place does affect health and warrants further research. Existing studies demonstrate that a range of characteristics of the built as well as the social and economic environment can and do affect health and health behaviors. Community context affects health, and choices that occur beyond the individual or household level also constrain individuals' opportunities. Although advantaged households may be able to move to more salutary environments, this opportunity is not available to all, and the selection process itself can contribute to increased disadvantage of poorer households over time.

Moreover, multiple recent studies indicate that place effects can and do differ by gender, although the gender differences are not universal and appear to vary by race/ethnicity and socioeconomic status. To fill in the gaps in our understanding of community effects on men's and women's health, research is needed to examine and elucidate the role of biology in these health outcomes to determine what is related to exposure to contextual factors versus vulnerability to particular factors. For example, it is critical to continually consider the extent to which biology and social factors contribute independently to men's and women's health outcomes and whether and how they interact to create, maintain, or exacerbate differences. Thus, in considering this literature, we have raised questions and suggested avenues for research that we hope would provide answers as to why gender differences exist.

rates of nonspecific symptoms compared to men. Moreover, recent research shows that women with known cardiovascular disease or diabetes (a primary risk factor for cardiovascular disease) were significantly less likely to receive appropriate care for high cholesterol (Bird, Fremont, Bierman, Wickstrom, Shah, et al., 2007; Chou, Scholle, Weisman, Bierman, Correa-de-Araujo, et al., 2007; Chou, Brown, Shih, Jensen, Pawlson, et al., 2007).

If we are to understand the potential impact of interventions designed to change neighborhood conditions, it may also be critical in some cases to examine both the relationships between objective measures of the neighborhood environment and residents' perceptions of those conditions (e.g., neighborhood safety) and health. To further tease out these findings, new interdisciplinary work is needed that examines how neighborhood characteristics are related to health behaviors, cumulative biological risk, and ultimately to health outcomes.

POLICY LEVERS

Although the range of community and neighborhood characteristics that have been linked to health is quite broad, most of the research does not include an examination of the policy decisions that affect these characteristics. Because the studies to date have not evaluated the impact of particular policies, they typically refer to the characteristics as amenable to policy intervention without making recommendations about specific policies that might alter the characteristics. Here we provide examples of some of the types of policies that affect specific community and neighborhood characteristics described above.

A wide range of policies affect the degree of disorder, disintegration, and disadvantage in a neighborhood or community. Not surprisingly, these broad overlapping categories include many factors that interact to affect health. Clearly policing is relevant, but these neighborhood conditions are also affected by the availability of affordable housing; the quality of the housing stock, which is related to the larger community's investment in the neighborhood; the degree to which state and local government support major institutions in the community, including schools, businesses, and public facilities; and the quality of mass transportation to and from the area.

In other words, many social policies shape the degree to which residents of a particular neighborhood experience opportunities for themselves and their children. Taken together, these opportunities and the other social institutions in the neighborhood contribute greatly to the sense of cohesion and trust within the community and the degree of social capital that the residents share together with which to represent their needs to the larger community. Thus, disorder and disintegration directly affect the extent to which a neighborhood, or even a community as a whole, has a voice and the power to be heard at the state and national level and thus to attract needed resources (e.g., poor minority neighborhoods in New Orleans after Hurricane Katrina as well as the entire affected region) to address short- or long-term problems.

Clearly, many communities also work to attract employers, but in so doing they vary greatly as to which employers are considered desirable (e.g., businesses that provide jobs with health insurance versus low-wage employers, such as Wal-Mart, which have been shown to increase the number of low-wage workers on Medicaid [Hicks, 2007a, 2007b]). Communities also vary in the compromises they are willing to make to attract new employers and in their efforts to bring employers to high-poverty neighborhoods. Without such broader efforts at the community and state level, areas of concentrated poverty may lack both the authority and the power to attract large employers.

Even the quality of public schools varies substantially across the United States, despite a degree of national funding, stated goals, and measurement tools for assessing performance. Moreover, communities also vary considerably in the extent to which they offer public preschool, half- or full-day kindergarten, the age at which children can enter kindergarten, and the cost and quality of after-school programs.[15] These differences are related in part to the amount of state and local funding for schools and the cost of living across the county. Communities and neighborhoods vary greatly in the extent to which they can and do subsidize schools through property tax, school bonds, and parental contributions. Even when efforts have been made to equalize the allocation of property tax money between schools in lower and higher income areas, the ability of parent-teacher organizations to raise funds through direct donations and various fundraising events continues to vary drastically. Communities also differ in the extent to which they provide publicly subsidized

---

[15] In Cambridge, Massachuestts, a child who is 4 years old by March 1st can start kindergarten the following September. Those who have not turned 5 by September 31st the following year will complete a second year of kindergarten. In contrast, in New Zealand students enroll in school throughout the year starting at or after their fifth birthday, with mandatory enrollment at age 6.

preschool and day care and whether they require or even encourage businesses to support child care; for example, by requiring or providing incentives to developers to include subsidized space for child care in new office construction. Together these community choices shape the quality of local primary and secondary education and the demand and cost for child care for younger children.

These are but a few examples of the extent to which communities vary in their efforts and effectiveness in creating environments that provide men and women the opportunities to pursue healthy lives.

WHERE DO WE GO FROM HERE?

Health education has to be not only about changing behavior but also about changing environments and informing people about the links between their environment and health. As discussed in this chapter, these links extend beyond the commonly recognized effects of pollution and even the risk of victimization from crime to the relative affluence and resources of a neighborhood or community. We have illustrated many ways in which these aspects of the community shape both stress levels and health-related choices and behaviors. Clearly, individuals and families need more information about how choices they make about where to live affect their health. At the very least this information would enable those who are planning to move to adequately compare their neighborhood options in terms of creating a healthy life. However, such opportunities are relatively few and far between for most individuals and their families. For individuals and decision makers to make creating and supporting state and local policies that foster health a priority, they need both information on the health consequences of specific policies and actions and a voice in the political process.

The ideal community is not just planned by decision makers at higher levels; it has to be one where people can participate and have a voice and where their dialogue with policymakers at the neighborhood and community level is taken into account in policy decisions. To achieve this end, we need to shift the focus of the public health dialogue from the individual to the community in order to create new opportunities for men and women to pursue a healthy life. Current community research provides an excellent foundation for change, but because it has typically focused on more traditional avenues of health behavior modification, additional studies are needed to assess and demonstrate the value of such neighborhood, community, and even state-level interventions. Yet, information alone is rarely sufficient to instigate change. In this case, efforts are needed to affect the process by which policy is developed and enacted so that the health impact is routinely considered in major and minor decisions at this level.

Our primary concern extends beyond this general and ambitious agenda. Relatively few studies have systematically examined whether these community and neighborhood factors affect men's and women's health similarly or differently. We have attempted to shed light on the types of research that are needed to understand the extent to which these community and neighborhood characteristics contribute to good and poor health as well as their effects on gender differences in health. Moreover, this research provides an opportunity to use these insights to understand gender differences in health and for communities to make better policy decisions in order to improve health. Simply put, understanding whether and how such factors contribute to differences in men's and women's health is essential to using this larger body of research to create state and local policies that foster improved health for both men and women.

References

Adler, N. E., Boyce, T., Chesney, M. A., Cohen, S., Folkman, S., Kahn, R. L., et al. (2002). Socioeconomic status and health: The challenge of the gradient. In J. T. Cacioppo et al. (Eds.), *Foundations in Social Neuroscience* (pp. 1095–1110). Cambridge, MA: MIT Press.

American Heart Association (AHA). (2005). *Heart Disease and Stroke Statistics – 2005 Update.* Dallas: American Heart Association.

Bird, C. E., Finch, B., Do, P., Escarce, J., Lurie, N., & Seeman, T. E. (2006). *Gender differences in the relationship between neighborhood socioeconomic characteristics and allostatic load.* Paper presented at the Academy Health Annual Meeting, Seattle, WA.

Bird, C. E., Fremont, A. M., Bierman, A. S., Wickstrom, S. L., Shah, M. M., Rector, T., et al. (2007). Does quality of care for cardiovascular disease and diabetes differ by gender for enrollees in managed care? *Women Health Iss., 17*(3), 131–138.

Bond-Huie, S. A., Hummer, R. A., & Rogers, R. G. (2002). Individual and contextual risks of death among race and ethnic groups in the United States. *J Health Soc Behav, 43*(3), 359–381.

Bornstein, R., & Lin, Q. (2000). Urban heat islands and summertime convection thunderstorms in Atlanta: Three case studies. *Atmos Environ, 34*, 507–516.

Browning, C. R., & Cagney, K. A. (2002). Neighborhood structural disadvantage, collective efficacy, and self-rated physical health in an urban setting. *J Health Soc Behav, 43*(4), 383–399.

Browning, C. R., & Cagney, K. A. (2003). Moving beyond poverty: Neighborhood structure, social processes, and health. *J Health Soc Behav, 44*(4), 552–571.

Bruhn, J. G., & Wolf, S. (1979). *The Roseto Story: An Anatomy of Health.* Norman: University of Oklahoma Press.

Chou, A. F., Scholle, S. H., Weisman, C. S., Bierman, A., Correa-de-Araujo, R., & Mosca, L. (2007). Gender disparities in the quality of cardiovascular disease care in private managed care. *Women Health Iss., 17*(3), 120–130.

Chou, A. F., Brown, A. F., Shih, S., Jensen, R., Pawlson, G., & Scholle, S. H. (2007). Gender and racial disparities in the management of diabetes mellitus among Medicare patients. *Women Health Iss., 17*(3), 150–161.

Cohen, S., Frank, E., Doyle, W. J., Skoner, D. P., Rabin, B. S., & Gwaltney Jr., J. M. (2002). Types of stressors that increase susceptibility to the common cold in healthy adults. In J. T. Cacioppo et al. (Eds.), *Foundations in Social Neuroscience* (pp. 1225–1240). Cambridge, MA: MIT Press.

Collier, C. G. (2006). The impact of urban areas on weather. *Quart J Royal Meteorol Soc, 132*(614), 1–25.

Cubbin, C., Hadden, W. C., & Winkleby, M. A. (2000). Neighborhood context and cardiovascular disease risk factors: The contribution of material deprivation. *Ethn Dis, 11*(4), 687–700.

Diez Roux, A. V., Merkin, S. S., Arnett, D., Chambless, L., Massing, M., Nieto, F. J., et al. (2001). Neighborhood of residence and incidence of coronary heart disease. *N Engl J Med, 345*(2), 99–106.

Do, D. P., Dubowitz, T., Bird, C. E., Lurie, N., Escarce, J. J., & Finch, B. K. (2007). Neighborhood context and ethnicity differences in body mass index: A multilevel analysis using the NHANES III survey (1988–1994). *Econ Human Biol, 5*(2), 179–203.

Duncan, C., Jones, K., & Moon, G. (1995). Psychiatric morbidity: A multilevel approach to regional variations in the UK. *J Epidemiol Comm Health, 49*(3), 290–295.

Earls, F., & Carlson, M. (2001). The social ecology of child health and well-being. *Annu Rev Pub Health, 22*, 143–166.

Egolf, B., Lasker, J., Wolf, S., & Potvin, L. (1992). The Roseto effect: A 50-year comparison of mortality rates. *Am J Pub Health, 82*(1), 89–92.

El-Shaarawi, A. H., Cherry, W. H., Forbes, W. F., & Prentice, R. L. (1976). A statistical model for studying regional differences in observed mortality rates, and its application to Ontario during 1964–68. *J Chron Dis, 29*, 311–330.

Ellaway, A., & Macintyre, S. (2001). Women in their place: Gender and perceptions of neighborhoods and health in the West of Scotland. In I. Dyck, N. Davis Lewis, & S. McLafferty (Eds.), *Geographies of Women's Health* (pp. 265–281). London: Routledge.

Eng, C., Pedulla, J., Eleazer, G. P., McCann, R., & Fox, N. (1997). Program of All-inclusive Care for the Elderly (PACE): An innovative model of integrated geriatric care and financing. *J Am Geriatr Soc, 45,* 223–232.

Ewing, R., Schmid, T., Killingsworth, R., Zlot, A., & Raudenbush, S. (2003). Relationship between urban sprawl and physical activity, obesity, and morbidity. *Am J Health Promot, 18*(1), 47–57.

Farquhar, J. W., Fortmann, S. P., Maccoby, N., Haskell, W. L., Williams, P. T., Flora, J. A., et al. (1985). The Stanford Five-City Project: Design and methods. *Am J Epidemiol, 122,* 323–334.

Feldman, P. J., & Steptoe, A. (2004). How neighborhoods and physical functioning are related: The roles of neighborhood socioeconomic status, perceived neighborhood strain, and individual health risk factors. *Ann Behav Med, 27*(2), 91–99.

Fisher, J. K., Li, F., Michael, Y., & Cleveland, M. (2004). Neighborhood-level influences on physical activity among older adults: A multilevel analysis. *J Aging Phys Act, 12*(1), 45–63.

Forsyth, A. (2005). *Reforming Suburbia: The Planned Communities of Columbia, Irvine, and The Woodlands.* Berkeley: University of California Press.

Fox, A. J., Goldblatt, P. O., & Jones, D. R. (1985). Social class mortality differentials: Artefact, selection, or life circumstances? *J Epidemiol Comm Health, 39,* 1–8.

Frank, L. D., Engelke, P. O., & Schmid, T. L. (2003). *Health and Community Design: The Impact of the Built Environment on Physical Activity.* Washington, DC: Island Press.

Fremont, A. M., & Bird, C. E. (2000). Social factors, physiological processes, and physical health. In C. E. Bird, P. Conrad, & A. M. Fremont (Eds.), *The Handbook of Medical Sociology* (pp. 334–352). Englewood Cliffs, NJ: Prentice Hall.

Haan, M., Kaplan, G. A., & Camacho, T. (1987). Poverty and health: Prospective evidence from the Alameda County Study. *Am J Epidemiol, 125,* 989–998.

Hendler, S. (2005). Towards a feminist code of planning ethics. *Plan Theory Pract, 6*(1), 53–69.

Hicks, M. J. (2007a). *The Local Impact of Wal-Mart.* Youngstown, NJ: Cambria Press.

Hicks, M. J. (2007b). Wal-Mart's impact on local revenue and expenditure instruments in Ohio, 1988–2003. *Atl Econ J, 35*(1), 77–95.

Hume, D., & Womersley, J. (1985). Analysis of death rates in the population aged 60 years and over of greater Glasgow by postcode sector of residence. *J Epidemiol Comm Health, 39,* 357–363.

Jackson, S. A., Anderson, R. T., & Johnson, N. J. (2000). The relation of residential segregation to all-cause mortality: A study in black and white. *Am J Pub Health, 90,* 615–617.

Jones, K., & Duncan, C. (1995). Individuals and their ecologies: Analyzing the geography of chronic illness within a multilevel modeling framework. *Health Place, 1,* 27–30.

Karoly, L. A., Kilburn, M. R., & Cannon, J. S. (2005). *Early Childhood Interventions: Proven Results, Future Promise.* Santa Monica, CA: RAND Corporation.

Kiecolt-Glaser, J. K., McGuire, L., Robles, T. F., & Glaser, R. (2002). Psychoneuroimmunology: Psychological influences on immune function and health. *J Consult Clin Psychol, 70*(3), 537–547.

King, W. C., Brach, J. S., Belle, S., Killingsworth, R., Fenton, M., & Kriska, A. M. (2003). The relationship between convenience of destinations and walking levels in older women. *Am J Health Promot, 18*(1), 74–82.

Kirby, J. B., & Kaneda, T. (2006). Access to health care: Does neighborhood residential instability matter? *J Health Soc Behav, 47*, 142–155.

Krause, N. (1996). Neighborhood deterioration and self-rated health in later life. *Psychol Aging, 11*(2), 342–352.

Lasker, J. N., Egolf, B. P., & Wolf, S. (1994). Community social change and mortality. *Soc Sci Med, 39*(1), 53–62.

LeClere, F. B., Rogers, R. G., & Peters, K. D. (1997). Ethnicity and mortality in the United States: Individual and community correlates. *Soc Forces, 76*, 169–198.

LeClere, F. B., Rogers, R. G., & Peters, K. D. (1998). Neighborhood social context and racial differences in women's heart disease mortality. *J Health Soc Behav, 39*, 91–107.

Leighton, A. (1959). *My Name is Legion: Foundations for a Theory of Man in Relation to Culture.* New York: Basic Books.

Leighton, D. C., Hardings, A. S., Maclin, D. B., Macmillan, A. M., & Leighton, A. H. (1963). *The Character of Danger: The Stirling County Study.* New York: Basic Books.

Levanthal, T., & Brooks-Gunn, J. (2001). Moving to better neighborhoods improves health and family life among New York families. *Pov Res News, 5*, 1576–1582.

Lloyd, O. L., Smith, G., Lloyd, M. M., Holland, Y., & Gailey, F. (1985). Raised mortality from lung cancer and high sex ratios of births associated with industrial pollution. *Br J Indust Med, 42*, 475–480.

MacIntyre, S. (2001). Inequalities in health: Is research gender blind? In D. A. Leon & G. Walt (Eds.), *Poverty, Inequality, and Health* (pp. 283–293). Oxford: Oxford University Press.

MacIntyre, S., & Ellaway, A. (2000). Neighbourhood cohesion and health in socially contrasting neighbourhoods: Implications for the social exclusion and public health agendas. *Health Bull, 58*(6), 450–456.

MacIntyre, S., Ellaway, A., & Cummins, S. (2002). Place effects on health: How can we conceptualise, operationalise and measure them? *Soc Sci Med, 55*, 125–139.

Mackenbach, J. P., Looman, C. W. N., Kunst, A. E., Habbeman, J. D. F., & vander Maas, P. J. (1988). Regional differences in decline of mortality from selected conditions: The Netherlands. *J Epidemiol Comm Health, 45*, 231–237.

Malmstrom, M., Sundquist, J., & Johannson, S. E. (1999). Neighborhood environment and self-reported health status: A multilevel analysis. *Am J Pub Health, 89*(8), 1181–1186.

Marmot, M., & McDowall, M. E. (1986). Mortality decline and widening social inequalities. *Lancet, 2*, 274–276.

McEwen, B. S. (2002). *The End of Stress as We Know It.* Washington, DC: John Henry Press.

McEwen, B. S., & Stellar, E. (1993). Stress and the individual: Mechanisms leading to disease. *Arch Intern Med, 153*, 2093–2101.

Molinari, C., Ahern, M., & Hendryx, M. (1998). The relationship of community quality to the health of women and men. *Soc Sci Med, 47*(8), 1113–1120.

Morenoff, J. D., Diez Roux, A. V., Osypuk, T., & Hansen, B. (2006). *Residential environments and obesity: What can we learn about policy interventions from observational studies?* Paper presented at the National Poverty Center's "Health Effects of Non-Health Policy," Bethesda, MD.

Morenoff, J. D., & Lynch, J. (2004). What makes a place healthy? Neighborhood influences on racial/ethnic disparities in health over the life-course. In N. B. Anderson, R. A. Bulatao, & B. Cohen (Eds.), *Critical Perspectives on Racial and Ethnic Differences in Health in Late Life* (pp. 406–449). Washington, DC: National Academies Press.

Mui, A. C. (2001). The Program of All-Inclusive Care for the Elderly (PACE): An innovative long-term care model in the United States. *J Aging Soc Policy, 13*, 53–67.

Patrick, D., & Wizicker, T. M. (1995). Community and health. In B. C. Amick, S. Levine, A. R. Tarlov, & D. C. Walsh (Eds.), *Society and Health* (pp. 46–92). New York: Oxford University Press.

Puska, P., Nissinen, A., & Tuomilehto, J. (1985). The community-based strategy to prevent coronary heart disease: Conclusions from the ten years of the North Karelia Projects. *Am Rev Pub Health, 6*, 147–193.

Raleigh, V. A., & Kiri, V. (1997). Life expectancy in England: Variations and trends by gender, health authority, and level of deprivation. *J Epidemiol Comm Health, 51*(6), 649–658.

Reeves, D. (2002). Mainstreaming gender equality: An examination of the gender sensitivity of strategic planning in Great Britain. *Town Plan Rev, 73*(2), 197–214.

Robert, S. A. (1998). Community-level socioeconomic status effects on adult health. *J Health Soc Behav, 39*, 18–37.

Robert, S. A. (1999). Socioeconomic position and health: The independent contribution of community socioeconomic context. *Annu Rev Sociol, 25*, 489–516.

Ross, C. E. (2000). Walking, exercise, and smoking: Does neighborhood matter? *Soc Sci Med, 51*(2), 265–274.

Sampson, R. J., Morenoff, J. D., & Earls, F. (1999). Beyond social capitol: Spatial dynamics of collective efficacy for children. *Am Sociol Rev, 64*, 633–660.

Sampson, R. J., Morenoff, J. D., & Gannon-Rowley, T. (2002). Assessing "neighborhood effects": Social processes and new directions in research. *Annu Rev Sociol, 28*, 443–478.

Sampson, R. J., Raudenbush, S. W., & Earls, F. (1997). Neighborhoods and violent crime: A multilevel study of collective efficacy. *Science, 277*(5328), 918–924.

Seeman, T. E., Singer, B. H., Rowe, J. W., Horwitz, R. I., & McEwen, B. S. (1997). Price of adaptation–allostatic load and its health consequences: MacArthur Studies of Successful Aging. *Arch Intern Med, 157*(19), 2259–2268.

Shaw, M., Gordon, D., Dorling, D., Mitchell, R., & Smith, G. D. (2000). Increasing mortality differentials by residential area level of poverty: Britain 1981–1997. *Soc Sci Med, 51*(1), 151–153.

Silver, E., Mulvey, E. P., & Swanson, J. W. (2002). Neighborhood structural characteristics and mental disorder: Faris and Dunham revisited. *Soc Sci Med, 55*, 1457–1470.

Singer, B., & Ryff, C. D. (1999). Hierarchies of life histories and associated risks. *Ann NY Acad Sci, 896*, 96–115.

Stafford, M., Cummins, S., Macintyre, S., Ellaway, A., & Marmot, M. (2005). Gender differences in the associations between health and neighborhood environment. *Soc Sci Med, 60*, 1681–1692.

Stone, B., & Norman, J. M. (2006). Land use planning and surface heat island formation: A parcel-based radiation flux approach. *Atmos Environ, 40*(19), 3561–3573.

Sturm, R., & Cohen, D. A. (2004). Suburban sprawl and physical and mental health. *J Royal Inst Pub Health, 118*(7), 488–496.

Sundquist, K., Theobald, H., Yang, M., Li, X., Johansson, S.-E., & Sundquist, J. (2006). Neighborhood violent crime and unemployment increase the risk of coronary heart disease: A multilevel study in an urban setting. *Soc Sci Med, 62*(8), 2061–2071.

Taylor, S. E., Repetti, R. L., & Seeman, T. E. (1997). Health psychology: What is an unhealthy environment and how does it get under the skin? *Annu Rev Psychol, 48*, 411–447.

van Poppel, E. W. A. (1981). Regional mortality differences in western Europe: A review of the situation in the seventies. *Soc Sci Med, 15D*, 341–354.

Veugelers, P. J., Yip, A. M., & Kephart, G. (2001). Proximate and contextual socioeconomic determinants of mortality: Multilevel approaches in a setting with universal health coverage. *Am J Epidemiol, 154*(8), 725–732.

Waitzman, N. J., & Smith, K. R. (1998). Phantom of the area: Poverty, residence, and mortality in the US. *Am J Pub Health, 88*, 973–976.

Winkleby, M. A., & Cubbin, C. (2003). Influence of individual and neighborhood socioeconomic status on mortality among black, Mexican-American, and white women and men in the United States. *J Epidemiol Comm Health, 57*, 444–452.

Wnuk-Lipinski, E. (1990). The Polish country profile: Economic crisis and inequalities in health. *Soc Sci Med, 31*, 859–866.

Wolf, S., Herrenkohl, R. C., Lasker, J., Egolf, B., Philips, B. U., & Bruhn, J. G. (1988). Roseto, Pennsylvania 25 years later – highlights of a medical and sociological survey. *Transact Am Clin Climatol Assoc, 100*, 57–67.

Yen, I. H., & Kaplan, G. A. (1999). Neighborhood social environment and risk of death: Evidence from the Alameda County study. *Am J Epidemiol, 149*(10), 898–907.

Yen, I. H., & Syme, S. L. (1999). The social environment and health: A discussion of the epidemiological literature. *Annu Rev Pub Health, 20*, 287–308.

FIVE

Priorities and Expectations

Men's and Women's Work, Family Life, and Health

In this chapter, we examine how work and family life are related to men's and women's health. Many of the differences in men's and women's lives that we have considered in earlier chapters have their roots in their family roles and in their jobs. Family and work are the two arenas where the constraints on choice are most readily apparent and frequently experienced, because they involve a myriad of routine decisions that occur on a daily basis. Consequently, in these arenas it is clear that individuals are making choices actively or at least by default. Moreover, both work and family roles are associated with some activities, as well as stresses, that tend to occur along gender lines. For example, occupations, careers, and family life each carry with them expectations derived from men's and women's social roles. Thus, as one of the mothers Judith Warner interviewed for her recent book on motherhood aptly noted, "These are choices that don't feel like choices at all. They are the harsh realities of family life in a culture that has no structures in place to allow women – and men – to balance work and child rearing" (Warner, 2005). Many of these choices are forced by time or financial constraints, which as this mother's comment illustrates can often leave individuals with a sense that they had little if any freedom to choose among the competing priorities, tasks, and goals. Both families and work also create routines and establish norms that can promote health, in part by discouraging negative health behaviors.

There is no road map for how to make choices that enhance health while taking on and managing the obligations of work and family. Despite the abundance of health information and recommendations, no reference or tool systematically lays out the potential or likely health implications of different career and family choices and role combinations. Of course, some occupations are known to be highly stressful or to have associated health hazards, such as an increased risk of particular injuries or hazardous exposures. Similarly, it is clear that many single parents experience exceptionally high stress levels because of the time, financial, and emotional demands they face. Conflicts between work and family issues are widely discussed, as are the most important health behavior admonitions (e.g., maintain a healthy weight, eat a proper diet, exercise regularly, minimize chronic stress, limit alcohol consumption, and do not smoke). However, little evidence-based advice is available on how individuals can apply even this well-established health knowledge effectively when attempting to engage in multiple roles at work and home. Information on how to assess potential health implications could be particularly valuable, for example, when making major decisions such as planning a career or considering a possible move. The degree of interdependence that occurs in families, and for some at work, can reduce autonomy and affect men's and women's choices. Thus, because of the quantity and nature of the constraints presented by work and family roles and responsibilities, examining choice at the level of work and family may shed new light on men's and women's health-related behavior.

This chapter illustrates many of the ways in which men's and women's lives are constrained. Much of our time is spent carrying out our work and family roles, where our everyday decisions occur. On a day-to-day basis, many of the constraints imposed on individuals at the community and society level are largely invisible. For example, we typically accept the extent to which public transportation, parental leave, and elder care are available, even though access to these resources can create opportunities for individuals to organize their time and responsibilities in ways that reduce stress and facilitate positive health behaviors. Within the constraints established by the lack or availability of such resources at the society and community level, individuals make decisions and assert control over their daily activities, including those related to their health.

Here we consider the choices men and women face regarding how to fulfill their roles and obligations at work and at home. In ideal circumstances, individuals have substantial decision latitude and the opportunity to act autonomously and creatively to organize their work and their time. However, decision latitude and autonomy vary substantially across jobs and occupations in the workplace and across roles and responsibilities in the home. In addition, individuals typically endeavor to maintain positive work and family relations. Consequently, individual choices are embedded with a range of power and other social dynamics in the family and the workplace. If health improvement is a goal, then it is critical to understand both the options available to the individual and those that could be provided by decision makers at other levels to increase opportunities to choose health.

As we examine the constraints faced by individuals within their work and family roles, it is necessary to consider the ways in which employers and families also find themselves in a bind. Although both groups value health, it is not their sole objective. Families need at a minimum to feed, clothe, and house their members, whereas employers need to create a productive and profitable business. In Chapters 3 and 4, we examined some of the responsibilities and obligations that the state and communities have delegated to families and employers. In the United States, these responsibilities include the provision of health insurance, child care, and many other family caregiving responsibilities. Although there are many ways in which employers and families might help men and women create healthier lifestyles and day-to-day choices, they are constrained (or burdened) by the cost of health care or insurance, maternity and other parental leaves, and so on. In fact, the cost of health insurance and of some other supports that might facilitate healthy choices motivates employers to have two tiers of workers, limiting expensive benefits to higher wage workers.[1] Because the cost of benefits do not increase for longer hour workers even if they earn overtime pay, and those on an annual salary are typically exempt from overtime pay, employers often encourage or require longer hours of work. This practice puts employers at odds with the preferences of many dual-earner couples to reduce their time spent in

---

[1] Some companies create this division in part by subcontracting some work to other businesses that do not pay benefits. Others keep a pool of skilled workers at less than full-time hours so that they do not qualify for benefits and they are available to meet varying demands of work flow.

paid work and thus their total work hours, thereby limiting the chronic stress many face in trying to juggle work and family demands.

Similarly, both individuals and families are caught between the demands on their time; the need to earn sufficient income to provide for the household, including paying for day care and health care costs; and the desire to maximize the quality of life in both the short and long term for all of the family. Family constraints are not limited to those who are married or have children. For example, most single adults are embedded in families, meaning that they have responsibilities toward extended family members, and vice versa (Allen & Pickett, 1987; Connidis, 2001).[2] Families use a range of approaches to make choices in the face of competing demands on time and money.[3] Some workplaces have also developed work-family policies to reduce and ameliorate stress, worry, and strain so as to maximize the well-being, quality of life, and productivity of their employees.

Work and family relations display and re-create gender roles in the division of labor and the expectations that are held for men and women over the life cycle. The norms, expectations, and responsibilities attached to work and family roles can positively or negatively shape and constrain men's and women's choices and in turn their health. In particular, individuals face time and financial constraints that often necessitate tradeoffs among their priorities. For example, barriers to health might include long and demanding work hours that are stressful and reduce opportunities to exercise or to eat a healthy diet, whereas becoming a parent brings a wide range of new responsibilities and with them far greater time and financial demands, including the need to spend much more time in less desirable

[2] Moreover, single as well as married adults find their choices constrained by their employment options, and depending on their occupation may be compelled to work longer or less desirable hours than they would prefer in order to provide for themselves and obtain essential benefits.

[3] When finances are very tight, individuals faced with high costs for insurance, especially those who perceive themselves to be in good health, are likely to at least consider the possibility of going without coverage either temporarily (for example, between jobs or during a move) or for longer periods. Similarly, those in poor health who lack pharmaceutical or other coverage may consider skipping much needed and often highly cost-effective medications and preventive care. Thus, the cost of care or of insurance may cause people to consider making choices that they know are contradictory to pursuing a healthy life.

ways (such as cleaning house or settling disagreements). However, families and workplaces can also have a positive influence on health behaviors by making nutritious food available or offering exercise classes or facilities at the worksite, and by intentionally or unintentionally constraining unhealthy options or even requiring healthy behavior, such as through prohibiting smoking in the workplace or the home (Weden, Astone, & Bishai, 2006). Thus, decisions in the family and the workplace can constrain choices in ways that make it easier or harder to choose health.

Clearly, work and family establish many of the specific, and often gendered, responsibilities and obligations that can facilitate or compete directly with decisions about prioritizing health and carrying out the actions necessary to do so. For example, many have argued that women's greater responsibility for organizing the medical care of other family members contributes to their awareness and prioritizing of both health advice and preventive care, which in turn contribute to their higher use of medical care compared to men. At the same time, women's greater responsibility for children may increase both financial and time demands in ways that compete more directly with opportunities to exercise or to get sufficient sleep for mothers compared to fathers.

Some constraints are related to the priorities mandated by the needs of one's particular family structure (for example, being a single-wage earner nearing retirement age, a married professional with elderly dependents, or a member of a dual-earner couple with young or school-aged children) or the demands of one's occupation and how the work is organized and scheduled. For those who are employed full-time, work itself consumes many of their waking hours. Similarly, routine household activities (including shopping, cooking, cleaning, doing laundry, and maintaining a home) take a considerable amount of time whether one is single or married and whether or not one has children. Operating within these constraints may involve major decisions and actions, but everyday events and choices also affect the activities that people engage in on a daily basis. Moreover, work and family life involve ongoing effort, prioritizing, and actions, as well as coordination with the needs, efforts, and schedules of coworkers or family members, whether one's objective is to maintain a home or a job, advance at work, or devise a new way to combine one's roles. Although it is possible to choose to make different tradeoffs in order to expand one's options, decisions involving restructuring work and family arrangements cannot typically be made unilaterally.

CHANGES IN MEN'S AND WOMEN'S WORK AND FAMILY ROLES AND RESPONSIBILITIES

To fully understand the impact of work and family responsibilities on men's and women's health, we need to consider their distribution across the related social roles and role combinations. This distribution has changed considerably over time, leading to more similar role exposure for men and women and possibly decreasing any gender differences in the effects of particular roles as they have become more normative for either gender. In fact, comparisons of the effects of particular social roles and responsibilities of men and women only became feasible as larger numbers of men and women entered roles and work that were traditionally held primarily or exclusively by members of one gender. Thus, although many of the theories are long standing, empirical investigations are more recent, and differences in findings over time may relate to the decreasing stigma of holding what were once atypical gender roles.

Whereas in 1940 only the husband was employed in 67% of married couples in the United States, by 1992 only 18% of couples were made up of employed husbands and stay-at-home wives. As the proportion of traditional single-earner households decreased, those in which both spouses were employed increased from less than 10% to more than 40% of couples. The trend is more striking among married-couple families with children under age 18. In 1975, only the father was in the labor force in 52.6% of these families, whereas both parents worked in 43.4%. By 1988 this pattern had reversed to 32.7 and 63.0%, respectively (Hayghe, 1990). In fact, in 2005, these numbers were largely the same: 30.9 and 61.3%, respectively (U.S. Department of Labor, 2006a). To date, this convergence represents a greater range of normative options for women than men.[4] Thus, in the past women faced substantial constraints on

---

[4] For an overview of key issues of gender work and health in a broader array of industrialized countries, see the World Health Organization's report on this topic by Messing and Östlin (2006).

entering professional and managerial occupations, but many though not all of those barriers have been broken down. In contrast, men in most parts of the country still face considerable barriers to being the primary caregiver for their own children or even to being the secondary wage earner to a higher earning spouse. Moreover, both men and women in dual-earner families are ultimately affected in many ways by the absence of a stay-at-home spouse and the consequent increases in time demands for working adults both with and without children.

Despite the rapid change in women's employment patterns over recent decades, gender differences in jobs and roles still persist, as do the expectations related to each. Although the roles of father and mother have become far less distinct, they are not identical.

Yet, as a result of changes in gender roles, many men and women grew up in homes with a different division of paid and unpaid work than the households they go on to create. The shifts in women's employment have produced new role expectations and increased demands on both men's and women's time, even as a new goal of work–family balance has emerged. In an outstanding study of trends in time use among Americans over the past four decades, Bianchi, Robinson, and Milkie (2006) suggest that normative expectations may be changing in ways that contribute to an increased sense of time pressure. Their data suggest that parents are giving themselves over to parenting to the greatest extent possible, even as the post-adolescence period of dependence on parents' resources has extended into a third decade for many children. These growing and competing demands make life less predictable and require creative problem solving as individuals, families, and even employers need to invent new ways of arranging work and family life.

Therefore, we explore in this chapter how these challenges make it difficult for men and women to choose health. We begin by discussing the health impact of work and family separately and then consider the ways in which the interplay between work and family affects men's and women's health. In the final sections of this chapter, we consider some of the strategies that families and workplaces use to encourage healthy lifestyles and facilitate men's and women's efforts to balance work and family life.

HOW DO MARRIAGE AND FAMILY AFFECT HEALTH?

Marriage

Overall in 2004, 55% of adults age 18 and above in the United States were currently married and living with their spouse (U.S. Census Bureau, 2005). That married adults have better physical and mental health than single adults is well documented (Berkman, 1962; Gove, 1973; Hemstrom, 1996; Lillard & Waite, 1995; Rogers, 1995; Ross, Mirowsky, & Goldsteen, 1990; Schoenborn, 2004; Verbrugge, 1979). A large body of research indicates that currently married men and women are on average healthier than their never-married, widowed, and divorced peers and that the differences vary with age. At issue is the extent to which these patterns reflect health benefits of being married, negative effects of divorce, and the selection of healthier individuals into marriage (P. M. Eng, Kawachi, Fitzmaurice, & Rimm, 2005; Lee et al., 2005; K. Williams & Umberson, 2004).

On average, married people have advantages in terms of economic resources, social and psychological support, as well as support for healthy lifestyles, all of which may contribute to better health compared to those who are never married, divorced, or widowed. Among married individuals, poorer physical and mental health may lead to greater selection out of marriage.[5] Thus, the observation that married adults are on average healthier than those who are not currently married reflects in part these selection processes into and out of marriage.[6] However, marriage presents its own tensions and potential sources of conflict as spouses engage in negotiations about roles and responsibilities.

[5] In a study examining whether psychological distress at age 23 explained marital transitions between ages 23 and 33, Hope, Power, and Rodgers (1999) found that the increased psychological distress of divorced men and women involved both selection and causation. In addition to possible effects of poor mental health on the risk of divorce, because couples often share many of the same health exposures and behaviors such as diet or smoking, those with poorer physical health may also be at greater risk of becoming widowed.

[6] The term "differential selection" does not imply that everyone who gets married is healthier than everyone who remains single. Rather it suggests that healthier individuals are on average somewhat more likely to enter marriage and somewhat less likely to exit marriage or become widowed.

Negative Effects

Not surprisingly, the quality of communication and the level of support within a marriage are associated with its potential positive or negative health effects. Marriage may have negative effects, particularly if it brings high demands and low levels of control, or high levels of interpersonal conflict. A recent study of the relationship between marital quality and self-rated health indicates that adults in poor relationships experience more rapid declines in self-rated health compared to those with better marriages (Umberson, Williams, Powers, Liu, & Needam, 2006). The authors found that the association between marital quality and self-rated health was stronger for older adults, indicating that it is not only younger adults who are vulnerable to health effects of marital quality. Consequently, ending a marriage that has high levels of conflict may be beneficial and can have fewer short-term negative effects than ending a more supportive relationship.

Our interest focuses one layer deeper to consider whether and how marriage and its combination with parenthood are related to differences in men's and women's health and their opportunities to make choices that improve or maintain their health. Another long-standing finding is that men appear to experience greater health benefits from marriage than do women (Mirowsky & Ross, 2003). However, there is some evidence that poor mental health is a greater barrier to marriage and employment for women than men and that it leads more rapidly or more frequently to divorce and either unemployment or selection out of the labor force. Longitudinal research by Williams and Umberson (2004) suggests that for self-rated health, the marital status differences reflect the strains of marital dissolution more than any benefits of marriage and that these strains undermine the self-assessed health of men but not women. However, researchers have not studied whether this finding extends to other measures of physical or mental health.[7]

---

[7] Self-assessed or self-rated health is measured by an individual's response to the question, "How would you rate your health: excellent, very good, good, fair or poor?" Consequently, the measure captures aspects of both one's mental and physical state. Self-rated health has been shown to be associated with subsequent mortality risk above and beyond independent health assessments. However, research using a wider array of health assessments is needed to fully examine the social and biological processes that link experiences to health outcomes.

Gender differences in the effects of entering and ending marriages could occur because there are differences in the resources men and women bring to marriage, the types or amounts of support husbands and wives provide each other, the constraints they experience in marriage, or the consequences of social support or marital conflict. For example, some evidence suggests that financial stress may be associated more strongly with depressive symptoms for wives than for husbands (Ross & Huber, 1985), perhaps because wives are more often responsible for maintaining the family budget, doing the shopping, making sure there is food on the table, and paying the bills (Huber & Spitze, 1983). However, financial strains have been linked to poorer health among both men and women (Lynch et al., 1994; Lynch, Kaplan, & Shema, 1997). For example, Kahn and Pearlin (2006) confirmed that the number of periods of past financial strain experienced was independently associated with poorer self-rated health, number of serious health conditions, illness symptoms, depressive symptoms, and functional impairment.[8] Therefore, in the discussion below, we consider men's and women's roles and experiences inside and outside of marriage.

Parenting

The relationship between parenting and health is both interesting and complex. Given the rewards of parenting and the conscious effort typically involved in becoming a parent, one might expect it would impart substantial health benefits. However, particularly when children are young or are still living at home, there are many social and economic demands associated with parenting that can place considerable constraints on parents' time, finances, and patience. Consequently, those who choose not to have children may have far more freedom to pursue activities they enjoy or, for example, to exercise, whether they enjoy it or not. Thus, one might expect negative effects of parenthood on health and health behaviors as competing demands make one's health a lower priority.

[8]   Although they examined whether the effects differed for African Americans compared to whites, they did not test for gender differences in effects.

Although parenthood does not necessarily lead to poor health or a decrease in quality of life, research indicates that parents face many tradeoffs between the rewards of parenting and the greater amount of time they spend on less desirable activities (Bird, 1997). Among married parents, the birth of a child is typically associated with a move toward a more traditional gendered division of labor in the household (Belsky & Hsieh, 1998; Entwisle & Doeringer, 1981), with mothers decreasing their employment levels and fathers becoming increasingly committed to the breadwinner role (Blau, Ferber, & Winkler, 1998; Lundberg & Rose, 2002); this process continues with the birth of a second child (Klerman & Leibowitz, 1999). Due in part to mothers' tendency to reduce their hours of employment after having children, a wage penalty continues to be associated with motherhood (Budig & England, 2001). In general, adding a child to the household decreases per capita income and can reduce wealth (Gove & Hughes, 1984; Qvortrup & Christofferson, 1990), which may lead to increased economic hardship and psychological distress (Mirowsky & Ross, 1992; Ross & Huber, 1985).

Research on whether parents with children at home have higher levels of psychological distress than adults without children has produced mixed results. Numerous studies have found that, after an initial period of adjustment, parents whose children have entered adulthood and moved out of the family home (sometimes referred to as having an empty nest) were less depressed than adults without children. However, Evenson and Simon (2005) found that although some types of parenthood were associated with more depression than others, there was no type of parent (e.g., single, married, step, custodial, and those with or without their adult children or adult stepchildren living in their home) who reported less depression than adults without children. Moreover, although there were no gender differences in the association between parenthood and depression, women were more likely than men to experience the particular types of parenting such as single parenthood most associated with depression. Thus, part of the gender differences in depression appear to be related to the structure of households, including the greater prevalence of single parenthood among women compared to men. Fewer studies have examined whether parenting affects physical health, in part because the combination of any positive and negative health effects of being a parent likely plays out over a very long time frame, particularly since most people enter parenthood in their relatively healthy years.

Negative aspects of parenthood are more likely to outweigh the positive for those mothers and fathers who face the greatest financial and time constraints. Consider, for example, poor parents with a child who is sick or has special needs due to developmental, behavioral, emotional, or physical health problems. State-funded programs provide assistance with therapeutic, medical, and special education needs of seriously ill and developmentally delayed children. Yet, taking advantage of these programs usually requires a family member to take on the role of case manager for the child, which may include keeping up with the latest medical research, coordinating physician visits and therapy schedules, arranging for educational programming, and filing insurance paperwork (Porterfield, 2002). These circumstances can also place considerable strain on marriages, thus increasing the likelihood of separation or divorce. However, single parents of special needs children and those with other substantial caregiving obligations may face the greatest challenges (Lundberg, 1988).[9]

HOW DOES WORK AFFECT HEALTH?

It is well established that employed adults experience better health than those who are not working for pay (Matthews, Hertzman, Ostry, & Power, 1998; McDonough & Amick, 2001; Ross & Bird, 1994). This is not surprising given that employed people experience both intrinsic and extrinsic benefits of work that can contribute to good health. The former include pay and other benefits, such as insurance and sick leave, whereas the latter include any positive aspects of the work. However, as in the case of marriage, debate continues regarding the extent to which this pattern

---

[9] Whereas reducing work hours may not generate financial hardship for married parents, it can be financially devastating for single parents. Even previously employed single mothers face multiple barriers to full-time employment, particularly if their child requires ongoing medical care. Porterfield (2002) found that decreased labor force participation of single mothers of children with special needs is limited to those whose child is under age 6. This pattern may be due to high costs and less availability of preschool or day care for children with special needs, as well as the greater pressure or need for single mothers to assume a breadwinner role once school or day care becomes available.

reflects the selection of healthier adults into the labor force and into jobs and their greater success in maintaining employment compared to those with poorer mental or physical health (Chandola, Bartley, Sacker, Jenkinson, & Marmot, 2003; Hammarström & Janlert, 2005).[10]

A health selection effect on employment might be more conspicuous in men, in part because men are less likely than women to leave the labor force for reasons other than health. Yet, evidence of health selection is limited even among men. For example, in a longitudinal study using data from the Panel Study of Income Dynamics to follow a sample of employed adults until they left the labor market, McDonough and Amick (2001) found evidence that, among 25- to 39-year-olds, men were more vulnerable to labor market effects of poor health than women. However, there was no gender difference among those who were aged 40 to 61. It is unclear to what extent the gender difference among younger workers is related to the types and prevalence of particular health problems that men and women experience versus differences in the jobs they perform and the expectations put on them. Some have speculated that men's jobs may provide them greater access to disability insurance and other benefits that can support them in exiting the labor force if their health declines. Thus, to the extent that differential selection out of the labor force occurs, it may not be due purely to men's and women's relative risks of injury or declining health, but rather to differences in the jobs men and women tend to hold and thus men's better access to disability insurance, which enables them to leave the workforce in the event they become disabled.

---

[10] Moreover, contrary to the health selection hypothesis, studies find limited evidence linking physical and mental health status to advancement among the employed. For example, Chandola and colleagues (2003) examined longitudinal data from the White-hall II study (initially consisting of 10,308 men and women aged 35–55 in the British civil service) collected over a 10-year period to assess the relative impact of health on changes in social position (health selection) and of changes in social position on changes in health (social causation). They found no evidence for an effect of mental or physical health on changes in employment grade. When financial deprivation was used as a measure of social position, there was a significant effect of mental health on changes in social position among men, although this health selection effect was more than two and a half times smaller than the effect of social position on changes in health. The results to date suggest that the development of social gradients in health cannot be primarily explained in terms of health selection.

Trends in Work Segregation by Gender

The degree to which men and women are segregated into different occupations declined considerably between 1960 and 1990 as increasing numbers of women entered the work force, and it then plateaued in the 1990s (Cohen, 2004; England, 2005).[11] As a result of the occupational segregation that remains and of differences in pay across jobs in the United States, women who were employed full-time year-round in 2004 earned an average of 76.5 cents on the dollar compared to men (based on the ratio of median female to median male earnings; DeNavas-Walt, Proctor, & Lee, 2005). Thus, men and women are exposed to different types of work as well as to differences in pay and other benefits. In part these differences in earnings reflect differences in both educational and employment opportunities and role expectations for men and women (Reskin & Padovic, 1994).

Economists have long argued that women's segregation into particular jobs reflected choices to pursue work with lower costs for absences from the labor force due to mothering responsibilities. However, the data do not support this explanation as men's and women's jobs have similar costs related to absences (England, 2005). It is less clear whether gender segregation reflects early gender socialization leading men and women to differ in their educational choices and job aspirations and choices. Sociologists also point to socialization as a lifelong process whereby men and women continually receive feedback from others as to whether their behavior makes sense and is deemed appropriate. Failure to conform to social norms may lead to reprisals for what is seen as gender-atypical behavior, dress, or even communication style.[12] Thus, rather than simply enacting internalized social norms, we are actively responding to some degree of social constraints as we select our clothing, care for our families, choose particular jobs, or even express dissatisfaction

---

[11] Gender segregation occurs within occupations as well. For example, although women's representation among physicians has increased rapidly in recent decades, women remain highly concentrated in primary care and pediatrics relative to men, who are more highly represented among highly paid medical specialties including surgeons.

[12] Marlo Thomas is often quoted as having said, "For a man to be called ruthless, he has to be Mussolini. All a woman has to do is put you on hold."

or disagreement (West & Fenstermaker, 1993; West & Zimmerman, 1983).[13]

Gender segregation varies considerably cross-nationally. Yet, contrary to what one might expect, gender segregation is lower in reputably "gender-traditional" countries, such as Italy, Japan, and Portugal, than in "progressive" Sweden or the United States.[14] Perhaps this unexpected finding occurs because Sweden and other Nordic countries did not address gender segregation; rather they focused on pay equity. Based on data from 10 industrialized countries, Charles (2003) examined this seemingly anomalous pattern by considering two aspects of segregation: horizontal (manual vs. nonmanual labor occupations) and vertical (in terms of status of nine major occupational categories ranging from laborers to professionals). Her results confirm that men are overrepresented in manual work cross-nationally. In addition, there are status differentials between men's and women's positions within both manual and nonmanual occupations. Together these two types of segregation account for a considerable share of occupational gender inequality. Gender-egalitarian cultural norms were associated with lower levels of vertical segregation in the nonmanual sector, whereas postindustrial economic structures coincided with greater horizontal segregation (and more vertical segregation of nonmanual occupations).[15] England (2005) also demonstrates that far greater declines in gender segregation of the U.S. labor force have occurred

---

[13] Although it is clear that there are gender differences in what behavior and choices are seen as normative and that males and females tend to aspire to different jobs from very early ages, it is difficult to tease out the extent to which early versus ongoing socialization and pressures for conformity explain segregation in employment and in social roles (England, 2005). To address this issue, Epstein (2004) examined how time ideologies integrate with gender and work ideologies to constrain an individual's ability to transgress gender role boundaries regarding their lives and their activities.

[14] In addition the pro-natalist policies in progressive welfare states (the United States being an exception) tend to encourage women to be in part-time employment, which leads to greater vertical segregation – which in turn delays women's progress in careers. However, because they have a structure of benefits that make family life easier, people who become parents in these countries experience fewer challenges combining work and family and appear to be somewhat healthier than otherwise similar parents in the United States.

[15] Cross-national research indicates that pro-natalist national child care and leave policies affect women's employment and that the age and number of children also have independent effects on women's employment that vary across countries.

among those with a college education than among the less educated, with clerical and blue-collar jobs remaining far more highly gender segregated. As a result of gender segregation, men and women tend to experience work that differs in terms of health consequences (Weden, Astone, & Bishai, 2006), as well as in direct intrinsic and extrinsic rewards.

Intrinsic and Extrinsic Rewards of Work

One explanation of the better health of employed adults compared to those who are not working for pay is that work itself has benefits that lead directly or indirectly to better health. In particular, work can offer the opportunity to learn new skills, to be creative and self-expressive, and to make decisions about one's own activities (autonomy) and about the use of resources or the activities of others (authority). Levels of autonomy and authority are related to the ability to schedule one's own time and work activities and to come and go from work as needed; such latitude can reduce the stress associated with high levels of demands at work as well as from boredom associated with more routine work. High levels of autonomy and authority are associated with the higher status jobs that are held more often by men. In addition, work can offer extrinsic rewards, including prestige or status, as well as income and acknowledgment of one's contribution.

Creative and rewarding work has been linked to lower levels of psychological distress among employed persons. These characteristics also affect the impact of the unpaid work involved in parenting, household labor, volunteer work, and other types of tasks (Bird, 1999; Bird & Ross, 1993). Work can be interesting and intrinsically rewarding whether or not it is done for pay (Bird & Ross, 1993; Mirowsky & Ross, 2003). Interestingly, employed individuals report lower levels of autonomy and higher levels of creativity in their daily activities than those who are outside the labor force, including those who are retired (Ross & Mirowsky, 2006; Ross & Wright, 1998). Consequently, there appears to be a tradeoff between the autonomy available to those not working for pay and the creativity, income, and other rewards associated with employment.

Some types of work can be inordinately stressful. In particular, work with high demands and low control has been linked to stress and illness, as well as higher levels of mortality. The combination of low job decision latitude and high psychological job demands has been characterized as high-strain work and is a confirmed risk factor for cardiovascular diseases (Kristensen, 1995; Schnall & Landsbergis, 1994; Theorell & Karasek, 1996).

Decision latitude has proven repeatedly to be an important predictor of the physical and mental health effects of jobs with low psychological demands as well as those with high psychological demands. The theory underlying this research suggests that active work characterized by high psychological demands and high levels of decision latitude allows workers not only to exert control over their work but can also influence their choices and responses to other life experiences. Consequently, by engaging in active work, one can over time acquire feelings of mastery of situations that arise (Theorell & Karasek, 1996). In contrast, passive work, characterized by low psychological demands and low decision latitude, fails to provide the learning and motivation to develop additional decision-making skills and constructive behavior patterns. Individuals who perform passive work are left more susceptible to work overload and strain in the face of more demanding situations that arise at work or elsewhere. Thus, the degree of latitude one has in organizing and carrying out tasks and responsibilities at work and at home affects both problem-solving abilities and psychological resilience to cope with the stressful situations that invariably arise.

Although we are focusing here on the characteristics of paid work, unpaid work including household labor and other activities and responsibilities can also be considered in terms of the level of demands placed on the individual and the amount of latitude he or she has in deciding when and how to do the work. Time sensitivity of tasks relates to the degree of latitude one has in choosing when or whether to complete the task. For example, whereas the family has to be fed every day and laundry needs to be tended to frequently, the lawn may only need to be mowed and the bills paid once or twice a month and the car may only need an oil change a few times a year. Thus, the tasks differ in the amount of time involved, the frequency with which they need to be accomplished, and the discretion one typically has as to whether to attend to them immediately. To the extent that these tasks are divided along gender lines, men have traditionally had greater responsibility for those tasks that were less frequent and had somewhat more discretion as to when they would be performed (Gjerdingen, McGovern, Bekker, Lundberg, & Willemsen, 2000).

Work Hours and Scheduling

In addition to the effects of the type of work one does, working extended hours or on either undesirable or unpredictable schedules may have a range of negative effects on men's and women's ability to pursue health and engage in positive health behaviors. Despite the overall positive association between employment and health, numerous authors have expressed concerns over the possibility that Americans are now overworked (Schor, 1991). Some have pointed out that control over one's work hours may be as important psychologically as control over other aspects of one's work.

Americans are now working more hours per year than at the end of World War II (Leete & Schor, 1994; Mishel & Bernstein, 1994; Rones, Ilg, & Gardner, 1997), and the use of overtime has increased (Hetrick, 2000). However, the average work week has remained essentially unchanged in recent decades (Coleman & Pencavel, 1993a, 1993b; Leete & Schor, 1994; Rones, Ilg, & Gardner, 1997; U.S. Department of Labor, 1999, 2006b). Yet, there is growing diversity in the number and schedule of hours people work (Smith, 1986; U.S. Department of Labor, 2002), as well as the amount of flextime (U.S. Department of Labor, 1998). Between 1970 and 2000, the portion of adults who reported working 40 hours the prior week declined by about 10 percentage points among both men and women (Jacobs & Gerson, 2004). Over the same period, an increasing proportion of both men and women reported working less than 30 hours or 50 or more hours. By the late 1990s, less than a third of employed Americans worked a "standard work week," defined as 35 to 40 hours a week. Only slightly more than half regularly worked a fixed day-time schedule on all five weekdays for a specific number of hours. Similarly, the European Union Survey on Working Conditions carried out in 2000 found that only 24% of the working population engaged in standard day work, defined as working between 7:30 a.m. and 6 p.m. from Monday to Friday (Boisard, Cartron, & Valeyre, 2002). Moreover, in Europe, 50-hour and longer work

weeks are comparatively rare and in many countries are simply not per-
mitted. Thus, although nonstandard hours are likely an issue for workers
in many countries, the United States is an outlier among industrialized
countries in the percentage of long-hour workers, a fact that likely exacerbates the constraints of work and the complexities both men and women
face in attempting to manage both work and family responsibilities.[16]

Jacobs and Gerson (2004) note that the persistence in the average
work week in the United States masks two competing trends: (1) the
increasing length of the work week for professionals and other highly
educated workers and (2) decreases in work hours for other workers
due in part to the growth in part-time and contingent employment.
Among nonprofessionals, they find a growth in both overtime work and
in underemployment whereby many workers are kept at less than full-
time hours in part to avoid the expense of having to provide them benefits
and other protections given to full-time employees.

Over recent decades, a wide range of industries have succeeded in
transferring much of the burden of uncertainty in the flow of work (or
in demand) to workers. Whereas manufacturing traditionally managed
short-term increases in demand by offering or requiring overtime work,
the service industry has addressed uncertainty in day-to-day demand by
asking workers to leave when business is slow and expecting or requiring
them to stay when things are unusually busy, or even to come in for
unscheduled shifts to meet demand (Leidner, 1993). Where employers
used to shoulder the burden and cost of unpredictability in work demand
for professionals and primarily shifted it only onto lower skilled workers,
increasingly more highly paid workers in competitive industries, such
as flight attendants and nurses, are given little choice in schedules and
are expected or required to meet unanticipated demand. The impact of
unpredictable work schedules likely complicates life for those with family
or other caregiving responsibilities while serving as a potential barrier to
many positive health behaviors even for those who are single.

---

[16] Many European countries also have average work weeks of 35–38 hours, greater options
for parental leave and leave to care for a sick child, and a shorter work year due to more
weeks of vacation time. Not surprisingly, shorter work hours are associated with lower
take-home pay and less discretionary income than in the United States. However, the
higher levels of social supportive programs and policies combined with shorter work
hours mean that families also have lower expenses, particularly for child care and
after-school "extended-day" programs.

Health Effects of Long-Hour and Shift Work

Certain work schedules have been linked to poorer health. In particular, long, night-shift, and rotating-shift work hours can present a variety of health hazards. For example, illness and injury rates are higher among people who work more than 12 hours a day or more than 60 hours per week (Dembe, Erickson, Delbos, & Banks, 2005). Working overtime has also been linked to an increased injury rate compared to those who do not work overtime, even after adjusting for age, gender, occupation, industry, and region (Dembe et al., 2005). In addition, a substantial body of work documents significant health consequences of working the night shift or rotating shifts. Shift work, either working odd hours or rotating shifts, has been linked to an increased risk of cardiovascular disease and decreased sleep time for both men and women (Caruso, Hitchcock, Dick, Russo, & Schmit, 2004). There are also effects on emotional health. Night shifts and rotating shifts disrupt circadian rhythms, producing sleep disturbances, fatigue, digestive troubles, and irritability, which can reduce both mental agility and performance efficiency (Akerstedt, 1990; Barton, 1994; Kawachi et al., 1995); for an excellent review of health disorders of shift workers see Knutsson (2003). Sleepiness has been shown to be a contributing factor to increased rates of work accidents and injuries (see a review by Folkard & Tucker, 2003). In addition, strong evidence exists for an association with peptic ulcer disease, coronary heart disease, and an increased risk of compromised pregnancy outcomes (for a review, see Knutsson, 2003). Moreover, a British study demonstrated that working very long hours was negatively associated with women's health behavior (O'Connor, Conner, & Jones, 2005). Women, but not men, who worked longer hours consumed more high-fat and high-sugar snacks, exercised less, and, if smokers, smoked more. In addition, their findings indicated that individuals who worked in highly demanding, low-control work environments consumed more snacks when they experienced one or more daily hassles.

To assess whether the diversity of work schedules poses greater problems for American workers than in the past, Fenwick and Tausig (2004) analyzed 1977 and 1997 data from representative samples of the U.S. labor force. Consistent with prior research, they found nonstandard shifts, especially evening or night, and rotating shifts to be disruptive to family and social life, but unlike prior studies they found no substantial effects on health outcomes at either time point. Moreover, benefits from working a "flexible" schedule extended to all workers with either children or a spouse or partner. Working a flexible schedule reduced disruptions to family and social life as well as levels of stress and burnout (see also Presser, 2003). Schedule control also proved beneficial to all workers, and the effects were independent of job schedule. They argue that the ability to choose a work schedule and to control starting and ending times within that schedule may reflect the underlying issue of autonomy in the workplace with consequences for the well-being for all workers. Thus, having the latitude to choose work hours may help prevent or decrease the risk of some of the negative health effects found in other studies.

The combination of long and unpredictable work hours may interact with the lingering gender segregation of the labor force. Consider again the predominantly female occupation of flight attendant. Although flight attendants work alongside the almost exclusively male airline pilots, they tend to have even less autonomy in setting their schedules. Flight crews typically have to work a 14-hour period and have no say on which shift to work, issues that often arise in contract negotiations. Because pilots have traditionally commanded substantially higher salaries than flight attendants, they are more likely to be the primary breadwinner in their household and thus to be able to shift some family responsiblities to their spouse (or hire household help) so as to limit or reduce some of the disruptions in family life that inevitably result from this unpredictability. Although numerous studies have examined the high miscarriage rate among flight attendants (Aspholm et al., 1999; Daniell, Vaughan, & Millies, 1990), little attention has been paid to the consequences of this unusually unpredictable long-hour shift work for family life and health (Ballard et al., 2006).

WORK AND FAMILY ROLES INTERACT TO AFFECT HEALTH

Men's and women's work and family roles increasingly overlap and are far less differentiated than in the past, which has created for many a cultural lag between the norms and roles observed in childhood and those experienced and enacted in adulthood. Both the underlying gender roles and lags in expectations tend to leave women feeling greater responsibility for the care of their children than do men, and thus women are somewhat more stressed and conflicted when difficulties arise regarding day care and after-school care (Barnett & Rivers, 2005; Thoits, 1992). Moreover, as a result of these rapid and continued changes, as well as the large array of financial and caregiving responsibilities left to the family, entire cohorts of men and women are left to grapple with and attempt to resolve the multiple demands on their time without clear role models or examples of successful approaches or "best practices."

One consequence of the lag between change and solutions is that men and women may experience different degrees of responsibility for addressing various family concerns. Furthermore, they may find their various roles and obligations more or less compatible, for example, in terms of their physical and psychological demands or the total time commitment or scheduling related to both routine and unexpected events. Although being the sole or primary breadwinner can offer some protection from tedious and unrewarding household duties, it clearly brings its own responsibilities and burdens that may include longer work hours and possibly a long commute either to minimize housing costs or maximize housing size, quality, and location for the money. Moreover, as a result of changing norms, adults now place greater value on balancing time spent on work and on family; work–family balance has gained increasing popularity in part as a potential solution to the absence of a homemaker spouse and the growing time demands on employed adults. Clearly, some fathers as well as mothers may be conflicted by not being able to participate fully in both domains. However, the standards of full participation in each realm are not identical for mothers and fathers.

Does Gender Affect Combining Work and Family Roles?

Although both husbands and wives are obviously exposed to economic shortfalls faced by the household, men are more likely to feel responsible for being the primary breadwinner and are far less likely to have expected to be a stay-at-home parent (Belsky & Hsieh, 1998; Belsky & Kelly, 1994). Thus, employed mothers, in comparison both to working women without children and to stay-at-home moms, typically have a wider range of roles at which they may feel the need to be successful. In contrast, fathers may feel little need or pressure to compare the quantity or quality of time spent with their children to that of stay-at-home dads. At the same time, however, men may feel they have fewer ways in which to pursue alternative arrangements of their roles and time. For example, although it has become accepted that some women in the professions will seek part-time work while their children are young, there is considerably less understanding of or support for men who seek less than full-time work in medicine (Bird, Lang, Chertoff, & Amick, 2002), law, and other professions (Epstein, 2004) so that they can spend more time with their families. These standards and expectations are normative as well as internalized. Consequently, men who frequently work long hours when their children are young may be seen by their employers as good workers as well as good fathers because they are being good breadwinners. In contrast, a woman working the same schedule may not be seen as equally successful and accomplished as a worker and a mother. Such perceptions and implicit assumptions may affect whether, or when, she is considered for promotion to a position with increased responsibility, irrespective of her own preferences or those of her family.

Interestingly, there is some evidence that husbands and wives make decisions differently regarding whether and when to relocate for work. Bielby and Bielby (1992) found that, whereas husbands decided whether to move for work or to follow their wife in a work-related move based on the impact on their own careers, wives made their decisions based on the impact on the finances of the household. Consequently, couples were more likely to make a move that benefited the husband's career but not the household than to do so for a move that benefited the wife's career but not the household. Other research indicates that, among couples within the United States and Great Britain, wives who moved long distances with their husbands (greater than 30 km) were more likely to be unemployed or otherwise out of the labor force than wives who were nonmigrants, wives who had moved shorter distances, or husbands whether or not they had moved (Boyle, Cooke, Halfacree, & Smith, 2001). These studies illustrate one of the ways in which differences in men's and women's lives and resources constrain and shape their options and decision making related to work and family.

Despite the potential conflicts among multiple social roles, there is considerable evidence that fulfilling several roles can result in role enhancement for those who are not experiencing a level of time pressure that produces role overload. In the simplest case, multiple roles can be beneficial because one is able to draw on both individual successes and resources available in each role to find satisfaction. For example, one role may provide more creativity, whereas another provides greater social or economic rewards. In addition, having multiple areas in which to measure one's success, productivity, or effectiveness can be particularly helpful when work or responsibilities in one area present substantial challenges. In a study of British women's experiences in combining roles, McMunn and colleagues (2006) found better health among those who are married, parents, and working than among those with fewer roles.

A related issue is whether and to what extent positive and negative experiences in work and family roles spill over into other areas of life. In an ideal circumstance, one would be able to leave the frustrations of work at work and return to a satisfying home life, or leave the challenges of a particular family or parenting problem at home and return to a successful work life. At issue is whether and under what circumstances either negative or positive experiences carry over from one role to another, thereby creating additional stress and problems. Not surprisingly, both positive and negative spillover can and does occur, particularly negative spillover for those experiencing role overload (Crouter, Bumpass, Head, & McHale, 2001). Similarly, findings regarding job strain and family life indicate that negative experiences in either realm can, and often do, spill over into other areas of one's life.

Finally, holding too many demanding or conflicting roles can lead to role overload (Gjerdingen et al., 2000). In this case the time and energy or psychological demands of multiple roles are overwhelming and stressful and can undermine positive health behaviors (see Grzywacz and Marks, 2000, on the risk of problem drinking). One of the most obvious potential effects on health is in the area of sleep. Clearly, both short- and long-term loss of sleep and frequent disruptions to sleep can undermine both physical and mental health. Moreover, getting adequate sleep is important to working efficiently and to engaging in effective problem solving; consequently, sleep loss may exacerbate feelings of overload. Although single individuals without children may be somewhat less likely to face such role overload, the demands of work and self-care may still at times come into conflict for those working long hours, whether they do so routinely or to meet occasional deadlines. However, the complexity of scheduling and meeting competing time-sensitive demands increases for those with young children or other caregiving responsibilities while also making it more difficult to find the time to catch up on any lost sleep. Hislop and Arber (2003) have written on how gender relations affect the amount of sleep women and men get. They argue that women's unpaid work extends through the night as they often have caregiving demands and carry out other household responsibilities then (see also Dzaja et al., 2005).

Jacobs and Gerson (2004) observed that, even though the average number of hours worked annually has not increased substantially in the United States over the past several decades, as a result of the rapid increases in mothers' employment, families with children now have more total hours of labor force participation. Whether or not single parents and adults in dual-earner households are experiencing greater demands on their time than in the past, they now make up a significantly larger share of the population (Bianchi et al., 2006). Consequently, the problems that these two groups of parents face are becoming more prevalent, which presents new challenges both for employers and families. For example, single parents and those in dual-earner households have a greater need for child care, which creates an increased demand for public preschool and kindergarten, as well as after-school care and summer educational and child care programs. The shift in the composition of households has also affected businesses that provide goods and services to households. For instance, single-parent and dual-earner families are less likely to have someone at home to shop for and prepare food during the workday. As a result, the needs of these households contribute to the demand for processed and prepared foods, as well as evening and weekend primary medical care and dental appointments.

Managing both work and family life presents substantial challenges for so many due to constraints in the availability of work arrangements that mesh well with the demands of family life. A significant proportion of American workers, and especially those who have very long work weeks, would prefer to work less (Jacobs & Gerson, 2004). Yet, there is also considerable evidence that many U.S. employees would like to work more hours. In a study of workers' actual and preferred hours, Reynolds (2003) found that, although 37% wanted to reduce their hours, 22% wanted to work more. Interestingly, preferences were associated with worker, job, and family characteristics, with family responsibilities associated with wanting to work *more* rather than *fewer* hours. An equal proportion of employed men and women were content with their work hours (42%), but men were more likely to want to work more hours and women were more likely to want fewer hours. Moreover, Reynolds found that eliminating such hour mismatches would require the creation of many part-time jobs because 16% of full-time workers reported a preference for part-time work versus only 5% of part-time workers who reported a preference for full-time work. Not surprisingly, the results also suggest that work–family conflict may be more likely to produce a desire for fewer hours among employees who are well off economically.

Jacobs and Gerson (1998) noted that, although workers can make choices about their work hours, these are often "forced choices between unpalatable alternatives" or what we describe as *constrained choices* resulting from having to balance two limited resources: time and income. Other authors find that a variety of workers face similar tensions. For example, a study of married-couple families found a considerable disparity between couples' self-reports of preferences and actual behavior, suggesting that long work hours result from constraints and demands imposed by the workplace, rather than from workers' preferences for employment (Clarkberg & Moen, 2001). Men and women who work longer hours than they prefer to are more likely to feel overworked and in turn to make mistakes at work, experience work–family conflict, and have poorer health (Galinsky, Kim, & Bond, 2001). Furthermore, there is good reason to believe that employers have the upper hand in establishing work hours and the length of the work week (Golden, 1996).

The challenges that nonstandard work hours and shift work present to various aspects of family functioning differ somewhat by gender and whether there are children in the household. In fact, based on a study of workers in the United States, Presser (2003) found some positive effects of nonstandard work hours and spouses working different shifts, such as a more equal gender division of household labor and increased parental time with children, as well as the obvious negative social consequences, such as increased marital instability and complex child care patterns. Thus, it appears that there are considerable tradeoffs that Americans make when working nonstandard schedules. However, because of the lack of information and variability in effects, Presser (2004) called for additional research on the costs and benefits of working nonstandard schedules, a point we would expand to include the effects on family life, workers' health, and the ability to make informed individual and policy choices.

In an analysis of the effects of shift work and job schedule control on the family life and health of American workers, Fenwick and Tausig (2001) found that working shifts other than Monday through Friday was associated with increased family conflict and worker burnout. However, the evening or night, and rotating shifts thought to produce the greatest problems for workers and their families had no such effects. Thus, they conclude that, given the diversity of schedules and reasons for working them, general statements about the stressful nature of shift work for all workers are unwarranted. Control over scheduling significantly affects family and health outcomes for both men and women, regardless of family status and whether they work standard or nonstandard shifts (Fenwick & Tausig, 2001, 2004). Although the challenges presented by nonstandard work hours and shift work differ by gender and family status, control over one's work hours appears to be beneficial for all workers.

FLEXIBILITY AND CHOICE AS CRITICAL RESOURCES

Decision making is an ongoing process. Over time, families employ a variety of strategies to manage work and social roles and create a high quality of life. These range from deciding whether to have a stay-at-home spouse, invest more heavily in one career, hire help with housework and child or elder care, stagger work hours to shorten children's day care hours by having one spouse drop off the children and the other pick them up, or even working opposite shifts to maximize parental time with children or minimize child care expenses. Among the many effects of juggling these competing demands of employment and parenthood are decreased time for sleep and exercise and often a decreased prioritization of one's own health over that of the children. Because parenthood typically occurs in early to middle adulthood, the effects of poorer health behaviors are not as readily apparent or understood as they are in older or frailer individuals, who may experience physical reminders of the effects of lack of sleep or exercise. Moreover, the challenges of balancing work and family life or other caregiving responsibilities are not limited to those with children.

The many approaches to the division of labor within the household and family decision making have cost-benefit tradeoffs for men and women that add to the complexity of creating healthy lives. For example, for parents with the flexibility to slightly stagger their work hours, such an arrangement can provide increased time with the children at meals and limit the amount of child care that needs to be purchased or obtained from family members or other adults. However, working opposite shifts or having a parent working rotating shifts can have considerable costs in terms of marital quality. Yet, parents who pay for child care so that they can work similar hours must earn more to cover the cost and typically pay more to obtain high-quality care and longer hours of child care. Consequently, in an attempt to buy sufficient child care help, some parents may feel pressed to work longer hours to obtain or retain jobs that pay sufficiently more than day care salaries. Others may conclude that it is impossible to come out ahead by working more and instead shift to having a primary breadwinner and a stay-at-home parent, despite the long-term costs of an absence from the labor force. Clearly, men's and women's lives, resources, and opportunities can contribute to differences in their priorities and choices on these issues.

Although most families have multiple options for earning sufficient income and dividing responsibilities, the range of possibilities is obviously larger for those households of greater means. Similarly, the options vary depending in large part on where one lives. Comparative studies have not examined the experience of parenting and its health consequences cross-nationally. However, we contend that neither the social policies of the United States nor those of states and cities in the United States have been designed to ease the competing demands of work and family. Rather, a wider range of responsibilities have been left to individuals and families than in other countries. As a result many men and women cannot effectively make their own health a priority because they are distracted or overwhelmed by obligations that compete for their resources, energy, and attention.

We have yet to realize the health consequences of the growing complexity of balancing work and family and the related chronic stress that many adults experience over extended periods. Both the prevalence and growing age range of adults with multigenerational responsibilities suggest that demands on families are increasing and that both families and employers will be faced with multiple challenges in managing these demands (Spillman & Pezzin, 2000). Although earlier research found minimal effects of multigenerational responsibilities on caregivers' well-being, Wolff and Kasper (2006) found that those caring for older adults are now responsible for an increasingly disabled segment of the population. Moreover, among caregivers to older adults, women are more likely than men to be over age 65, to be the primary caregivers, and to provide more intensive and complex care. Women caregivers are also more likely than men to report difficulty with care provision and with balancing caregiving with other family and employment responsibilities, to suffer from poorer emotional health secondary to caregiving, and to cope with caregiving responsibilities by forgoing respite participation and engaging in increased religious activities (Navaie-Waliser, Spriggs, & Feldman, 2002).

Work-Life Programs and Policies

Given the limited range of work–family policy in the United States compared to Europe, an increasing number of employers in the United States have some form of work-life programs and policies designed or intended to create a supportive workplace environment. One set of work-life policies allows employees to work shorter hours, nonstandard schedules, or even flexible schedules. These accommodations can allow workers to better coordinate their schedules with the school day or day care hours. Employees without children are often attracted to nonstandard schedules that may allow them to avoid rush hour traffic and possibly even work fewer days per week (e.g., four 10-hour days or nine 9-hour days over a 2-week period). Having a weekday off on a weekly or biweekly basis allows workers to manage a range of responsibilities during normal business hours (including shopping, errands, and medical appoint-ments), to have time to volunteer or otherwise be involved in their child's activities, or to exercise or engage in other leisure-time activity. By allow-ing workers to better fit their work schedule to their lives, flexible sched-ules can reduce the need to use vacation time in a piecemeal fashion, leaving workers greater opportunity to take time off over holidays, for vacations, or during school breaks for those with children. In addition, some employers offer other job benefits that can help address the demands of work and family. Most common among these are health insurance benefits for a spouse and children. Other benefits include assistance with "work-life planning" such as access to information on formal caregiver services to help accommodate those with new or changing responsibili-ties, the ability to purchase long-term care insurance for parents or other relatives, or advice on how to use or develop a flexible schedule to mini-mize absenteeism.

In an innovative study of management practices and work-life balances practices in medium-sized manufacturing firms in the United States, France, Germany, and the United Kingdom, Bloom, Kretschmer, and Reenen (2006) assessed whether work-life balance is associated with pro-ductivity. They examined family-friendly policies: part-time to full-time flexible working schedules, shorter hours, more holidays, subsidized child care, job sharing, and home-working entitlements. These policies were associated with better management (as indicated by modern business practices in the areas of operations, monitoring, targets and incentives) and with larger, typically more global firms. More productive firms and those with more competitive environments did not have significantly less family-friendly policies. There was no systematic relationship between work-life policies and productivity after taking into account good man-agement. They conclude that work-life polices are on average neutral, rather than being associated with either higher levels of productivity (win–win) or inherently costly in terms of productivity. However, they note that the programs are costly to implement and maintain and that they may result in lower profitability.

Sharing responsibility for health across the levels of decision making as we have discussed can provide new and more effective ways to invest in health efficiently. As illustrated in Chapters 4 and 5, multiple factors outside of an individual's control affect his or her ability to act on opportunities to pursue a healthy life. Moreover, some of these constraints appear to operate differently for men and women. Although individuals may be able to use this information to help inform their choice of work environments and families may use it to make decisions regarding whether and how to accommodate the preferences and needs of two breadwinners, additional population health benefits are attainable if employers consider these health effects when evaluating workplace policies and organization.

References

Akerstedt, T. (1990). Psychological and physiological effects of shift work. *Scand J Work Environ Health, 16*, 67–73.

Allen, K. R., & Pickett, R. S. (1987). Forgotten streams in the family life course: Utilization of qualitative retrospective interviews in the analysis of lifelong single women's family careers. *J Marr Fam, 49*(3), 517–526.

Aspholm, R., Lindbohm, M. L., Paakkulainen, H., Taskinen, H., Nurminen, T., & Tiitinen, A. (1999). Spontaneous abortions among Finnish flight attendants. *J Occup Environ Med, 41*(6), 486–491.

Ballard, T. J., Romito, P., Lauria, L., Vigiliano, V., Caldora, M., Mazzanti, C., et al. (2006). Self perceived health and mental health among women flight attendants. *J Occup Environ Med, 63*(1), 33–38.

Barnett, R. C., & Rivers, C. (2005). *Same Difference: How Gender Myths Are Hurting Our Relationships, Our Children, and Our Jobs.* New York: Basic Books.

Barton, J. (1994). Choosing to work at night: A moderating influence on individual tolerance to shift work. *J Appl Psychol, 79*, 449–454.

Belsky, J., & Hsieh, K.-H. (1998). Patterns of marital change during the early childhood years: Parent personality, coparenting, and division-of-labor correlates. *J Fam Psychol, 12*, 511–528.

Belsky, J., & Kelly, J. (1994). *The Transition to Parenthood.* New York: Delacorte Press.

Berkman, J. (1962). Mortality and marital status: Reflections on the derivation of etiology from statistics. *Am J Pub Health, 52*(8), 1318–1329.

Bianchi, S., Robinson, J. R., & Milkie, M. A. (2006). *Changing Rhythms of American Family Life.* New York: Russell Sage Foundation.

Bielby, W. T., & Bielby, D. D. (1992). I will follow him: Family ties, gender-role beliefs, and reluctance to relocate for a better job. *Am J Sociol, 97*(5), 1241–1267.

Bird, C. E. (1997). Gender differences in the social and economic burdens of parenting and psychological distress. *J Marr Fam, 59*(4), 809–823.

Bird, C. E. (1999). Gender, household labor, and psychological distress: The impact of the amount and division of housework. *J Health Soc Behav, 40*, 32–45.

Bird, C. E., Lang, M. E., Chertoff, J., & Amick, B. C. (2002). Organizational supports for and barriers to part-time work arrangements for professionals: The case of radiology. *Res Sociol Health Care, 20,* 159–182.

Bird, C. E., & Ross, C. E. (1993). Houseworkers and paid workers: Qualities of the work and effects on personal control. *J Marr Fam, 55,* 913–925.

Blau, F. D., Ferber, M. A., & Winkler, A. E. (1998). *The Economics of Women, Men, and Work* (3rd ed.). Upper Saddle River, NJ: Prentice-Hall.

Bloom, N., Kretschmer, T., & Reenen, J. V. (2006). *Work-Life Balance, Management Practices and Productivity.* London: London School of Economics, Center for Economic Performance.

Boisard, P., Cartron, D., M., G., & Valeyre, A. (2002). *Temps et travail: La Durée du Travail.* Dublin, Ireland: European Foundation for the Improvement of Living and Working Conditions.

Boyle, P., Cooke, T. J., Halfacree, K., & Smith, D. (2001). A cross-national comparison of the impact of family migration on women's employment status. *Demography, 38*(2), 201–213.

Budig, M. J., & England, P. (2001). The wage penalty for motherhood. *Am Sociol Rev, 66*(2), 204–225.

Caruso, C. C., Hitchcock, E. M., Dick, R. B., Russo, J. M., & Schmit, J. M. (2004). *Overtime and Extended Work Shifts: Recent Findings on Illnesses, Injuries, and Health Behaviors* (No. 2004–143). Washington, DC: U.S. Department of Health and Human Services.

Chandola, T., Bartley, M., Sacker, A., Jenkinson, C., & Marmot, M. (2003). Health selection in the Whitehall II study, UK. *Soc Sci Med, 56*(10), 2059–2072.

Charles, M. (2003). Deciphering sex segregation: Vertical and horizontal inequalities in ten national labor markets. *Acta Sociol, 46*(4), 267–287.

Clarkberg, M., & Moen, P. (2001). Understanding the time squeeze: Married couples' preferred and actual work-hour strategies. *Am Behav Scien, 44*(7), 1115–1135.

Cohen, P. (2004). The gender division of labor: "Keeping house" and occupational segregation in the United States. *Gen Sociol, 18*(2), 239–252.

Coleman, M. T., & Pencavel, J. (1993a). Changes in work hours of male employees 1940–1988. *Indust Labor Rel Rev, 46,* 264–283.

Coleman, M. T., & Pencavel, J. (1993b). Trends in market work behavior of women since 1940. *Indust Labor Rel Rev, 46,* 653–676.

Connidis, I. A. (2001). *Family Ties and Aging.* Thousand Oaks, CA: Sage.

Crouter, A. C., Bumpass, M. F., Head, M. R., & McHale, S. M. (2001). Implications of overwork and overload for the quality of men's family relationships. *J Marr Fam, 63,* 404–416.

Daniell, W. E., Vaughan, T. L., & Millies, B. A. (1990). Pregnancy outcomes among female flight attendants. *Aviat Space Environ Med, 61*(9), 840–844.

Dembe, A. E., Erickson, J. B., Delbos, R. G., & Banks, S. M. (2005). The impact of overtime and long work hours on occupational injuries and illnesses: New evidence from the United States. *Occup Environ Med, 62*(9), 588–597.

DeNavas-Walt, C., Proctor, B., & Lee, C. H. (2005). *Income, Poverty, and Health Insurance Coverage in the United States, 2004. Current Population Reports.* Washington, DC: U.S. Government Printing Office.

Dzaja, A., Arber, S., Hislop, J., Kerkhofs, M., Kopp, C., Pollmächer, T., et al. (2005). Women's sleep in health and disease. *J Psychiatr Res, 39*(1), 55–76.

Eng, P. M., Kawachi, I., Fitzmaurice, G., & Rimm, E. (2005). Effects of marital transitions on changes in dietary and other health behaviours in U.S. male health professionals. *J Epidemiol Comm Health, 59*, 56–62.

England, P. (2005). Gender inequality in labor markets: The role of motherhood and segregation. *Soc Polit, 12*, 264–288.

Entwisle, D., & Doeringer, S. (1981). *The First Birth: A Family Turning Point.* Baltimore: Johns Hopkins University Press.

Epstein, C. F. (2004). Border crossings: The constraints of time norms in transgressions of gender and professional roles. In C. F. Epstein & A. L. Kalleberg (Eds.), *Fighting for Time: Shifting Boundaries of Work and Social Life* (pp. 317–340). New York: Russell Sage Foundation.

Evenson, R. J., & Simon, R. W. (2005). Clarifying the relationship between parenthood and depression. *J Health Soc Behav, 46*(4), 341–358.

Fenwick, R., & Tausig, M. (2001). Scheduling stress: Family and health outcomes of shift work and schedule control. *Am Behav Scien, 44*(7), 1179–1198.

Fenwick, R., & Tausig, M. (2004). The health and family social consequences of shifting work and schedule control: 1977 and 1997. In C. F. Epstein & A. L. Kalleberg (Eds.), *Fighting for Time: Shifting Boundaries of Work and Social Life* (pp. 77–112). New York: Russell Sage Foundation.

Folkard, S., & Tucker, P. (2003). Shift work, safety and productivity. *Occup Med, 53*, 95–101.

Galinsky, E., Kim, S. S., & Bond, J. T. (2001). *Feeling Overworked: When Work Becomes Too Much.* New York: Families and Work Institute.

Gjerdingen, D., McGovern, P., Bekker, M., Lundberg, U., & Willemsen, T. (2000). Women's work roles and their impact on health, well-being, and career: Comparisons between the United States, Sweden, and the Netherlands. *Wom Health, 31*(4), 1–20.

Golden, L. (1996). The economics of worktime length, adjustment, and flexibility: A synthesis of contributions from competing models of the labor market. *Rev Soc Econ, 54*, 1–45.

Gove, W. (1973). Sex, marital status and mortality. *Am J Sociol, 79*, 45–67.

Gove, W. R., & Hughes, M. (1984). *Overcrowding in the Household: An Analysis of Determinants and Effects.* New York: Academic Press.

Grzywacz, J. G., & Marks, N. F. (2000). Family, work, work-family spillover, and problem drinking during midlife. *J Marr Fam, 62*, 336–348.

Hammarström, A., & Janlert, U. (2005). Health selection in a 14-year follow-up study: A question of gendered discrimination? *Soc Sci Med, 61*, 2221–2232.

Hayghe, H. V. (1990). Family members in the work force. *Month Labor Rev, 113*(3), 14–19.

Hemstrom, O. (1996). Is marriage dissolution linked to differences in mortality risks for men and women? *J Marr Fam, 58,* 366–378.

Hetrick, R. L. (2000). Analyzing the recent upward surge in overtime hours. *Month Labor Rev, 123*(2), 30–33.

Hislop, J., & Arber, S. (2003). Understanding women's sleep management: Beyond medicalization-healthicization? *Soc Health Ill, 25*(7), 815–837.

Hope, S., Power, C., & Rodgers, B. (1999). Marital status transitions and psychological distress: Longitudinal evidence from a national population sample. *Psychol Med, 29,* 381–389.

Huber, J., & Spitze, G. D. (1983). *Sex Stratification: Children, Housework, and Jobs.* New York,: Academic Press.

Jacobs, J. A., & Gerson, K. (1998). Toward a family-friendly, gender equitable work week. *U Penn J Labor Employ Law, 1,* 457–472.

Jacobs, J. A., & Gerson, K. (2004). *The Time Divide: Work, Family, and Gender Inequality.* Cambridge, MA: Harvard University Press.

Kahn, J. R., & Pearlin, L. I. (2006). Financial strain over the life course and health among older adults. *J Health Soc Behav, 47,* 17–31.

Kawachi, I., Colditz, G. A., Stampfer, M. J., Willett, W. C., Manson, J. E., Speizer, F. E., et al. (1995). Prospective study of shift work and risk of coronary heart disease in women. *Circulation, 92,* 3178–3182.

Klerman, J. A., & Leibowitz, A. (1999). Job continuity among new mothers. *Demography, 36*(2), 145–155.

Knutsson, A. (2003). Health disorders of shift workers. *Occup Med, 43,* 103–108.

Kristensen, T. S. (1995). The demand-control-support model: Methodological challenges for future research. *Stress Med, 11,* 17–26.

Lee, S., Cho, E., Grodstein, F., Kawachi, I., Hu, F. B., & Colditz, G. A. (2005). Effects of marital transitions on changes in dietary and other health behaviors in US women. *Int J Epidemiol, 34,* 69–78.

Leete, L., & Schor, J. B. (1994). Assessing the time-squeeze hypothesis: Hours worked in the United States, 1969–89. *Indust Relat, 33,* 25–47.

Leidner, R. (1993). *Fast Food, Fast Talk: Service Work and the Routinization of Everyday Life.* Los Angeles: University of California Press.

Lillard, L. A., & Waite, L. J. (1995). Till death do us part: Marital disruption and mortality. *Am J Sociol, 100,* 1131–1156.

Lundberg, S. J. (1988). Labor supply of husbands and wives: A simultaneous equations approach. *Rev Econ Stat, 70,* 224–235.

Lundberg, S., & Rose, E. (2002). The effects of sons and daughters on men's labor supply and wages. *Rev Econ Stat, 84*(2), 251–268.

Lynch, J. W., Kaplan, G. A., Cohen, R. D., Kauhanen, J., Wilson, T. W., Smith, N., et al. (1994). Childhood and adult socioeconomic status as predictors of mortality in Finland. *Lancet, 343,* 524–527.

Lynch, J. W., Kaplan, G. A., & Shema, S. J. (1997). Cumulative impact of sustained economic hardship on physical, cognitive, psychological, and social functioning. *N Engl J Med, 337*(26), 1889–1895.

Matthews, S., Hertzman, C., Ostry, A., & Power, C. (1998). Gender, work roles and psychosocial work characteristics as determinants of health. *Soc Sci Med, 46*(11), 1417–1424.

McDonough, P., & Amick, B. C. (2001). The social context of health selection: A longitudinal study of health and employment. *Soc Sci Med, 53,* 135–145.

McMunn, A., Bartley, M., Hardy, R., & Kuhet, D. (2006). Life course social roles and women's health in mid-life: Causation or selection? *J Epidemiol Comm Health, 60,* 484–489.

Messing, K., & Östlin, P. (2006). *Gender Equality, Work and Health: A Review of the Evidence.* Geneva: World Health Organization.

Mirowsky, J., & Ross, C. E. (1992). Age and depression. *J Health Soc Behav, 33*(3), 187–205.

Mirowsky, J., & Ross, K. (2003). *Education, Social Status, and Health.* Hawthorne, NY: Aldine De Gruyter.

Mishel, L., & Bernstein, J. (1994). *The State of Working America 1994–95.* Armonk, NY: M. E. Sharpe.

Navaie-Waliser, M., Spriggs, A., & Feldman, P. H. (2002). Informal caregiving: Differential experiences by gender. *Med Care, 40*(12), 1249–1259.

O'Connor, D. B., Conner, M. T., & Jones, F. (2005). *Effects of Stress on Eating Behaviour: An Integrated Approach.* Swindon, England: Economic and Social Research Council.

Porterfield, S. L. (2002). Work choices of mothers in families with children with disabilities. *J Marr Fam, 64,* 972–981.

Presser, H. (2003). *Working in a 24/7 Economy: Challenges for American Families.* New York: Russell Sage Foundation.

Presser, H. (2004). Employment in a 24/7 economy: Challenges for the family. In C. F. Epstein & A. L. Kalleberg (Eds.), *Fighting for Time: Shifting Boundaries of Work and Social Life* (pp. 46–76). New York: Russell Sage Foundation.

Qvortrup, J., & Christofferson, N. M. (1990). *Childhood as a Social Phenomenon.* Vienna: European Centre for Social Welfare Policy and Research.

Reskin, B. F., & Padovic, I. (1994). *Women and Men at Work.* Thousand Oaks, CA: Pine Forge Press.

Reynolds, J. (2003). You can't always get the hours you want: Mismatches between actual and preferred work hours in the U.S. *Soc Forces, 81*(4), 1171–1199.

Rogers, R. G. (1995). Marriage, sex, and mortality. *J Marr Fam, 57,* 515–526.

Rones, P. L., Ilg, R. E., & Gardner, J. M. (1997). Trends in hours of work since the mid-1970s. *Month Labor Rev, 120*(4), 3–14.

Ross, C. E., & Bird, C. E. (1994). Sex stratification and health lifestyle: Consequences for men's and women's perceived health. *J Health Soc Behav, 35,* 161–178.

Ross, C. E., & Huber, J. (1985). Hardship and depression. *J Health Soc Behav, 26*(4), 312–327.

Ross, C. E., & Mirowsky, J. (2006). *Creative Work and Health.* Austin, TX: Population Research Center.

Ross, C. E., Mirowsky, J., & Goldsteen, K. (1990). The impact of family on health: The decade in review. *J Marr Fam, 52*, 1059–1078.

Ross, C. E., & Wright, M. P. (1998). Women's work, men's work and the sense of control. *Work Occup, 25*, 33–55.

Schnall, P. L., & Landsbergis, P. A. (1994). Job strain and cardiovascular disease. *Ann Rev Pub Health, 15*, 381–411.

Schoenborn, C. A. (2004). *Marital Status and Health: United States, 1999–2002. Advance Data from Vital and Health Statistics, No. 351*. Hyattsville, MD: National Center for Health Statistics.

Schor, J. B. (1991). *The Overworked American: The Unexpected Decline of Leisure*. New York: Basic Books.

Smith, S. J. (1986). The growing diversity of work schedules. *Month Labor Rev, 109*, 7–13.

Spillman, B. C., & Pezzin, L. E. (2000). Potential and active family caregivers: Changing networks and the 'sandwich generation'. *Mil Q, 78*, 347–374.

Theorell, T., & Karasek, R. A. (1996). Current issues relating to psychosocial job strain and cardiovascular disease research. *J Occup Health Psychol, 1*(1), 9–26.

Thoits, P. A. (1992). Identity structures and psychological well-being: Gender and marital status comparisons. *Soc Psychol Q, 55*(3), 236–256.

Umberson, D., Williams, K., Powers, D. A., Liu, H., & Needham, B. (2006). You make me sick: Marital quality and health over the life course. *J Health Soc Behav, 47*(1), 1–16.

U.S. Census Bureau. (2005). *Current Population Reports*. Washington, DC: U.S. Census Bureau.

U.S. Department of Labor. (1998). *Workers on Flexible and Shift Schedules. Labor Force Statistics from the SPS, USDL98–119*. Washington, DC: U.S. Government Printing Office.

U.S. Department of Labor. (1999). *Report on the American Workforce*. Washington, DC: U.S. Government Printing Office.

U.S. Department of Labor. (2002). Over one quarter of full-time workers have flexible schedules. *Month Labor Rev*. Retrieved September 8, 2007, from http://www.bls.gov/opub/ted/2002/apr/wk3/art05.htm.

U.S. Department of Labor. (2006a). *Employment characteristics of families in 2005*. Retrieved September 8, 2007, from http://www.bls.gov/news.release/archives/famee_04272006.pdf.

U.S. Department of Labor. (2006b). *Labor force statistics from the current population survey: Household data annual averages (Table 19)*. Retrieved September 20, 2006, from http://www.bls.gov/cps/cpsaat19.pdf.

Verbrugge, L. (1979). Marital status and health. *J Marr Fam, 41*(2), 267–285.

Warner, J. (2005). *Perfect Madness: Motherhood in the Age of Anxiety*. New York: Riverhead Books.

Weden, M. M., Astone, N. M., & Bishai, D. (2006). Racial, ethnic, and gender differences in smoking cessation associated with employment and joblessness through young adulthood in the US. *Soc Sci Med, 62*, 303–316.

West, C., & Fenstermaker, S. (1993). Power, inequality, and the accomplishment of gender: An ethnomethodological view. In P. England (Ed.), *Theory on Gender/ Feminism on Theory* (pp. 151–157). New York: Aldine de Gruyter.

West, C., & Zimmerman, D. H. (1983). Doing gender. *Gen Soc, 1*, 125–151.

Williams, K., & Umberson, D. (2004). Marital status, marital transitions, and health: A gendered life course perspective. *J Health Soc Behav, 45*, 81–98.

Wolff, J. L., & Kasper, J. D. (2006). Caregivers of frail elders: Updating a national profile. *Gerontologist, 46*(3), 344–356.

SIX

Gender and Individual Health Choices

In Chapters 3 through 5 we explored the myriad ways in which larger social units including policy regimes, communities, families, and workplaces make decisions and establish policies and practices that structure men's and women's opportunities for pursuing health. In Chapter 2 we introduced the schematic framework of constrained choice Figure 2.2 to depict the various decision levels that influence men's and women's lives and individual choices. The diagram suggests that the decisions and actions at each of these levels are linked and that collectively they can impinge on men's and women's options over the course of their lives. One purpose of the diagram is to illustrate what is missing in explanations of gender differences and to emphasize that the connections between broader social contexts and individual choices are rarely transparent, and thus health consequences of prior personal and government decisions are often underestimated and frequently overlooked. The bottom of the diagram shows how the interaction between individual health behavior choices and biological processes can lead to subsequent gender differences in health outcomes. However, the linear form of the process displayed in the heuristic diagram oversimplifies a very complex dynamic and is not intended to imply there are known direct links between specific constraints at various levels and health behavior choices and biological processes. Although men's and women's life choices are constrained in ways that can lead to the gender and health differences discussed in Chapters 1 and 3, few if any researchers have attempted to marshal the data needed either to specify those connections or to clarify the role of biological processes in this dynamic. Another purpose of the diagram is to call attention to the need for such cross-disciplinary research that ultimately will allow us to answer the question, *Do men and women make everyday and life choices that contribute to gender differences in health?*

In this chapter the focus is on men and women as individuals and on the health behaviors they engage in over the life course. Here we are concerned with how social circumstances and biological factors might contribute to the variation in particular health behaviors that men and women adopt and that contribute to the observed disparities in their health. Although we recognize that health behaviors are intertwined with work and family gender roles and other socioeconomic realities, our argument impels us to raise the critical question: *Why are some individuals able to create and maintain healthy lifestyles, whereas others are not?* For many reasons this is a complex question to address. First, practical and ideological concerns affect how nations, communities, workplaces, and families define and prioritize health, and these broader considerations shape the environment in which individuals themselves come to value and pursue health. Second, there are knowledge gaps and debates in health behavior research regarding definitions of health practices and their relative risk, the relations among them, their mechanisms of action, how and why health practice rates vary across the life course both within and across nations, and how such practices differentially contribute to particular health outcomes (e.g., Newsom, McFarland, Kaplan, Huguet, & Zani, 2005; Sussman, 2005). Third, for some individuals, an existing health problem, family history, or known genetic vulnerability will affect their health behaviors and longevity.

Depending on the nature of their biological and physiological susceptibility, men and women can and do respond in both similar and different ways when exposed to the same risky practice. To illustrate, recent research shows how the smoking-related risk of lung cancer is differentially associated with race and gender (Haiman et al., 2006). The risk was similar among those who smoked 30 or more cigarettes a day, but among the men and women who smoked no more than 10 cigarettes a day, African Americans more than whites had an elevated lung cancer risk, and men had a higher risk than women. Although there is some uncertainty about the mechanism of action, Risch (2006) has suggested that family history, cultural ancestry, or gene frequencies can interact with unknown aspects of the environment and in a variety of ways affect both men's and women's physiological response to health-damaging practices and their health trajectory.

As we have indicated elsewhere in the book, health consciousness and risk judgments of the potential health effects of specific behaviors or some toxic aspect of the environment, even if they are accurate, are not always uppermost in most people's minds, especially in making small everyday choices. Nor is health often the main priority even in larger decisions, such as what career to pursue, where to live, or whether to marry or have children. It is not the way most people think about everyday life choices or about health-impairing behaviors unless their health status, as is the case with chronic conditions, dictates such vigilance. In addition, not everyone has the same demands on his or her time and other resources, so for some individuals other priorities and obligations compete with health, as is so often the case when trying to balance work and family. This is one reason why low-income single parents have poorer health status than higher income married couples with children. What is still debatable is whether most adults and adolescents misunderstand, ignore, or are simply unaware of the fact that many seemingly minor choices today can and do have a cumulative impact on health down the road. Even when women and men are fully informed about the health benefits of salutary behaviors such as exercise and about the health risks of certain behaviors (e.g., smoking), they still often engage in health-damaging practices both in adolescence and adulthood. These ostensibly voluntary actions and puzzling choices contribute to gender differences in such damaging lifestyle behaviors as smoking, lack of exercise, excessive drinking, poor eating habits, and reckless driving. Such differences could be a gendered response to constraints or a form of coping with existing vulnerabilities, job and family stress and strain, or social circumstances that make men and women feel insecure and overwhelmed. Although the precursors of health behaviors are not fully understood, data from longitudinal studies indicate that some health-damaging practices such as smoking and drinking emerge in early adolescence and often continue into and sometimes throughout adulthood (see, for example, Ellickson, Tucker, & Klein, 2003; Sussman & Sussman, 2001; Tucker, Ellickson, Orlando, Martino, & Klein, 2005).

In the discussion of constrained choice that follows, we explore both national and cross-national data on gender differences in health behaviors as a way to shed new light on why under certain circumstances some individuals can and do engage in health-promoting practices, which are seemingly under men's and women's individual control, whereas others do not or cannot. Although we consult an extensive multidisciplinary literature, this effort is hampered in some ways by the lack of conclusive evidence about the precursors, epidemiology, pathways, and outcomes of health behaviors for men and women. With that caveat in mind we use this chapter to generate different ways to think about the expansion of opportunities for individuals to pursue health.

SELECTED HEALTH BEHAVIORS IN THE UNITED STATES AND THE GENDER GAP IN LONGEVITY

The belief that an individual's choice of lifestyle behaviors can affect one's health and longevity is widespread, most notably among Western cultures. This assumption has generated numerous theories of health behavior benefits and an extensive and diverse body of research within the United States and cross-nationally. Considerable evidence and impressive successes from a range of disciplines validate the claim that choosing or adopting healthy behaviors – the earlier in life the better – can prevent or control diseases later in life. Lifestyle-related behaviors, such as smoking, drinking, exercise, and eating a balanced diet, are frequently cited as factors that contribute to health disparities and the gender gap in health. Yet as we noted earlier, understanding the psychological and social circumstances that underlie health behaviors in general and their association with gender in particular remains elusive. For instance, if we knew that there was a strong association among various health-impairing behaviors that either men or women might be more likely to engage in, then we would be able to target prevention efforts to a specific subgroup or to one behavior that triggers the others, and in this way perhaps close the gender gap and extend life. But knowledge of the associations among the health behaviors and their relation to the gender gap is surprisingly incomplete.

In fact, there are striking disagreements about the degree to which the health behaviors are interrelated or are independent, depending on the measures being used (e.g., individual level or population based). To illustrate, Newsom and colleagues (2005) examined individual-level data from three large epidemiological surveys in the United States and found that the major health behaviors (smoking, alcohol, diet, and exercise) are largely independent of each other. The researchers do cite studies that found associations between particular behaviors, such as smoking and alcohol abuse (see Jensen et al., 2003, cited in Newsom et al., 2005), and they acknowledge that measurement error or response bias could affect the lack of association among the health behaviors in the North American population. But Newsom and colleagues (2005) interpret the lack of association among the four health behaviors studied to mean that no single factor accounts for all four behaviors, and they go on to argue that the results challenge the underlying causal role attributed to motivation and health consciousness by many health behavior theories and researchers. Confirmation for the weak association among health behaviors is provided in a smaller study by Reeves and Rafferty (2005) that showed that only 3% of adults engaged in all of the four behaviors studied. These researchers used data from just one of the epidemiological surveys (BRFSS) and measured slightly different behaviors (smoking, body weight, diet, and physical activity). Various other studies have found evidence of patterns of health behaviors in narrower subgroups of the population defined by age, gender, and race (see, for example, Berrigan, Dodd, Troiano, Krebs-Smith, & Barbash, 2003; Gallant & Dorn, 2001; Kamimoto, Easton, Maurice, Husten, & Macera, 1999; Laaksonen, Luoto, Helakorpi, & Uutela, 2002; Pronk et al., 2004).

The debate about the nature of the interrelations and degree of independence among health behaviors is relevant because disease prevention and health promotion depend on comprehending the prevalence, antecedents, and underlying association among the health practices as the behaviors may have synergistic effects on disease. If this and other controversies in health behavior research were resolved, it would help explain how social and biological factors contribute to the behavioral choices men and women make and the health effects of those choices.

The principal behaviors most often cited as a health risk, especially for ischemic heart disease (IHD) and lung cancer, are cigarette smoking, excessive alcohol consumption, physical inactivity, and overeating or consuming an unbalanced diet (eating fewer fruits and vegetables and more fat) that leads to obesity. Smoking and alcohol are considered the two most preventable causes of premature death. These health practices are particularly relevant for understanding men's excess mortality rates in relation to women. Other influential health behaviors include driving safely, minimizing stress, getting sufficient sleep, engaging in safe sex practices, having good dental hygiene, complying with treatment for chronic conditions, and avoiding environmental hazards.

The following section summarizes trends among the four principal risk behaviors that are most amenable to measurement and research in both the United States and abroad and are therefore studied more extensively (U.S. Department of Health and Human Services, 2005). These gender comparisons provide a portrait of what different and similar types of health behavior choices men and women are making at various stages of the life course and highlight some of the health consequences for both adults and adolescents. We use these data to illustrate not only the gender pattern across these health practices but also to point out the differential biological and physiological response of men and women, for example, to substances such as nicotine and alcohol. This discussion is designed to illustrate the interaction among risky health behavior choices, biological processes, and the gender gap in longevity.

SMOKING

The good news is that the general decrease in cigarette smoking among adults over the last 10 years has contributed to a decline in mortality rates, especially male deaths from ischemic heart disease (IHD) all over the world (World Health Organization, 2002b). The decrease in smoking accounts in part for the increase in men's life expectancy in the United States (Pampel, 2002; Preston & Wang, 2006). Only slightly more men than women are smokers in the United States, but the magnitude of the smoking gender gap varies cross-nationally. Both the percent of smokers and the gender gap are greater, for example, in Korea, Hungary, and Russia than in Sweden, Norway, or the United States.[1] However, tobacco

---

[1] In general Central and Eastern European Countries (such as Bulgaria, The Czech Republic, Estonia, Latvia, Lithuania, Poland, Rumania, Slovakia and Slovenia) have a lower life expectancy and larger gender gap than the rest of Europe. In addition to negative natural growth (emigration and deaths exceed births), these countries have experienced dramatic regime changes, demographic transitions, and considerable social

use is still the leading risk factor for total disease burden in both the United States and Canada, whereas in other countries in the Americas, alcohol is the leading risk factor (Ezzati, Lopez, Rodgers, Vander Hoorn, & Murray, 2002; World Health Organization, 2002b). In other countries in the Americas, men and women are smoking less but have more alcohol-related deaths.

Both men and women are thus making choices and these choices are associated with a variety of factors that impair their health and longevity in different ways. For example, Weden and colleagues (2006) show how men's and women's choices are differentially affected by joblessness and other social factors. Even the choice of whether to smoke or to be around others who smoke appears to put women at increased risk of lung cancer compared to men (Haiman et al., 2006). In fact, the U.S. incidence rates for all cancers combined declined for males but not females. Although lung cancer deaths are still higher for males, lung cancer has also become the leading cause of cancer mortality for women.

In the United States, in 1965, 50% of men and 33% of women were daily smokers, in contrast to 24% of men and 19% of women in 2003 (U.S. DHHS, 2005, Figure 12 and Table 60). Smoking rates are strongly associated with levels of educational attainment. Adults with less than a high school education were three times as likely to smoke compared to those with a bachelor's degree or more education (see U.S. DHHS, Table 64, 2005). There has also been a decline in pregnant women and mothers who smoke (down to 11% in 2002) across all racial and ethnic groups, but some differences persist. The highest maternal smoking rates are among American Indian and Alaskan native mothers (20%), non-Hispanic white mothers (15%), and Hawaiian mothers (14%; USDHHS, 2005, Figure 10). These gender and status differences indicate that there is something about the social circumstances of an individual's life that puts him or her at risk for unsafe health behavior.

Among high-school students (grades 9–12), smoking rates also decreased from 1997 to 2005 (Johnston, O'Malley, Bachman, & Schulenberg, 2006; U.S. DHHS, 2005). In 2002, 22% of high-school

insecurity. Men's longevity is lower than women's, and men smoke and consume alcohol in greater numbers, although there is some variation in rates among these countries (World Health Organization, 2002b).

students reported any current smoking (1 or more days in the last 30) and 10% smoked frequently (20 days or more) (U.S. DHHS, 2005). Smoking is more prevalent by both measures among white adolescent girls than among Hispanic and non-Hispanic black girls. Among boys, smoking prevalence varies less by race and ethnicity. By the 12th grade, 29% of boys and 23% of girls were current smokers, with one-half of both groups smoking frequently, which is slightly higher than the adult rate for current smokers but parallels the gender difference in adult prevalence. Many of the frequent adolescent smokers had already become nicotine dependent (U.S. DHHS, 2005). Thus, smoking behavior does vary by gender, race, and SES, and to some extent these differences could be viewed as a negative response to different constraints confronting these adolescents.

But the data are insufficient to fully understand all the reasons why specific groups of adolescents and adults initiate and continue to smoke, whether this behavior has the same meaning for men and women, or what the most effective way is to get them to stop.[2] Thus, the progress made in reducing the general level of smoking in the population is offset by the fact that adolescents are still engaging in this detrimental practice, as are a significant percent of adult men and women in the United States and around the world. Most individuals have a general understanding of the health effects of smoking, so these practices would appear to be informed choices based perhaps on a faulty perception or judgment of their own personal risk.

The discussion of constrained choice in Chapter 2 addressed the issue of whether individuals who value health but fail to choose healthy behaviors or are unable to make health a priority could still be considered as acting rationally. We paraphrase that question here: *What puts individuals at risk for smoking, and are they being irresponsible or irrational for not effectively making their health a priority?* The association between some risky behaviors and the SES gradient in health (Banks, Marmot, Oldfield, &

---

[2] There is extensive research linking smoking and nicotine to weight control, especially among women. As a result many smoking cessation programs incorporated weight control procedures into their intervention efforts. For examples of reviews of this field, see work by Filozof, Fernandez Pinilla, and Fernandez-Cruz, 2004; Li, Kane, and Konu, 2003.

Smith, 2006) leads us to ask this question: *Does someone who has fewer resources and options have the same opportunity to act on information about risky practices related to a potentially unhealthy or foreshortened future compared to someone with more resources and options?* Since it is known that early use of alcohol and cigarettes can lead to addiction, we also need to ask this: *If someone started smoking and drinking in adolescence, to what degree are such actions voluntary as an adult?* Although there are no clear answers to these questions, we raise them at this juncture to illustrate the different type of questions that might be addressed in a constrained choice framework.

ALCOHOL CONSUMPTION

The gender pattern for alcohol consumption differs from that for smoking, in which men's and women's smoking rates have become more similar over the past decade. In contrast, in the United States, male adolescents and adults consume more alcohol than do females, and this is the case in most of the world (World Health Organization, 2002a). However, in the United States and much of the industrialized world, females' alcohol consumption has increased. A meta-analysis of international longitudinal surveys found, consistently across cultures, that men drank more than women and that marriage and aging reduced both men's and women's drinking (Filmore et al, 1997). Depression predicted subsequent increases in drinking among women but not among men.

There is an emerging line of research bringing together epidemiology and genetics and demonstrating variation in the prevalence of a specific genotype, apolipoprotein E (EPOE). This genotype is associated with the impact of a range of health behaviors (such as dietary intake of antioxidants or consumption of excess amounts of alcohol) on health outcomes, such as cognitive function, cholesterol levels, and life expectancy (see, for example, Ewbank, 2004; Hu et al., 2006; Seeman et al., 2005). Genetic variations likely explain some of the differences in the effects of health behaviors across studies and may be useful for understanding racial/ethnic dissimilarities in the risk for different diseases. It may also be worthwhile to explore whether specific genes affect men's and women's alcohol risk similarly. Moreover, there are reliable studies that suggest that small amounts of some kinds of alcohol contribute to better health, although it is not known how the risks and benefits vary by gender across the life-span (see, for example, the special issue of *Alcohol Health and Research World*, 1996, especially articles by Dufour and Valliant and Hiller-Sturmhofel; also see Greenfield and Kerr, 2003, about issues and limitations of measures of alcohol trends).

Those who drink to excess may not be aware of the evidence showing that in addition to men's and women's different body mass, they may metabolize alcohol differently. Women reach higher blood alcohol levels than men when consuming equivalent weight-adjusted amounts of alcohol (Wilsnack & Wilsnack, 2002), indicating a physiological basis for alcohol response and some alcohol-related health effects.[3] Recent studies have introduced a gender correction factor (giving the same weight to a smaller number of drinks per day for women) in reporting consumption, although this is still controversial. Wilsnack and Wilsnack (2002) argue that although there is considerable variation in alcohol consumption across regions, international comparisons of men's and women's differential drinking behavior rates can help determine whether such differences can be attributed to biological and/or to social factors. In an article discussing the sex differences in genetic risk for alcoholism, Prescott (2002) suggests, "An understanding of the mechanisms influencing sex differences in risk can help illuminate not only the differences in men's and women's drinking behavior and related problems but also the biological and cultural basis for variability within each sex" (p. 264).

---

[3] Alcohol (ethanol) is a central nervous system depressant, and it is this system that is most severely affected by drinking. Central nervous system impairment depends on the concentration of alcohol in blood. Ability to metabolize alcohol quickly diminishes with age. In terms of body weight and type, the less you weigh, the more you will be affected by a given amount of alcohol. For people of the same weight, a well-muscled individual will be less affected by alcohol than someone with a higher percentage of fat, since fatty tissue does not contain water (alcohol has an affinity for water) and will not absorb much alcohol.

Women tend to have a higher percentage of body fat and thus a lower percentage of body water. If a man and woman of the same body weight ingest the same amount of alcohol, the woman will attain a higher blood-level of alcohol (which is not case when a woman is fit and the man obese). Total water volume tends to decrease with age. Women also tend to eliminate alcohol from their bodies at a rate of 10% greater than men (information adapted from http://www.intox.com/physiology.asp, accessed September 17, 2007).

Yet, men do drink more than women, and for men under the age of 64 this behavioral practice in part contributes to their excess mortality from cirrhosis of the liver and lower life expectancy compared to women. Men's higher rate of alcohol consumption is reflected in the age-adjusted death rates for liver cirrhosis that, like lung cancer, vary by race and sex. Both black and white men die at twice the rate of women. In 2001 the age-adjusted liver cirrhosis death rate per 100,000 population for white males and females was 13.4 vs. 6.5, and for black males and females it was 14.1 vs. 5.8. Although all liver cirrhosis mortality rates are decreasing, the rate for blacks is decreasing even more because it had previously been much higher than the rate of whites (Yoon, Yi, & Hilton, 2005). The age-adjusted death rate from all types of cirrhosis shows a similar pattern: the rate for males is consistently higher and almost twice the rate for females. About 43.6% of the mortality rate from cirrhosis is alcohol related, so the health-damaging effects of excessive alcohol consumption are quite direct.

In addition to liver cirrhosis, accidents are another direct health effect of alcohol consumption, especially for adolescents. Although the rates of motor vehicle (MV) injuries declined by 40% for teens and young adults in 2003, young adults 15–24 years of age have the highest rate of MV injuries for any age group (U.S. DHHS, 2005). One-third of deaths in this age group are the result of MV accidents. Twenty percent of those 16–20 years of age involved in fatal accidents in 2003 were intoxicated. In 2002, 75% of young drivers who had been drinking and were killed in car accidents were not wearing seatbelts (22% of males and 15% of females report never using a seatbelt in 2003); states with strong seat belt laws have higher rates of compliance, illustrating the positive impact of state regulations and policies on individual health behavior. Male students in grades 11 and 12 were almost twice as likely as their female peers to drink and drive (22% vs. 12%).

The increase in women's rates of drinking is therefore a worrisome trend as it suggests that women who live like men (in terms of their alcohol consumption) are thus more likely to die prematurely like men (Wilsnack & Wilsnack, 2002). This trend could in the long run conceivably reverse the gender pattern in alcohol-related deaths (a similar reversal occurred as women took up smoking in the last century and decades later lung cancer became the leading cause of cancer mortality for females).

As discussed in Chapter 5, the structure of gender roles both at work and in the family has put men and women in a bind about how to combine the two. Rates for drinking to excess vary with the normative context, family history, severity of liquor laws, economic circumstances, and, as we contend, a host of personal constraints and opportunities confronting men and women. The consumption of alcohol may be one counterproductive strategy for coping with the stress and strain arising from conditions of social and personal uncertainty. Although some men and women smoke and also drink to excess, the two behaviors are independent, meaning they do not always occur in combination, nor does one predict the other.

DIET AND WEIGHT

In reviewing the typical U.S. diet and eating behaviors (especially the trend in super-sizing containers and portions), none of the news is particularly good. Poor eating habits in terms of the type and amount of food consumed lead some individuals to become overweight or obese. Among adults, excess weight elevates the risk of CHD and diabetes and increases the severity of symptoms associated with hypertension, arthritis, and musculoskeletal problems. Although women and girls are more likely to report eating more fruits and vegetables and lower fat foods than men and boys (Reeves & Rafferty, 2005; U.S. DHHS, 2005), there has been little improvement in rates of overweight, obesity, and physical activity among adults and adolescents and little significant difference by gender. A main problem associated with excess weight in children and adolescents, particularly obesity, is its persistence into adult life and its link with the risk of both diabetes and cardiovascular disease.

The longitudinal National Health and Nutrition Study (NHANES) showed an increase in being overweight and obesity among adults from the 1988–1994 to the 1999–2002 surveys (U.S. DHHS, 2005). The upward weight trend since 1980, which has received considerable attention in the United States in recent years, reflects the increase in the percentage of obese adults 20–74 years of age (U.S. DHHS, 2005, Table 73, Figure 15). In the 1999–2002 survey, 65% of adults were classified as overweight and 31% as obese (28% of men and 34% of women are obese). Rates differed slightly by race and ethnicity in women; among the obese, half were non-Hispanic blacks and one-third were non-Hispanic whites. For obese men, the prevalence differed very little by race or ethnicity. Among children 6–11 years of age and adolescents aged 12–19, 16% of both groups were overweight in 1999–2002; this percentage among both age groups varies by race and ethnicity, with 14% of non-Hispanic whites, 21% of non-Hispanic blacks, and 23% of those with Mexican origins being overweight. The distribution of increased weight among adults and children across the life-span suggests that the distal factors and eating habits affecting weight gain could be similar for both men and women.

Although there are some gender differences in diet and exercise behaviors, there is no obvious pattern. Clearly, exercising regularly and maintaining a healthy diet do not necessarily co-occur. People may eat nutritious food or make poor dietary choices in part because of the short-term rewards of eating what they please or what is readily available without considering the long-term health consequences. It is unclear how gender socialization itself might influence weight gain and lack of exercise, but sex-related physiological processes may contribute to some of the health consequences of excess weight. For example, men and women store fat in different parts of their bodies, and this physiological process makes gender a risk factor for various kinds of health conditions, such as diabetes, elevated serum cholesterol, and CVD, among other conditions. Poor diet, limited opportunity to engage in physical activity and participate in organized sports,[4] genetic factors, physiology, and existing health conditions are associated with excess weight both in men and women as well as children and adolescents.

PHYSICAL ACTIVITY

The predicted benefits of regular physical activity include a reduced risk of premature mortality, CHD, diabetes, colon cancer, hypertension,

---

[4] The rapid change brought about by enactment in 1972 of Title 9 mandating that girls and women were entitled to participate in the same organized sports as men certainly increased their participation in structured physical activity.

and osteoporosis. Exercise also improves symptoms associated with musculoskeletal problems and with mental health conditions such as depression and anxiety. Along with a healthy diet, exercise reduces the risk of being overweight and obese, although there are hereditary factors associated with obesity.

According to *Health United States, 2005* (U.S. DHHS, 2005), male high-school students were more likely than female students to be physically active in 2003. Only 50% of non-Hispanic black female students reported being physically active, which if it is a continuing behavior pattern may contribute later in adulthood to the higher rates of obesity and hypertension in black females. However, the percentage of all high-school students participating in regular physical activity declines with advancing grade (from 73% in 9th grade to 60% in 12th grade). This decline is explained in part by decreasing enrollment in and availability of physical education (PE) classes. In 2003, only 28% of high-school students attended daily PE, whereas 38% watched 3 or more hours of TV each day. Such adolescent practices may continue into adulthood and account for the increasing rates of overweight and obese adults of both genders.

The level of physical activity for adult men and women remained stable over the past decade (U.S. DHHS, 2005, Table 72). About 3 in 10 adults report some physical leisure-time activity, whereas 4 in 10 report being sedentary. Men are more likely than women to have regular physical leisure-time activity. Until retirement, the availability of regular leisure time decreases with age, and the amount of that time and the age of retirement vary by economic status. Those individuals with higher status and greater wealth have more leisure time. As noted in Chapter 5, making or finding time for routine exercise is a health behavior choice that is related directly to the structure of workplaces and families and attempts to achieve some balance between them.

Decisions at the community level in making available safe parks, running tracks, playgrounds, and swimming pools or taking the actions needed to make lakes and oceans fit for recreational use clearly affect the constraints and opportunities that individuals have to make choices about outdoor exercise, as discussed in Chapter 4. Weather is both a constraint and opportunity as well. For example, the level of exercise and outdoor leisure-time activity is greater in the states along the West Coast than in parts of the United States without temperate climates and where people rely primarily on indoor facilities over long winter months. Yet, those who live in cold weather climates have the option to engage in winter sports, such as downhill skiing, cross-country skiing, and snow shoeing, although the earlier sunsets of northern winter climates tend to limit after-school outdoor activities. Opportunities to take advantage of both indoor and outdoor exercise facilities also vary by income and time constraints; thus, decision makers at different government levels play an important role in establishing policies and regulations to provide safe, healthy environments for exercise that enhance everyone's capacity to choose health.

CROSS-NATIONAL COMPARISONS OF INDIVIDUAL HEALTH BEHAVIORS

In Chapter 3 we used the framework of constrained choice to explore the proposition that different types of policy regimes formulate policies and regulations that could increase the options and opportunities for men and women to pursue health (see Abramovitz, 1996, for a social history of women and welfare policy). The cross-national comparisons showed that countries with social democratic regimes generally have a higher overall life expectancy and a smaller gender gap in longevity than other types of regimes. Here we extend that reasoning to again compare policy regimes, but with a focus on the level of individual men's and women's health behaviors and choices. We undertake these comparisons to determine whether there are discernible gender patterns in health behaviors across regimes and, if so, whether such differences might be associated with the gender gap in longevity.

Although there are numerous benefits to using cross-national aggregate data to examine gender differences in health behaviors, there are considerable challenges as well. The benefits include being able to (1) detect comparative trends across or within entire populations or with specific subgroups such as men and women (or boys and girls); (2) examine the antecedents and health consequences of such patterns; and (3) develop an understanding of the policy changes or other social issues that create circumstances that encourage men and women to pursue healthy practices. We are especially interested in those practices linked to diseases that are known to contribute to the gender gap in mortality and life expectancy.

The challenges of using cross-national data are best illustrated by the difficulties researchers encounter in tracking alcohol consumption. Here the main issues revolve around what data researchers are measuring. Are they measuring individual-level data, such as reports of the amount and type of alcohol individuals consume and how drinking is socially organized, including whether alcohol is used on special occasions, consumed routinely with most meals, or imbibed frequently and excessively? Or are they measuring the alternative – aggregate population data – in which drinking culture and norms are the focus, as well as sales data and per capita consumption of alcohol? When conducting studies, alcohol researchers can choose to rely solely on individual data or aggregate data at a population level, or a combination of the two. In addition, in terms of comparability, it matters whether researchers are using the same designs, measures, time points, and data sources, such as cross-sectional, longitudinal, or panel surveys. Greenfield and Kerr (2003) discuss these issues in relation to alcohol consumption trends and provide a list of surveys in the United States tracking alcohol and related data (see Appendix 1). We have added a second list (see Appendix 2) of the numerous international surveys tracking alcohol consumption across nations and regions that we encountered while conducting research for this book. The lists displayed in Appendices 1 and 2 are provided so the reader may have access to the variety of data sources to better understand the variation in analysis and findings in cross-national alcohol research. Whether one is studying adults or adolescents, the same issues of definition, measurement, and comparability will affect the collection and analysis of cross-national data on all health behaviors, including current and lifetime patterns of smoking, diet, and physical exercise.

Using the same policy regimes discussed in Chapter 3, Table 6.1 shows a cross-national comparison of male and female differences in health behaviors based on data from a variety of international studies. It includes the countries previously designated by the following three types of policy regimes, with the addition of Japan:

1. *Liberal:* United States, Canada, Australia, and the United Kingdom
2. *Conservative-Corporatist:* France, Austria, Germany, Italy, the Netherlands, and Japan[5]
3. *Social Democratic:* Sweden, Denmark, Norway, and Finland

Table 6.1 includes smoking, alcohol consumption, and obesity, as well as the incidence of lung cancer (the leading cause of cancer mortality) to illustrate the direct health effects associated with gender differences in smoking. As the table shows, men have higher smoking rates than women across all policy regimes, but the gender gap is significantly larger among the conservative-corporatist countries. Sweden is the only country in which the smoking rate of men and women is nearly similar. Even though Japan has the highest life expectancy of any country (see Table 6.2), it is surprising to see that Japanese men have the highest smoking rate (48%), and Japan has the largest smoking gender gap (34%). The gender gap in smoking rates is consistent with the large differences in lung cancer incidence for men (38.1%) and women (12.3%) in Japan, a pattern found in other countries as well. Men's lung cancer incidence rates in Japan are three to five times greater than are women's, but there is some cross-national variation; men's lung cancer incidence rates are much lower in the social democratic countries than in the other two regime types. For example, the percentages range from 21–45% in the social democratic countries versus 39–61% in the liberal and conservative-corporatist countries. These figures provide some validation for our contention that the family-friendly social and workplace policies enacted in the social democratic countries have a positive effect on men's smoking behavior and ability to pursue health.

Women's smoking rates vary across the regimes, but they are not that far behind the men's rates, especially in the liberal and social democratic countries. The magnitude of the smoking gap between men and women

---

[5] Japan is also included in Table 6.1 because Japanese women and men have the highest life expectancy of any country in the world.

Table 6.1. *Regime Type and Gender Differences for Selected Health Behaviors*

Regime Type	Smoking[1]		Alcohol[2,3]			Obesity[4]		Lung Cancer Incidents[5]	
	Female	Male	Female	Male Heavier & Binge Drinking	Per capita consumption	Female	Male	Female	Male
Liberal									
United States	16	19	8.4	7.3	8.5	33.3	27.8	36.1	61.9
Canada	14	19	–	–	8.3	13.9	16.0	31.6	55.8
Australia	18	21	–	–	9.2	21.4	21.9	16.8	39.5
United Kingdom	24	28	22	40	10.4	22.8	22.1	24.9	48.1
Social Democratic									
Sweden	18	17	18	33	6.9	9.8	11.0	14.4	21.4
Denmark	25	31	–	–	11.9	9.1	9.8	29.8	45.3
Norway	25	27	–	–	5.8	8.2	8.4	18.7	36.4
Finland	19	26	17	29	10.4	11.7	14.0	10.1	33.4
Conservative-Corporatist									
France	22	32	5	9	13.5	9.1	9.7	8.8	52.6
Austria	–	–	–	–	12.6	9.1	9.1	14.3	42.6
Germany	19	30	7	14	12.9	12.3	13.6	12.7	46.7
Italy	18	31	11	13	9.1	8.4	8.8	10.7	58.0
Netherlands	28	36	–	–	9.7	11.0	9.0	17.9	59.7
Japan	14	48	–	–	7.4	3.8	3.4	12.3	38.1

[1] OECD % adults smoking daily (2003), aged 15 and older.

[2] BD as % of all drinking in past 12 months (WHO, 2000) and heavier drinking BD = UK, Sweden, France, Germany, and Italy (WHO, 2000), U.S. = 18 and older age adjusted. U.S. (2003) heavier drinking in 2003 (U.S. DHHS, 2005).

[3] WHO – Alcohol consumption per capita.

[4] *OECD Factbook, 2005*, different dates from 1999–2003.

[5] Cancer Mondial-estimated lung cancer incidence (2002), age standardized rate per 1,000 population (International Agency for Research on Cancer).

Table 6.2. *Disease Mortality and Other Factors*

Regime Type	Cerebrovascular Mortality[1]		Lung Cancer Mortality[2]		Employment Rates[3] 2003		Life Expectancy[4]	
	Female	Male	Female	Male	Female	Male	Female	Male
Liberal								
United States	39.1*	43.2*	26.8	48.7	65.7	76.9	80.1	74.6
Canada	33.3*	40.4*	25.6	48.5	67.7	76.5	82.1	77.2
Australia	42.2*	47.5*	13.8	34.7	62.2	76.4	82.8	77.8
United Kingdom	59.6*	67.2	21.1	42.9	66.3	79.3	80.7	76.2
Social Democratic								
Sweden	48.1*	59.0*	12.9	22.6	72.8	75.6	82.4	77.9
Denmark	51.9*	63.2*	27.8	45.2	70.5	71.7	79.5	74.9
Norway	46.8*	58.5*	13.5	32.7	72.9	78.8	81.9	77.0
Finland	51.5	63.2	8.2	34.4	65.7	79.7	81.8	75.1
Conservative-Corporatist								
France	30.6*	43.0*	8.0	47.5	56.7	69.0	82.9	75.8
Austria	42.2	47.5	12.1	37.7	61.5	76.0	81.0	75.0
Germany	47.9*	61.3*	10.8	42.4	58.7	68.9	81.3	75.5
Italy	49.8*	64.1*	8.5	58.0	42.7	69.7	82.9	76.9
Netherlands	43.9	52.6	15.6	57.6	64.9	80.2	80.9	76.2
Japan	43.5*	71.3*	9.6	32.4	56.8	79.8	85.2	78.3

[1] OECD Health Data, 2005 – standardized death rates per 100,000 population, *denotes previous 1, 2, or 3 years.

[2] GLOBECAN, 2002, International Agency for Research on Cancer, Age-standardized rates per 100,000 population.

[3] *OECD Factbook, 2005*, men and women in employment as percent of working-aged population.

[4] OECD Health Data, 2005.

parallels the gender gap in life expectancy. However, the gender differences in lung cancer incidence are far greater than the gap in smoking behavior, which suggests that biological processes may compound the picture. In fact, research on the gender and race variation in lung cancer mortality rates discussed earlier in the chapter (Haiman et al., 2006; Risch, 2006) attributes the discrepancy, when controlling for the number of cigarettes smoked, in part to physiological differences in how men and women metabolize nicotine. Recent research (Thunet al., 2006) shows that even among nonsmokers men have higher rates of lung cancer than women.

Table 6.2 provides additional evidence for the potential indirect impact of the policy regime environment on the health effects of smoking behavior. Although there is no general pattern across regimes, it does show that lung cancer mortality rates are lower for both men and women who smoke less. But there is still a difference in magnitude: men's lung cancer mortality rates are three to five times greater than women's in the conservative-corporatist countries, but only twice as high as women's in the liberal and social democratic countries. Even though it is possible that other toxic environmental substances may be contributing both to men's lung cancer and mortality rates, having this information would not help us understand why men and women choose initially to smoke. However, exploring the behavior from the perspective of constrained choice does give us some insight into that question: a country confronted with an uncertain or declining economy and political instability creates an environment that contributes to an overall sense of (in)security in people's lives, and this in turn can affect smoking and other health behavior decisions of both men and women. In fact, such a scenario could be relevant for understanding the extremely high rates of smoking and alcohol consumption in Eastern European countries, for example, and in those countries that formed the former Russian Federation. The point is that the social organization of men's and women's lives and the social roles they perform are structured partly by such country-level factors, and particularly by the policies and measures enacted by different policy regimes, including access to day care, retirement benefits, education, health care, and employment (Cockerham, 2005; Cockerham, Rütten, & Abel, 1997). Although the population level of analysis does not fully explain why individual men and women choose to smoke and how much this practice contributes to men's excess mortality at younger ages, it does make a plausible case that distal policy decisions can indirectly affect individual behavior.

Cross-national comparisons for alcohol consumption are more difficult to obtain and to interpret because countries do not report these data in similar ways. Table 6.1 presents the per capita consumption rates using alcohol sales data. These data show that the general rate of sales/consumption varies by country, with Sweden and Norway having the lowest per capital consumption rates (6.9 and 5.8, respectively), and France, Austria, and Germany the highest rates (13.5, 12.6, and 12.9, respectively). These sales/consumption rates also reflect cultural differences in the type of alcohol consumed and how it is consumed on a social basis (Bordieu, 1984). For example, wine is mostly consumed in France, whereas beer is the drink of choice in Germany, and both the serving size and alcohol content vary with the type of beverage. Of course, sales/consumption data do not necessarily indicate anything specific about rates of alcoholism or actual drinking prevalence.

Except for Italy and the United States, men are nearly twice as likely as women to engage in heavy or binge drinking, as shown in Table 6.1. This disparity may be the result of different gender norms for drinking patterns or that alcohol is consumed for reasons that are related to gender role expectations. For instance, Courtenay (2000a, 2000b) and others suggest that drinking behavior is a marker of masculinity and manliness (Sabo, 1999; White & Cash, 2004). Our purpose in presenting these figures is to illustrate the kind of analysis that would be useful if more complete data on gender differences could be obtained and examined from a constrained choice perspective (see also World Health Organization, 2002a).

Table 6.2 also displays the cerebrovascular disease (CVD) mortality rates for men and women as well as life expectancy rates. Although men have higher CVD mortality rates, the gender difference is not as dramatic as for lung cancer rates. The liberal regime countries (with the exception of the United Kingdom) have lower CVD mortality rates than the other two policy regimes. The rates for both men and women tend to be higher in countries with more binge drinking and higher smoking rates. The association between these two behaviors and the fact that men both drink to excess and smoke more than women suggest that these practices contribute to men's excess mortality rates, as well as the life expectancy gender gap. These data clearly only provide a partial view of the complex connections among policy regimes, individual health behavior choices, and the gender health gaps.

Interestingly, although the rates of obesity shown in Table 6.1 are higher for both men and women in the liberal regime countries, there is little difference between men and women in the other two regimes. The employment figures listed in Table 6.2 show that higher percentages of men than women are employed and that this gender gap varies across policy regimes, with the social democratic countries having more equal employment percentages and the conservative-corporatist countries the largest employment gap. Japanese women's lower lung cancer mortality, CVD rates, low smoking, and obesity rates are consistent with their higher life expectancy (see Tables 6.1 and 6.2). These figures again suggest that distal environmental factors beyond the individual can shape men and women's health choices and ability to maintain their health.

Further confirmation is provided by a recent study of Banks and colleagues (Banks, Marmot, Oldfield, & Smith, 2006) that compared the health status of residents aged 55–64 in the United States and England using both disease biomarkers and self-reports of illness. The authors found that the U.S. population of men and women was less healthy in terms of diabetes, hypertension, heart disease, myocardial infarction, stroke, lung disease, and cancer. Although the researchers found an SES/health gradient within each country and the largest health disparities at the bottom of the education and income hierarchy, the health differences between the two countries were not driven solely by this distribution. The differences between the two countries persisted even after controlling for standard risk behaviors (including smoking, overweight, obesity, and alcohol drinking). For many diseases, individuals at the top of the SES distribution are less healthy in the United States than their English counterparts. Banks and colleagues suggest that the greater association between health and economic resources in the United States may be due to the lack of extensive social welfare policies needed to protect individuals from the impact of poor health on work, family income, and wealth.

TO WHAT EXTENT CAN INDIVIDUAL HEALTH CHOICES AND BEHAVIORS BE EXPLAINED?

Numerous models exist to explain why some people maintain healthy lifestyles while others are either unable to or appear to willfully adopt a health-destructive life course. In contrast to constrained choice, most of these perspectives rely on health-related consciousness and motivation as the explanation for health behavior choices (Newsom et al., 2005; Sussman, 2005). The long-standing public health model discussed in Chapter 2, which is one of the most prominent approaches to population health research in the United States, still focuses mainly on interventions intended to reduce proximal levels of exposure and thereby modify individual health risks. Such models are critically important because they provide the research evidence both for interventions designed to alter health-damaging behavior and for protective policies intended to regulate behavior. But targeted approaches that modify individual risks by changing attitudes or motivating someone to never start or to stop smoking, reduce alcohol consumption, eat a low-fat diet, or engage in regular exercise are only effective with some individuals. In fact, some researchers argue that individual-based interventions of this type can actually increase health disparities because they are more effective with higher status individuals who can more easily marshal the resources to change their behavior and are less effective with those populations with scarce resources and fewer options (see, for example, Banks et al., 2006; Graham, 2004; Mechanic, 2005; Williams, 2002, 2003). Alternatively, broad measures that mandate clean air, smoking bans, seatbelt laws, minimum ages for purchasing and drinking alcohol, safe drinking water, and sanitary food management and distribution are examples of protective public health measures that do not rely on individual motivation or social capital. Although such measures do restrict individual rights, they can be both an effective and efficient way to bypass social inequalities and also protect and improve population health.

In the rest of this chapter, we explore the role of childhood and adult socialization and experiences in creating, maintaining, and exacerbating health behavior differences between men and women. We contend that both gender roles and social policies not only differentially affect men's and women's access to protective health resources but also influence the adoption of both positive and negative health-related behaviors and coping strategies (Taylor et al., 2000). In addition, we consider again the potential biological contribution to gender differences in health effects of behaviors such as alcohol consumption and smoking. We also discuss the physiological and social impact of early life exposure to harmful circumstances or events (e.g., physical or sexual abuse) that can alter men's and women's health in various ways across the life course; see, for example, Carmen and Rieker (1989); Volpicelli, Balaraman, Hahn, Wallace, and Bux (1999); and the special journal issue edited by Zarit and Pearlin (2005) on health inequalities across the life course, especially articles by O'Rand and Hamil-Luker (2005); Wickrama, Conger, and Abraham (2005); and Hatch (2005).

Education and Motivation

Various explanations and theories have been developed to define and predict risky behaviors and practices in the hope of reducing and preventing their occurrence. Although some researchers consider the impact of school, family, and peer influences, the primary focus of these theories is on individual factors, such as attitudes, intentions, skills, emotions, self-standards, self-efficacy, and internalized norms and motivation; some researchers do advocate ecological models that incorporate different levels of environmental influences as well.[6] Many of the psychological theories of behavioral change that guide interventions targeted to individuals, particularly the health belief model and models of readiness to change, assume that there are logical steps to educating and motivating people. Once motivated and armed with the knowledge of how to make the best (most rational) choices for maintaining or regaining their health, individuals, these theories presume, will then take the recommended actions. The continual barrage of health information and advice is predicated on such a model. Yet as we noted in Chapter 1, often health information and advice are both inconsistent and confusing to even the most well educated; with few exceptions what constitutes the "best" choice is far from clear particularly because specific risks, benefits, and other considerations appear to vary considerably across and within race and gender groups.

---

[6] These include: self-regulation theory (Kanfer, 1970); health belief model (Rosenstock, 1974); theory of reasoned action (Fishbein & Ajzen, 1975); interpersonal relations and subjective culture theory (Triandis, 1997); protection motivation theory (Maddux & Rogers, 1983); theory of planned behavior (Ajzen, 1985); self-determination theory (Deci & Ryan, 1985); transtheoretical model of behavior change (Prochaska, DiClemente, & Norcross, 1992); social cognitive theory (Bandura, 2001); and the ecological models (Marshall & Biddle, 2001; Sallis & Owen, 1999).

To illustrate, in an effort to provide diet information tailored on the basis of age, gender, and level of activity, the U.S. Department of Agriculture created a website (mypyramid.gov) that generates detailed diet recommendations. Although this a laudable effort to personalize the informational guidelines, the educational attempt has not achieved the desired response. Our personal critique of this tool is that its limited impact is due to the inaccessibility of the information to large segments of the population and the complexity of the planning and record keeping required for implementing the recommendations once they are obtained.[7] The same could be said of recent attempts in the United States to provide information through health logos on food packages and the lack of uniform standards for designating a product as nutritious.

Research updates from the biomedical disciplines only add to the health advice conundrum.[8] For instance, the recent results from two longitudinal clinical trials from the Women's Health Initiative (WHI) question the value of two widely accepted diet recommendations. The two studies are the largest ever to test the effects of low-fat diets and calcium and vitamin D supplements on heart disease, fractures, and cancer. The low-fat diet study followed nearly 49,000 women aged 50–79 for almost 8 years and found no significant effects on heart disease, stroke, or breast and colorectal cancer rates, although there were some differences among subgroups (Beresford et al., 2006; Howard et al., 2006; Prentice et al., 2006). The calcium study, which followed 36,282 women, likewise showed the supplements did not prevent hip and other bone fractures, heart disease, or colorectal cancer (Jackson et al., 2006; Wactawski-Wende et al., 2006). These important and surprising findings are just one illustration

---

[7] Although knowing what food categories to eat in what proportion is useful, the detailed information on the number of times to eat specific categories of vegetables each week calls for a combination of advance planning and record keeping for most people to determine whether they are in fact following the recommended dietary guidelines, and that is a daunting task.

[8] In a recent *New York Times Magazine* article, Gary Taubes (2007a) examined the evidence from epidemiological research and asked the question "Do we really know what makes us healthy?" He attributes the health advice confusion to the limitations in science and offers suggestions about how to make sense of health news and research (see also Taubes, 2007b).

of the predicament for both physicians and individual women about what health practices to recommend or follow.

Despite evidence of its limited effectiveness with large and diverse populations, the health belief model continues to dominate the development of interventions to alter health practices. Likewise, the flow of information intended to inform people of their options to stay healthy never diminishes. We have argued elsewhere (Rieker & Bird, 2005) that what is missing from this model is the idea that men's and women's individual choices and options for pursuing health are constrained in different ways.

Gender Role Socialization and Health Behaviors

Women's and men's health behaviors cannot be understood without considering the gender roles that underlie the social organization of their lives and that interact with the biological and socioeconomic factors discussed earlier in the presentation of data on gender differences in health behaviors. Although men and women share many similar roles, such as spouse, parent, or child in the United States and to a greater or lesser degree in all countries, their roles and responsibilities still differ by gender. As noted in Chapter 5, the degree of differences has fluctuated and narrowed over time, but the range of expectations, responsibilities, and activities still vary somewhat for husbands versus wives, mothers versus fathers, and daughters versus sons. The variation allows considerable room for overlap, such that among some individuals or groups the gender role differences may be larger or almost nonexistent, but for the most part some differences remain. For example, differences in the time and labor intensity of being a mother versus a father to an infant may affect the low priority some mothers place on self-care. Thus, for women with high levels of caregiving responsibility, and especially those with limited financial resources, this role often becomes a barrier to engaging in exercise or in any leisure-time pursuit.

The mismatch between men's social role expectations and shifting notions of masculinity, along with uncertain economic opportunities and the rapidly changing skill set required for occupational success in today's knowledge-driven society, may also contribute to the kind of stress and pressure that lead to health-damaging behaviors, such as alcohol abuse, smoking, or overeating (Courtenay, 2000a, 2000b). For example, the main explanation offered by Courtenay (2000a, 2000b, 2003, 2004) for men's shorter lives and excessive drinking focuses on men's risky behaviors, their attitudes about health, and conflicts about the connection between manliness and health behaviors. This explanation is prevalent in the men's health movement. Although the emphasis on individual responsibility and internal psychological processes may be a part of the complex dynamic underlying men's shorter life expectancy, this narrow perspective still ignores both constrained choice and biological processes when recommending individual counseling and psychotherapy as solutions for all men. Although such a focus may be effective for those men who are receptive to this approach, this labor-intensive and costly option does not address the larger social issues nor does it change the social organization of the vast majority of men's lives. Ironically, both men's and women's roles are restricted in ways that can undermine making health a priority. Consequently, gender roles may interact at times with the opportunity structure created by decisions and policies at other levels in the constrained choice framework (described in Chapters 3 and 5) in ways that exacerbate the differences in the organization of men's and women's lives.

Young men and women may expect to take on specific gender roles and anticipate the ease or difficulty of combining those with particular educational, occupational, or career pursuits, as was the case with John and Susan's attempts to balance work, family, and careers described in previous chapters. Prior choices and goals can often affect later options and choices. For example, women who enter demanding professional careers are less likely than their male colleagues to have children or they tend to have fewer children (Mason & Goulden, 2002, 2004). In part this reflects the fact that women in the professions are more apt than their male colleagues to be married to a spouse with an equally demanding career and less likely to have a spouse who takes primary responsibility for child care and other domestic tasks. Moreover, both the demands and benefits of combining work and family differ somewhat for men and women (as we saw with John and Susan) because mothers are responsible for taking time from paid work to have a child and for both organizing and carrying out more of the domestic work and activities related to caring for children and families (DeVault, 1991). There is some work showing that change in family responsibilities is taking place (Hofferth, Pleck, Stueve, Bianchi, & Sayer, 2002).

Although gender role expectations are persistent across national borders, they vary by race, class, and ethnicity within countries. For instance, when immigrant women are required to leave their families and seek employment in other countries for extended periods of time, they are still expected by both their spouses and children to be the social/emotional caretaker from a distance while their breadwinner role goes largely unacknowledged; see Parrenas' work (2005) on Philippina migrant workers. Moreover, often these are the women who are hired by dual-career households to take up the slack in domestic responsibilities left undone by both men and women pursuing demanding careers. The discussion in Chapter 5 illustrates some of the health effects associated with these constrained choices.

Choosing not to get married or have children does not necessarily provide an escape route from this conundrum. Both because of the societal value placed on marriage and children and the ability to continue to revisit such a choice over several decades (or longer for men or for those who consider adoption), these are not simple choices for most people. Likewise, there are consequences in terms of costs and benefits both to having a spouse and not having a spouse and, in fact, to all gendered roles and role combinations. Further, the range of specific costs (in terms of narrowed options) and benefits (in terms of increased options) associated with each of these combinations differs somewhat by gender. Furthermore, although one may choose whether to become a parent or spouse, many of the caregiving responsibilities and relationships to the rest of one's family (including one's own parents) still fall disproportionately on women, and frequently on single adults or childless, married women. As a long line of labor history and other research has documented, when the caregiving and domestic responsibilities are hired out, the job is usually performed by low-paid immigrant women or more recently by low-paid immigrant men as well (Parrenas, 2005).

BEHAVIORAL HEALTH RISKS AND PROTECTIONS

Gender and health behaviors are related in complicated ways. The association among them varies by life-course stage, the specific behavior being addressed, and social economic status (SES). For instance, both education and income are associated with patterns of men's and women's health behaviors, particularly smoking and alcohol consumption (Banks et al., 2006). At this stage in the development of research knowledge, the relationship between gender and health behavior is more one of association than causal, as most of the health behavior studies are cross-sectional, although some are both prospective and longitudinal as discussed earlier in this chapter.

For example, a recent British study demonstrated that very long work hours are negatively associated with women's health behavior (O'Connor, Conner, & Jones, 2005). Women, but not men, who worked longer hours consumed more high-fat and high-sugar snacks, exercised less, and, of those who smoked, smoked more. In addition, their findings indicated that individuals who worked in highly demanding, low-control work environments consumed more snacks when they experienced one or more daily hassles. Although individuals may be able to use this information to help inform their choice of work environments, additional population health benefits are attainable if employers consider these health effects when evaluating workplace policies and organization.

As Chapter 5 demonstrates, marriage (depending on the quality) confers a general health benefit for both men and women. Transitions in and out of marriage and other status passages also affect the association between gender and negative or positive behaviors. Married individuals in general have a higher prevalence of positive health behaviors, with the exception of higher weight gain compared to single adults. The positive impact of a good marriage may be due to spousal social support, a collective pooling of options, a feeling of personal responsibility for the well-being of the partner, and the greater visibility of health-damaging behaviors in intimate relationships. Individuals with diminished options and less decision-making latitude (e.g., lower SES, less education) definitely have fewer resources and less opportunity to make their health a priority. Yet, although higher SES individuals with more options and extensive resources may encounter less difficulty choosing healthy behaviors in some ways, they also have the opportunity and means to engage in different types of health-damaging behaviors, such as dangerous leisure pursuits or expensive forms of substance abuse. In addition, as discussed earlier there is also reliable evidence that biological processes compound this story as men and women may metabolize both nicotine and alcohol differently over the life course (Haiman et al., 2006; Risch, 2006; Wilsnack & Wilsnack, 2002). Thus, the question remains: *What are the biological and/or social circumstances that place men and women at risk both for adopting unsafe health behaviors and that contribute to differential outcomes?*

Social and Economic Circumstances and Health Behaviors

No understanding of the complex link between gender and health behaviors would be complete without addressing the relationship of SES to health per se and to healthy lifestyles across the life course. To capture the larger context of people's lives, life-span researchers have attempted to deconstruct the global concept of social economic status (SES). Several researchers in this field have conceptualized the range and types of social circumstances subsumed by the concept of SES to illustrate that this indicator could conceal as much as it reveals (see, for example, Alwin & Wray, 2005; George, 1996; Oakes & Rossi, 2003; O'Rand, 2001). In contrast to the straightforward nature of the sociological approach of using education and income to measure SES, the life-span perspective tends to combine social, material, and psychological assets to provide a more comprehensive description of how individual advantages and constraints might vary. The life-span approach includes the following components: human capital (individual knowledge and skills); social capital (social resources and relationships); personal capital (resiliency, self-confidence, control, positive outlook, and coping strategies); cultural capital (beliefs, gender norms, and other values); material capital (owned resources, income, houses, cars, inherited wealth), and psychophysiological capital (genetic, hereditary, and acquired physical and mental vulnerabilities and strengths). However, there is little consensus across disciplines about the definition of various forms of capital (e.g., assets and disadvantages) conceptualized to be present in the lives

of individuals or families and how they are related to health maintenance.

We include this summary for two reasons: first, it provides a glimpse of
the complexity of capturing the interaction of biology and social environment, and second, it affords a concrete illustration of the way life-course
researchers view what we conceptualize as the constraints and opportunities that encourage or prevent individual men and women from pursuing
health. What matters here is that a substantial body of research shows
how one or more of these forms of *capital* can lead to either cumulative
adversity or provide protective resources or both, across different life-
course stages from childhood through adolescence and midlife to old age
and how they contribute to gendered health behaviors and their effects
(for specific examples, see Hatch, 2005; Kahn & Fazio, 2005; Moen, 2001;
Wray, Alwin, & McCammon, 2005; for a general overview of life-course
research, see Mortimer & Shanahan, 2003).

In 2005 the Centers for Disease Control and Prevention (CDC)
expanded the ecological model and incorporated ways to reduce risk and
improve health across the life course by developing a series of health protection goals and objectives. These are consistent with constrained choice
and include promoting healthy communities (e.g., safe food, water, side-
walks, parks); homes (e.g., smoke and radon detectors); schools (e.g.,
healthy food choices in vending machines, physical activity); workplaces
(e.g., smoke free, sponsored physical activity, stress reduction); health
care settings (e.g., reduction in associated infections and adverse events
associated with biological products); institutions (e.g., safe, equitable
environments); and travel and recreation (e.g., seatbelt use, safe playgrounds, and airplane air and water control; CDC, 2006). Both governmental agencies and researchers from different disciplines are employ-
ing both implicit and explicit ecological models to identify individual,
environmental, and population-based ways to reduce risk and promote
health; however, these models are seldom focused on gender.

A CONCLUDING QUESTION ON HEALTH BEHAVIORS AND CONSTRAINED CHOICE

From our constrained choice perspective, understanding the origin, nature, and health effects of differences in women's and men's

health-related behavior requires that we also comprehend the role of the social policy environment and a series of choices made at each level of our model. We are not asserting that individual health is fully determined by external social forces. But contained in our account of gender differences in health are more resonant questions. *Whose responsibility is health? Are protective measures, preventive behaviors, and the costs and consequences of poor health practices the province of individuals, families, the workplace, communities, states, or some combination of these?* How we answer these questions can have a variety of far-reaching ramifications. As most would agree, even in the context of constrained choice, teenaged and adult men and women are in charge, if not always in control, of the decisions they make on a routine basis about their health practices. However, priorities and prior decisions also can reduce the latitude individuals have and the options they perceive on a daily basis. For example, the decision not to drink heavily or smoke on any given day is affected by exposure and experience: whether one has ever done so in the past, has become addicted or was in the past, or is currently experiencing some critical life-disrupting circumstance, such as physical or sexual abuse (Carmen & Rieker, 1989). Likewise, choosing to exercise regularly is likely easier for those with sufficient resources and fewer time constraints and for those who already adhere to a routine exercise pattern. In addition to differences in values, motivation, and level of health consciousness, most individuals are unaware of their biological susceptibility and physiological response to various levels of exposure to health-damaging practices, such as drinking and smoking, and thus cannot always make an accurate judgment of their specific risk.

Making risk judgments is not a simple matter. Comprehending the distinction between the general link of smoking to lung cancer and one's personal risk requires specialized knowledge and information. Not everyone perceives the distinction nor necessarily possesses all of the specific or exact information needed to construct a personal risk assessment. Individuals tend either to overestimate or underestimate both the general and their personal risk for specific conditions, and health care providers are not always able to clear up the confusion. Underestimating both the general and personal risk associated with a particular behavior is also more likely when the behavior is prevalent or normative in a peer or reference group, such as adolescent smoking or drinking. Still, despite constrained choice, diminished latitude, and ambiguous risk information, each one of us at some point "decides" whether and how much to exercise, drink, smoke, or use other toxic substances.

In addition, individuals make decisions and day-to-day choices about how to moderate or minimize exposure to hazards (including toxins in the ground, in the home, or in the work environment) and how to reduce and manage transitory and chronic stress, especially once its negative effects are recognized or apparent. Fully understanding how to enable individuals to develop the kind of health consciousness or self-knowledge that helps them create and maintain healthy behaviors remains elusive.[9] This situation prevails in spite of the dedication of biomedical and social researchers who design the progressive research and generate the findings that shed light on many parts of this multifaceted cognitive and psychosocial process involved in pursuing health. Health behavior research to date reveals more about the antecedents and consequences of particular health behaviors than the most optimal and effective means to prevent or change negative practices once they have developed (Rothman, 2000; Sussman, 2005).

But the inclination to define the failure to either adopt positive health behaviors or to make choices that improve and protect health as simply faulty decision making by individuals vastly oversimplifies a complex process (Taubes, 2007). As alluded to in Chapter 2, such an outlook is embedded in a rational choice model of behavior that assumes that, in a free (unregulated) economy, everyone has the same degree of freedom or latitude, values, priorities, self-knowledge, and opportunity to maximize health. This perspective fails to take into account the broader context in which individual actions and policy measures intended to promote constructive health behaviors take place. Although all individuals should rationally place a high value on health, not everyone is equally able or motivated to engage in preventive behaviors or willing to agree to the tradeoffs between individual rights and protective public health

---

[9] Health promotion and intervention efforts proceed on the basis of both evidence and beliefs that men and women will respond to different sources of information or that gender-targeted approaches are a more effective way to bring about changes in health behaviors.

regulations. To illustrate, not everyone supports and obeys the evidence-based regulations shown to save lives, such as seatbelt and helmet laws, smoke-free workplaces, speed and blood alcohol limits for driving, and even traffic lights. As we showed, the prevalence of some of these behaviors differs considerably by gender as well as race and income. Thus, for the good of the public's health, social restraints on unhealthy behavior are enacted at local, state, and national levels and also promoted within families and workplaces. Finally, we recognize that there is an active dialectic if not an essential tension contained in the discussion throughout this book between constrained choice, which emphasizes diminished options resulting from prior personal choices and policy decisions at other levels, and the individual's responsibility and opportunity to pursue health across the life course. Clearly this conundrum poses a challenge not only for us as authors but also for those who make choices about health at all levels of decision making.

APPENDIX 1

Greenfield and Kerr (2003) list surveys that track alcohol consumption and a variety of other alcohol-related measures. These surveys include the following:

- *Gallup Survey.* Since 1939, this survey has frequently, but sporadically, measured the proportion of the population who drink alcohol. In 1950 and 1964, and more frequently since 1974, the survey has assessed whether drinking caused family problems. More information is available at www.gallup.com.
- *National Alcohol Survey (NAS).* This survey, conducted by the Alcohol Research Group, has measured many aspects of alcohol consumption, associated problems, and use of treatment approximately every 5 years since 1959. The most recent surveys were conducted in 1979, 1984 (with longitudinal follow-up in 1992), 1990, 1995, and 2000. The 1984, 1995, and 2000 surveys oversampled African American and Hispanic respondents. More information is available at www.arg.org.

- *Behavioral Risk Factor Surveillance System (BRFSS).* The objective of the BRFSS is to collect uniform state-specific and state-representative population data on risk behaviors and preventive health practices. Since 1984, this system has collected state-level representative measures of past-month abstinence, frequency of drinking, usual quantity per occasion, frequency of five or more drinks on one occasion, and frequency of drunk driving. The BRFSS covered 15 states when it began in 1984, increasing to 40 states in 1989, 48 in 1991, 50 in 1993, and adding the District of Columbia in 1996. Thirteen states have participated in all years. Alcohol consumption questions were included in the core survey every year from 1984 to 1993 and in 1995, 1997, and 1999. An optional alcohol consumption module was used by 17 states in 1996, 12 states in 1998, and 10 states in 2000. More information is available at http://ncadi. samhsa.gov/govstudy/bkd376/, downloaded September 17, 2007.
- *National Health Interview Survey (NHIS).* Since 1997, this annual survey has included questions on past-year and lifetime abstinence, past-year usual quantity, usual frequency, and frequency of five or more drinks. Before 1997, alcohol questions were included only sporadically. More information is available at http:// www.cdc.gov/nchs/nhis.htm, downloaded September 18, 2007.
- *Monitoring the Future (MTF) Survey.* Since 1975, this annual survey has tracked the national prevalence among 12th-grade students of monthly drinking and having five or more drinks on one occasion in the 2 weeks preceding the survey. Since 1991, it has also included 8th- and 10th-grade students and has added a question on the monthly prevalence of having been drunk. More information is available at www.monitoringthefuture.org.
- *National Household Survey on Drug Abuse (NHSDA).* This annual survey has collected information on alcohol use since 1974, and since 1994 it has included questions on lifetime, yearly, and 30-day abstinence; yearly and 30-day drinking frequency; 30-day usual quantity; 30-day frequency of five or more drinks; and yearly frequency of "getting very high or drunk" from alcohol. More information is available at www.samhsa.gov/oas/nhsda.htm, downloaded September 18, 2007.

APPENDIX 2

International Alcohol Research and Aggregate-Level Data (see Bloomfield et al., 2003):

- International Group on alcohol research (IRGGA) includes data on 35 or more countries using a standardized instrument.
- Gender, Alcohol and Culture (GENACIS) is an international study.
- World Health Organization (WHO) monitors alcohol consumption and related harm in the WHO Global Alcohol Database (most comprehensive source of per capital consumption data, which includes World Drink Trends [WDT] sponsored by the Dutch Distillers Association and provides sales and tax statistics).
- United Nations Food and Agriculture Organization (FAO) provides per capita consumption based on production data and includes not only beer, wine, and distilled spirits but also palm wine, maize, millet and sorghum beer, fruit wine, rice wine, and cider- and wheat-fermented beverages, some of which are relevant to developing countries.
- National Institute on Alcohol Abuse and Alcoholism (NIAAA) maintains the alcohol and alcohol problems science database (ETOH).
- The fourth wave of the Health Behavior of School-Aged Children (HBSC) survey conducted in 1997–1998 included children ages 11, 13, and 15 in 26 European countries, Canada, and the United States.
- European School Survey Project on Alcohol and Drugs (ESPAD) for the second time in 1999 surveyed 15-year-olds from 30 European countries.
- Other surveys include the European Alcohol Study (ECAS), Global Burden of Disease and Comparative Risk Assessment (CRA), Organization of Economic Cooperation (OECD) and the European Union (EU) surveys, and the International Collaborative Alcohol-Related Longitudinal Project.

References

Abramovitz, M. (1996). *Regulating the Lives of Women: Social Welfare Policy from Colonial Times to the Present*. Boston: South End Press.

Ajzen, I. (1985). From intentions to actions: A theory of planned behavior. In J. Kuhl & J. Beckman (Eds.), *Action Control from Cognition to Behavior* (pp. 11–39). New York: Springer-Verlag.

Alwin, D. F., & Wray, L. A. (2005). A life-span developmental perspective on social status and health. *J Gerontol Ser B, 60,* S7–S14.

Bandura, A. (2001). Social cognitive theory: An agentic perspective. *Annu Rev Psychol, 52,* 1–26.

Banks, J., Marmot, M., Oldfield, Z., & Smith, J. P. (2006). Disease and disadvantage in the United States and in England. *JAMA, 295*(17), 2037–2045.

Beresford, S. A. A., Johnson, K. C., Ritenbaugh, C., Lasser, N. L., Snetselaar, L. G., Black, H. R., et al. (2006). Low-fat dietary pattern and risk of colorectal cancer: The Women's Health Initiative randomized controlled dietary modification. *JAMA, 295*(6), 643–654.

Berrigan, D., Dodd, K., Troiano, R. P., Krebs-Smith, S. M., & Barbash, R. B. (2003). Patterns of health behavior in U.S. adults. *Prev Med, 36*(5), 615–623.

Bloomfield K, Stockwell, T., Gmel, G., & Rehn, N. (2003). International comparisons of alcohol consumption. *Alcohol Research & Health, 27,* 95–109.

Bordieu, P. (1984). *Distinction: A Social Critique of the Judgment of Taste.* Cambridge, MA: Harvard University Press.

Carmen, E. H., & Rieker, P. P. (1989). A psychosocial model of the victim-to-patient process: Implications for treatment. *Psychiatr Clin North Am, 12*(2), 431–443.

Centers for Disease Control. (2006). Retrieved September 17, 2007, from http://www.cdc.gov/about/goals.htm.

Cockerham, W. C. (2005). Health lifestyle theory and the convergence of agency and structure. *J Health Soc Behav, 46*(1), 51–67.

Cockerham, W. C., Rütten, A., & Abel, T. (1997). Conceptualizing contemporary health lifestyles: Moving beyond Weber. *Soc Quart, 38,* 321–342.

Courtenay, W. H. (2000a). Behavioral factors associated with disease, injury, and death among men: Evidence and implications for prevention. *J Men's Studies, 9*(1), 81–142.

Courtenay, W. H. (2000b). Constructions of masculinity and their influence on men's well-being: A theory of gender and health. *Soc Sci Med, 50,* 1385–1401.

Courtenay, W. H. (2003). Key determinants of the health and well-being of men and boys. *Int J Men's Health, 2*(1), 1–30.

Courtenay, W. H. (2004). Making health manly: Social marketing and men's health. *J Men's Health Gen, 1*(2–3), 275–276.

Deci, E. L., & Ryan, R. M. (1985). *Intrinsic Motivation and Self-Determination in Human Behavior.* New York: Plenum Publishing.

DeVault, M. (1991). *Feeding of the Family: The Social Organization of Caring as Gendered Work.* Chicago: University of Chicago Press.

Ellickson, P. L., Tucker, J. S., & Klein, M. S. (2003). Ten-year prospective study of public health problems associated with early drinking. *Pediatrics, 111*(5), 949–955.

Ewbank, D. C. (2004). The APOE gene and differences in life expectancy in Europe. *J Gerontol Biol Sci Med Sci, 59A*(1), 8–12.

Gender and Health

Ezzati, M., Lopez, A. D., Rodgers, A., Vander Hoorn, S., & Murray, C. J. L. (2002). Selected major risk factors and global and regional burden of disease. *Lancet, 360*(9343), 1347–1360.

Filmore, K. M., Golding, J. M., Leino, E. V., and et al. (1997). Patterns and trends in women's and men's drinking. In R. W. Wilsnack & S. C. Wilsnack (Eds.), *Gender and Alcohol* (21–48). New Brunswick, NJ: Rutgers Center of Alcohol Studies.

Filozof, C., Fernandez Pinilla, M. C., & Fernandez-Cruz, A. (2004). Smoking cessation and weight gain. *Obes Rev, 5*(2), 95–103.

Fishbein, M., & Ajzen, I. (1975). *Belief, Attitude, Intention, and Behavior: An Introduction to Theory and Research.* Reading, MA: Addison-Wesley.

Gallant, M. P., & Dorn, G. P. (2001). Gender and race differences in the predictors of daily health practices among older adults. *Health Edu Res, 16*(1), 21–23.

George, L. K. (1996). Missing links: The case for a social psychology of the life-course. *Gerontologist, 36*, 248–255.

Graham, H. (2004). Social determinants and their unequal distribution: Clarifying policy understandings. *Mil Q, 82*, 101–124.

Greenfield, T. K., & Kerr, W. C. (2003). Tracking alcohol consumption over time. *Alcohol Res Health, 27*(1), 30–38.

Haiman, C. A., Stram, D. O., Wilken, L. R., Pike, M. C., Kolonel, L. N., Henderson, B. E., et al. (2006). Ethnic and racial differences in the smoking-related risk of lung cancer. *N Engl J Med, 354*, 333–342.

Hatch, S. (2005). Conceptualizing and identifying cumulative adversity and protective resources: Implications for understanding health inequalities. *J Gerontol Ser B, 60*, 130–134.

Hofferth, S. L., Pleck, J. H., Stueve, J. L., Bianchi, S., & Sayer, L. The demography of fathers: What fathers do. In C. Tamis-Lemonda and N. Cabrera (Eds.), *The Handbook of Father Involvement* (pp. 63–90). Rathway, NJ: Erlbaum.

Howard, B. V., Van Horn, L., Hsia, J., Manson, J. E., Stefanick, M. L., Wassertheil-Smoller, S., et al. (2006). Low-fat dietary pattern and risk of cardiovascular disease: The Women's Health Initiative randomized controlled dietary modification trial. *JAMA, 295*(6), 655–666.

Hu, P., Bretsky, P., Crimmins, E. M., Guralnik, J. M., Reuben, D. B., & Seeman, T. E. (2006). Association between serum beta-carotene levels and decline of cognitive function in high-functioning older persons with or without apolipoprotein E4 alleles: MacArthur Studies of Successful Aging. *J Gerontol: Med Sci, 4*, 616–620.

Jackson, R. D., LaCroix, A. Z., Gass, M., et al. (2006). Calcium plus vitamin D supplementation and the risk of fractures. *N Engl J Med, 354*(7), 669–683.

Jensen, M. K., Sorensen, T. I., Andersen, A. T., Thorsen, T., Tolstrup, J. S., Godtfredsen, N. S., et al. (2003). A prospective study of the association between smoking and later alcohol drinking in the general population. *Addiction, 98*(3), 355–363.

Johnston, L. D., O'Malley, P. M., Bachman, J. G., & Schulenberg, J. E. (2006). *Monitoring the Future National Survey Results on Drug Use, 1975–2005, Vol. 1, Secondary School Students* (No. 06–5883). Bethesda, MD: National Institute on Drug Abuse.

Kahn, J. R., & Fazio, E. M. (2005). Economic status over the life course and social disparities in health. *J Gerontol: Soc Sci, 60B*, 76–84.

Kamimoto, L. A., Easton, A. N., Maurice, E., Husten, C. G., & Macera, C. A. (1999). Surveillance for five health risks among older adults: United States, 1993–1997. *MMRW CDC Surveil Sum, 48*(8), 89–130.

Kanfer, F. H. (1970). *Self Regulation: Research, Issues and Speculations.* New York: Appleton-Century-Crofts.

Laaksonen, M., Luoto, R., Helakorpi, S., & Uutela, A. (2002). Associations between health-related behaviors: A 7-year follow-up of adults. *Prev Med, 34*, 162–170.

Li, M. D., Kane, J. K., & Konu, O. (2003). Nicotine, body weight and potential implications in the treatment of obesity. *Curr Top Med Chem, 3*(8), 899–919.

Maddux, J. E., & Rogers, R. W. (1983). Protection, motivation theory and self efficacy: A revised theory fear appeals and attitude change. *J Exp Soc Psychol, 19*, 469–479.

Marshall, S. J., & Biddle, S. J. H. (2001). The transtheoretical model of behavior change: A meta-analysis of applications to physical activity and exercise. *Ann Behav Med, 23*, 229–246.

Mason, M. A., & Goulden, M. (2002). Do babies matter: The effect of family formation on the lifelong careers of academic men and women. *Academe, 88*(6), 21–27.

Mason, M. A., & Goulden, M. (2004). Marriage and baby blues: Redefining gender equity in the academy. *Ann Am Acad Polit Soc Sci, 596*(1), 86–103.

Mechanic, D. (2005). Policy challenges in addressing racial disparities and improving population health. *Health Aff, 24*(2), 335–338.

Moen, P. (2001). The gendered life course. In R. H. Binstock & L. K. George (Eds.), *Handbook of Aging and the Social Sciences* (5th ed., pp. 179–196). New York: Academic Press.

Mortimer, J. T., & Shanahan, M. J. (2003). *Handbook of the Life Course (Handbook of Sociology and Social Research).* New York: Kluwer Academic/Plenum Publishers.

Newsom, J. T., McFarland, B. H., Kaplan, M. S., Huguet, N., & Zani, B. (2005). The health consciousness myth: Implications of the near independence of major health behaviors in the North American population. *Soc Sci Med, 6*, 433–437.

Oakes, J. M., & Rossi, P. H. (2003). The measurement of SES in health research: Current practice and steps toward a new approach. *Soc Sci Med, 56*(4), 769–784.

O'Connor, D. B., Conner, M. T., & Jones, F. (2005). *Effects of Stress on Eating Behaviour: An Integrated Approach.* Swindon, England: Economic and Social Research Council.

O'Rand, A. (2001). Stratification and the life course. In R. H. Binstock & L. K. George (Eds.), *Handbook of Aging and the Social Sciences* (5th ed., pp. 197–213). New York: Academic Press.

O'Rand, A. M., & Hamil-Luker, J. (2005). Processes of cumulative adversity: Childhood disadvantage and increased risk of heart attack across the life course. *J Gerontol: Soc Sci, 60B*, 117–124.

Pampel, F. C. (2002). Cigarette use and the narrowing sex differential in mortality. *Popul Devel Rev, 28*(1), 77–104.

Parrenas, R. S. (2005). *Children of Global Migration: Transnational Families and Gendered Woes.* Stanford, CA: Stanford University Press.

Prentice, R. L., Caan, B., Chlebowski, R. T., Patterson, R., et al. (2006). Low-fat dietary pattern and risk of invasive breast cancer: The Women's Health Initiative randomized controlled dietary modification. *JAMA, 295*(6), 629–642.

Prescott, C. A. (2002). Alcohol research and health: Women and alcohol, an update. *Wom Alcohol, 26*(4), 264–273.

Preston, S. H., & Wang, H. D. (2006). Sex mortality differences in the United States: The role of cohort smoking patterns. *Demography 43*(4), 631–646.

Prochaska, J. O., DiClemente, C. C., & Norcross, J. C. (1992). In search of how people change: Applications to addictive behavior. *Am Psychol, 47*, 1102–1114.

Pronk, N. P., Anderson, L. H., Crain, A. L., Martinson, B. C., O'Connor, P. J., Sherwood, N. E., et al. (2004). Meeting recommendations for multiple healthy lifestyle factors: Prevalence, clustering, and predictors among adolescent, adult and senior health plan members. *Am J Prev Med, 27*(2), 25–33.

Reeves, M. J., & Rafferty, A. P. (2005). Healthy lifestyle characteristics among adults in the United States, 2000. *Arch Int Med, 165*, 854–857.

Rieker, P. P., & Bird, C. E. (2005). Rethinking gender differences in health: What's needed to integrate social and biological perspectives. *J Gerontol: Soc Sci, 60B*, 40–47.

Risch, N. (2006). Dissecting racial and ethnic differences. *N Engl J Med, 354*, 408–411.

Rosenstock, I. M. (1974). Historical origins of the health belief model. *Health Edu Monogr, 2*(4).

Rothman, A. J. (2000). Toward a theory-based analysis of behavioral mechanisms. *Health Psychol, 19*(Suppl 1), 64–69.

Sabo, D. (1999). *Understanding Men's Health: A Relational and Gender Sensitive Approach* (No. 99.14). Cambridge, MA: Harvard Center for Population and Development Studies.

Sallis, J. F., & Owen, N. (1999). *Physical Activity and Behavior Medicine*. Thousand Oaks, CA: Sage.

Seeman, T. E., Huang, M. H., Bretsky, P., Crimmins, E., Launer, L., & Guralnik, J. M. (2005). Education and APOE-e4 in Longitudinal Cognitive Decline: MacArthur Studies of Successful Aging. *J Gerontol: Psychol Sci, 60*(2), 74–83.

Sussman, S. (2005). Foundations of health behavior research revisited. *Am J Health Behav, 29*(6), 489–496.

Sussman, S., & Sussman, A. N. (2001). Praxis in health behavior program development. In S. Sussman (Ed.), *Handbook of Program Development in Health Behavior Research and Practice* (pp. 79–97). Thousand Oaks, CA: Sage.

Taubes, G. (2007a). Do we really know what makes us healthy? *New York Times Magazine*. September 16, 52–59, 74, 78, 80.

Taubes, G. (2007b). *Good Calories, Bad Calories: Challenging the Conventional Wisdom on Diet, Weight Control, and Disease*. New York: Knopf.

Taylor, S. E., Klein, L. C., Lewis, B. P., Gruenewald, T. L., Gurung, R. A., & Updegraff, J. A. (2000). Biobehavioral responses to stress in females: Tend-and-befriend, not fight-or-flight. *Psychol Rev, 107*(3), 411–429.

Thun, M. J., Henley, S. J., Burns, D., Jemal, A., et al. (2006). Lung cancer death rates in lifelong nonsmokers. *J Natl Cancer Inst, 98*(10), 691–699.

Triandis, H. C. (1997). *Interpersonal Behavior*. Monteray, CA: Brooks Cole.

Tucker, J. S., Ellickson, P. L., Orlando, M., Martino, S. C., & Klein, D. J. (2005). Substance use trajectories from early adolescence to emerging adulthood: A comparison of smoking, binge drinking and marijuana use. *J Drug Iss, 22*, 307–332.

U.S. Department of Health and Human Services. (2005). *Health United States, 2005, with Chartbook on Trends in the Health of Americans.* Hyattsville, MD: National Center for Health Statistics.

Volpicelli, J., Balaraman, G., Hahn, J., Wallace, M. A., & Bux, D. (1999). The role of uncontrollable trauma in the development of PTSD and alcohol addiction. *Alcohol Res Health, 23*(4), 256–262.

Wactawski-Wende, J., Kotchen, J. M., Anderson, G. L., Assaf, A. R., Brunner, R. L., O'Sullivan, M. J., et al. (2006). Calcium plus vitamin D supplementation and the risk of colorectal cancer. *N Engl J Med, 354*(7), 684–696.

Weden, M. M., Astone, N. M., & Bishai, D. (2006). Racial, ethnic, and gender differences in smoking cessation associated with employment and joblessness through young adulthood in the US. *Soc Sci Med, 62*(2), 303–316.

White, A. K., & Cash, K. (2004). The state of men's health in Western Europe. *J Men's Health Gen, 1*, 60–66.

Wickrama, K. A. S., Conger, R. D., & Abraham, W. T. (2005). Early adversity and later health: The intergenerational transmission of adversity through mental disorder and physical illness. *J Gerontol: Soc Sci, 60B*, 125–129.

Williams, D. (2002). Racial/ethnic variations in women's health: The social embeddedness of health. *Am J Pub Health, 92*, 588–597.

Williams, D. (2003). The health of men: Structured inequalities and opportunities. *Am J Pub Health, 93*, 724–731.

Wilsnack, S. C., & Wilsnack, R. W. (2002). International gender and alcohol research: Recent findings and future directions. *Alcohol Res Health, 26*(4), 245–250.

World Health Organization. (2002a). *WHO Gender Policy: Integrating Gender Perspectives in the Work of WHO.* Geneva: World Health Organization.

World Health Organization. (2002b). *The WHO Report: Reducing Risks, Promoting Healthy Life.* Geneva: World Health Organization.

Wray, L. A., Alwin, D. F., & McCammon, R. J. (2005). Social status and risky health behaviors: Results from the health and retirement study. *J Gerontol: Soc Sci, 60B*, 85–92.

Yoon, Y. H., Yi, H., & Hilton, M. E. (2005). *Surveillance Report #70: Liver Cirrhosis Mortality in the United States, 1970–2002.* Rockville, MD: NIAAA, Division of Epidemiology and Prevention Research.

Zarit, S. H., & Pearlin, K. I. (2005). Health inequalities across the life course. *J Gerontol Ser B, 60*(Special Issue II) 5–6.

SEVEN

Opportunities for Change

Both sex and gender-based differences and similarities in men's and women's physical and mental health are well documented. As we have shown throughout this book, these differences are not due solely to biological factors. In fact, many clinical and social science researchers now recognize that social and biological factors interact in complex ways and can affect the health of men and women differently. Still we contend that something is missing from the dominant explanations of those health differences. What is missing is an understanding of *constrained choice* – that is, how decisions made and actions taken at the family, work, community, and government levels differentially shape the health-related choices of individual men and women. In this chapter, we summarize the main points discussed in previous chapters and use that information to highlight opportunities for change. The change we advocate is for men and women, as well as decision makers at all levels, to consider health a priority in making major and everyday choices. Moreover, this is a strategic moment for researchers and policymakers to address the multifaceted aspects of gender differences in health. After more than a decade of gender-oriented research, members of the medical professions and some policymakers have begun to examine closely the social, biological, and psychological differences and similarities between men and women. The call for gender-specific medicine is just one example of the profound shift in thinking about how sex and gender matter when it comes to health.

So, how does this book differ from the vast streams of advice on how to be healthy? We contend that health is a shared responsibility and that decisions made at each of the levels described in our constrained choice

224

framework (Figure 2.2) can directly and indirectly enable or constrain men's and women's ability to pursue healthy lives. From our perspective, responsibility for health is necessarily the province of each of these levels and not solely that of individuals. Consider that health admonitions, which have become ubiquitous in the United States, do not appear to be helping individuals to effectively make health a priority in their everyday lives.[1] Rather than focusing on the role of individuals, we seek to identify opportunities to improve men's and women's health and reduce gender differences by bringing a new awareness to scientists, as well as decision makers at all levels, of the health implications of major and everyday choices.

As we stated in the Preface, we wrote this book to give researchers, policymakers, and others interested in understanding gender differences in health a new way to think about gender and health by recognizing how the choices of individuals, families, communities, and governments can enhance or undermine health. Our insights are intended to provide new avenues for intervention at each level of decision making to improve men's and women's health.

Taken together, the actions we recommend to increase men's and women's opportunities to pursue healthy lives constitute a new *platform for prevention* that would reap considerable benefits in terms of both individual and population health. Our intention is to generate a different kind of health consciousness, one that recognizes the role of *constrained choice* as an additional means of improving population health, both among individuals and among all levels of decision makers. Rather than increasing the medicalization of everyday life,[2] our approach focuses on the ways in which various decision contexts shape and constrain opportunities for men and women to pursue health. Although this process should complement the delivery of medical care and evidence based-health advice,

---

[1] This is ironic because two new comparative reports indicate that the health of Americans is worse than the health of the English (Banks, Marmot, Oldfield, & Smith, 2006) and the Canadians (Lasser, Himmelstein, & Woolhandler, 2006). Although the former study found that England's national health insurance did not explain the difference in health rates, in the latter study the ill health of uninsured Americans explained a large part of the difference.

[2] Medicalization refers to the process by which issues and problems come under the purview of medical professionals (Conrad, 2004, 2005; Conrad & Schneider, 1992).

our focus is not on these essential areas. This is not to suggest that health care delivery is an unimportant component of men and women's health status. Many complex gender differences in access to medical care, quality of care, and appropriateness are receiving much-needed attention from researchers and policymakers.[3] These issues clearly warrant further examination; however, they are beyond the scope of this book.

We conclude this chapter in two ways: first, by highlighting promising new advances in interdisciplinary research on the pathways between social and biological factors that affect men's and women's health outcomes, and second, by identifying actions that scientists and decision makers on all levels can take to reduce the constraints on men's and women's opportunities to pursue health.

NEW DIRECTIONS FOR INTEGRATING SOCIAL AND BIOLOGICAL RESEARCH

Gender differences in health persist across the life course despite attempts by many disciplines to explain this puzzling pattern. Clearly, in some cases health or longevity is determined by purely biological or social causes; for example, for individuals with particular genetic disorders or those whose deaths are due to interpersonal violence. However, we argue that generally both sets of factors are at play and may even interact such that social factors exacerbate or diminish the effects of biological factors. Although biological theories have long acknowledged environmental effects, only recently have large numbers of researchers begun to pursue interdisciplinary research examining a broad range of social and biological factors together. This work has led to numerous breakthroughs and advancement in many scientific disciplines.

Over the past decade the National Institutes of Health (NIH) have issued an increasing number of calls for grant applications to conduct

---

[3] Much of this work has focused on improving health care for women (see, for example, Anderson et al., 2002; Bird et al., 2007; Bird, Fremont, Wickstrom, Bierman, & McGlynn, 2003; Eisenman et al., 2007; Scholle, Weisman, Anderson, & Camacho, 2003; Sherbourne, Weiss, Duan, Bird, & Wells, 2004; Weisman, 1998; Weisman, Curbow, & Khoury, 1995). Consequently, the thinking about how to address gender inequities in care is more advanced regarding women's care than on issues regarding men's care, such as how to increase men's use of preventive services (Courtenay, 2000).

interdisciplinary research aimed at identifying the biological pathways through which social factors affect health. Yet, until recently, the research and policy dialogues in this area have focused almost exclusively on either social or biological explanations. Two Institute of Medicine reports (2001a, 2001b) – *Exploring the Biological Contributions to Human Health: Does Sex Matter?* and *Health and Behavior: The Interplay of Biological, Behavioral and Societal Influences* – moved in this direction, synthesizing diverse literatures, identifying knowledge gaps, and providing new directions for research on health. The first report distinguished between biological sex differences and socially acquired gender differences, reviewing evidence of the contribution of biological sex to men's and women's health and calling for evaluation of the contribution of sex in all biological and health research. The second examined the links between health and behavior, the influence of psychosocial factors on behavior, and the benefits of intervening at different levels to improve individual and population health. These two reports are invaluable resources because they advance a new way of thinking about human health.

Taken together, these two reports implicitly demand a third that would explore a more integrative approach. This gap represents a missed opportunity to examine the ways in which differences in men's and women's lives and in their physiology contribute to differences in their health. Although the report on the biological contributions to human health focuses on the effects of biological sex differences on health and the need to evaluate these biological differences in every study, it does not fully examine how these biological factors interact with social and cultural factors. Without assessing both biological and sociocultural influences, we cannot know their relative effects on men's and women's morbidity, mortality, and responsiveness to interventions including medical treatments.

Therefore, our framework of constrained choice is intended to set the stage for a new integrative research agenda to address this gap. To further this agenda it is necessary to understand sex and gender differences in health and their interaction (Bird & Rieker, 2002; Rieker & Bird, 2005). Researchers are beginning to create ways to study both biological and social factors simultaneously. A health advantage for one sex may arise from differences in men's and women's biology, in their social circumstances, or a combination of the two. By isolating research into social and biomedical domains, science policymakers and individual researchers maintain separate models of health and fail to explore the complex processes by which social and biological processes combine to affect health. Instead, integrative research could test competing hypotheses about the determinants of gender differences in health.

Although multiple links between chronic stress and poor health trajectories have been identified, the mechanisms by which stress produces a physiological impact remains elusive, as does the specific role of sex/gender in this dynamic. However, there is new interdisciplinary work theorizing and testing how stress affects health, for example, by modulating the rate of cellular aging (Epel et al., 2004).[4] Such interdisciplinary work provides a clearer understanding of the biological pathways that link social factors to health and whether the antecedents and outcomes differ for men and women. As we have noted throughout this book, increased attention has also been devoted to understanding racial/ethnic and socioeconomic disparities. Clearly this work will shed light on some possible explanations of gender differences in health, but these studies alone do not explain men's and women's health trajectories (Rieker & Bird, 2006).

The concept of allostatic load provides another example of an integrative approach. Allostatic load provides a multisystem explanation of the cumulative physiological toll that may be exacted on the body from attempts to adapt to or cope with life's demands (McEwen, 1998; McEwen & Stellar, 1993). This approach originates from the idea that healthy

---

[4] Epel and colleagues studied both perceived and event/environment-based stress in 58 healthy premenopausal women who were biological parents of either a healthy child or a chronically ill child. They found that psychological stress is associated with indicators of accelerated cellular and organismal aging including oxidative stress, telomere length, and telomerase activity in peripheral blood mononuclear cells (PBMCs). Although caregiving per se was not related to telomere length, the chronicity of caregiving stress was related to shorter telomere length. "Women with the highest levels of perceived stress have telomeres shorter on average by the equivalents of at least one decade of additional aging compared to low stress women" (p. 17312). The authors concluded that the findings have clinically significant implications for understanding how, at the cellular level, stress may promote earlier onset of age-related diseases.

functioning requires ongoing adjustments of the internal physiological milieu, with different physiological systems exhibiting fluctuating levels of activity as they respond and adapt to stressful environmental demands – a concept referred to as allostasis (Sterling & Eyer, 1988). Although healthy functioning involves ongoing fluctuation in physiological systems, these fluctuations should remain within optimal *operating ranges* of the physiological systems. So, for instance, one's blood sugar and blood pressure should not exceed the parameters considered to be normal.

Allostatic load has been used as a measure of the cumulative impact of adaptive physiological responses that chronically exceed optimal ranges, resulting ultimately in wear and tear on the body's regulatory systems such that they are no longer able to maintain normal parameters. Thus, this concept represents the role of biological mediators in an individual's physiological response to the circumstances of his or her life (McEwen, 1998). Consequently, allostatic load offers a useful approach to conceptualizing the biological impact of life experience and constrained choices on men's and women's health and longevity.

Although Seeman and colleagues (Seeman, McEwen, Singer, Albert, & Rowe, 1997) have used the allostatic load model to shed light on gender differences in health outcomes,[5,6] additional research is needed to assess whether and how the biological pathways between stress and health outcomes differ for men and women (Hale, 2003; Seeman, Singer, Ryff, Dienberg Love, & Levy-Storms, 2002).[7] There is growing evidence linking

---

[5] For examples, see Karlamangla, Singer, Greendale, & Seeman, 2005; Koivumaa-Honkanen et al., 2000; Loucks, Berkman, Gruenewald, & Seeman, 2006; Seeman et al., 2004; Seeman et al., 1997, 2002).

[6] Few studies have the sample size to examine gender differences in the relationship between total allostatic load and survival. In particular, research by Hale (2003) suggests that allostatic load predicts survival equally well for women compared to men, but there are some differences in the components through which these effects are achieved.

[7] For example, in an examination of two cohorts of men and women, Seeman and colleagues (2002) found that, among only the older of the two cohorts, men with strong social networks and emotional support had lower observed allostatic load than women. In the younger of the two cohorts, positive cumulative relationship experiences were associated with lower allostatic load for men and for women. Yet regardless of age, men tended to have higher total allostatic load scores, and in both men and women, higher scores were obtained through somewhat different patterns of biological dysregulation. For men, dysregulation in the cardiovascular parameters was observed, whereas high levels of the neuroendocrine parameters were observed in women.

aspects of the social and physical environment to health, yet understanding the biological pathways through which these aspects of the social and physical environment may affect health is still in its infancy. Insight into such patterns could inform efforts to improve individual and population health and help assure that such actions serve both men and women well.

Other examples of promising interdisciplinary work are the new and emerging fields that recognize interactions across physiological systems, such as neurocardiology, neuroendocrinology, neuroimmunology, neuropsychology, psychophysiology, immunopsychiatry, psychoneuroimmunology, and others that bridge the gap between the biomedical and social sciences. A groundbreaking transdisciplinary book, *Foundations in Social Neuroscience* (Cacioppo, Berntson, Taylor, & Schacter, 2002), brings together relevant collaborators and work in the neurosciences, the cognitive sciences, and the social sciences as a way of understanding the multilayered interactions among mind, behavior, and health.

In Chapter 1, we discussed the growing body of research that identified links between chronic stress and indicators of poor health, including disease outcomes and risk factors for cardiovascular disease and poor immune function. Yet for several decades, research on gender differences in stress and illness continued to focus on explaining women's excess psychological distress by examining sources of female disadvantage in resources and women's exposure to particular stressors. Recent work on the social organization of men's lives reveals a striking lack of cross-disciplinary attention to the health consequences of men's exposure and vulnerability to particular stressors (with some exceptions such as a new edited volume, *Textbook on Men's Mental Health* [Grant & Potenza, 2006]). By examining the differences in the social circumstances of men's and women's lives, we can clarify the multiple pathways through which gender shapes health across the life-span and identify new avenues for intervening to improve population health while also increasing health equity.

Another interesting direction worth pursuing is the research also discussed in Chapter 1 that demonstrates a connection between psychological states and physical health. Considerable evidence indicates a link between clinically diagnosed major depression and increased mortality. Although these studies do not show that depression is a predictor of mortality per se, symptoms of depression are associated with poor health and functional status, as well as increased disability, health care utilization, and cost of health services. A number of well-controlled studies link depression symptoms with cardiovascular disease; both serious depression and depressive symptoms put people in more jeopardy. Thus, gender differences in mental health may contribute in unknown ways to gendered patterns of physical health. Interdisciplinary research in this area will help demonstrate the net effects of gendered patterns of depression. In addition, the recently published *Textbook of Men's Mental Health* (Grant & Potenza, 2006) should help shed some light on these complex issues. The book brings together biomedical and social science research to help clinicians understand the role of gender in men's mental health, particularly how disorders manifest and treatment responses differ for men and women.

Although men and women share many physiological similarities, their relative genetic and hormonal vulnerabilities and strengths are poorly understood and perhaps underappreciated by clinicians as well as researchers. Gender-specific medicine[8] has an important role in health care delivery, but it cannot provide the comprehensive comparisons required to understand the antecedents of gender differences in health or the outcomes of specific interventions. Such comparisons will generate new insights and better tests of existing theories.

Only a focus on such sex and gender comparisons can advance our knowledge of the relative biological and social contribution to health and longevity. Both social and biological contributions to differences in men's and women's health must become more central to the scientific, biomedical, and social policy communities. Gender needs to have a prominent place figuratively and literally on both the research and policy agenda. Accomplishing this goal requires comparative, life-span, and longitudinal research on men's and women's lives.

---

[8] The fact that the majority of diseases afflicting both genders were only studied in men created the need for more knowledge about how the research findings applied to women. In an effort to translate research advances into clinical practice, the U.S. Public Health Service issued a report on women's health in 1985, which was followed by initiatives to create and implement new models of women's health care delivery (U.S. Department of Health and Human Services, 2002, 2004). This led many teaching hospitals and medical schools to establish gender-specific health care programs, such as Harvard Medical School's Center of Excellence in Women's Health and Columbia University's Partnership for Women's Health.

TAKING ACTION: MAKING CONSTRAINED CHOICE A PLATFORM FOR PREVENTION

Throughout the book, we have identified opportunities for intervention and change at various levels (the individual, the family, community, and social policy) to reduce health disparities. Only by systematically examining the social organization of men's and women's lives can we fully recognize these multiple health effects. For example, as we have shown, gender inequities in the family and in the labor force produce differences in men's and women's exposure and vulnerability to particular stressors and circumstances, which in turn affect their physical and psychological well-being. Ultimately, an understanding of these connections and consequences can inform the choices of individuals, families, communities, and societies. Moreover, because the experiences of individuals are intertwined with the social contexts in which they live and work, efforts to improve health and reduce gender differences require that we understand the ways in which individual behaviors, family and social context, and social policies interact.

To affect the majority of the population, any proposed intervention needs to consider and address the constraints on choices made at all levels, not simply those under the control of individual men and women. For example, data from workplace studies show that control and latitude over decisions related to one's work are essential to well-being. More generally, control and latitude over decisions related to a broader range of social roles and responsibilities are directly linked to individual men's and women's opportunities to pursue health or to make health a priority. Yet, over the life course the range of options available to an individual, or family, varies considerably by level of education and other economic circumstances. Consequently, less advantaged men and women bear an excess burden of premature death and disability.

Once recognized, constraints that ultimately affect health can be addressed at many levels, for example, by doing the following:

- recognizing how many everyday as well as major life choices affect health
- establishing health-protective national social policies

- developing healthy communities to provide incentives for positive health behaviors at the individual level
- increasing decision latitude in the workplace
- changing work and social environments through health-related regulations
- creating family arrangements and work environments that encourage and support less stressful lives
- choosing relationships that promote positive health behaviors

Thus, distributing responsibility for health and coordinating efforts across the levels of decision making can provide new, more effective, and perhaps more efficient ways to invest in health. As illustrated in Chapters 3 through 6, multiple factors outside of an individual's control affect his or her ability to act on opportunities to pursue a healthy life. Moreover, some of these constraints appear to operate differently for men and women.

Our emphasis on the population health benefits of augmenting health education efforts with organizational and policy interventions is not unique. For example, nutritionists, including Walt Willett and colleagues, have both argued for and demonstrated the health advantages of improving the quality of the food supply by labeling foods, so as to provide consumers the possibility of informed choice, and by establishing regulations that limit or prohibit the use of ingredients (such as trans-fats) that are shown to contribute to increased disease and mortality rates (Willett, Skerrett, & Giovannucci, 2001). However, to our knowledge, this dual approach of informing individual and family decision making while limiting the availability of poor choices through regulatory actions has not been specifically used to address the wide range of gender differences in health.

In the sections below, we propose specific actions that can be taken to make constrained choice a platform for prevention.

What the Medical and Scientific Communities Can Do

Working together, the scientific community can better inform decision makers at each of the levels of our model of constrained choice about health impacts. As we have argued throughout this book, both social and biological factors contribute to differences in men's and women's health. Neither the social nor the biological sciences alone can answer complex questions regarding the antecedents of gender differences in health and longevity. We contend that only a synthesis and specific actions can move interdisciplinary dialogues and research forward. Although there are many significant voices calling for such collaborative work around a variety of issues including racial/ethnic and socioeconomic disparities, far less attention is being devoted to using this approach to understand and address gender differences in health. A multidisciplinary approach would stimulate and advance creative dialogue across social and biological disciplines studying the same health conditions, including but not limited to cardiovascular disease, immune disorders, substance abuse, and depression (see Chapter 1). Without such work, the relative contribution of social and biological factors to men's and women's health cannot be assessed nor can optimal intervention points be identified. A clearer understanding of the combined effects of social and biological factors could provide the basis for a new agenda for research, intervention, and policy to address differences in men's and women's health. We may find that the most effective interventions include a combination of biomedical and social approaches or that additional efforts should be targeted at specific levels – the individual, work and family, community, or even nation.

As we have long contended, only multidisciplinary research can fully capture the *net consequences* of constrained choice for men and women by simultaneously studying a broad range of health outcomes (Bird & Rieker, 1999; Rieker & Bird, 2000, 2005). Ultimately, such work will provide a more complete model of the pathways between social and biological factors and gender differences in mental and physical health. Furthermore, research based on our constrained choice framework would better inform policy by determining the optimal conditions and most cost-effective ways to invest in physical and mental health improvement.

Advancing Interdisciplinary and Transdisciplinary Research. Typically, social scientists emphasize the contribution of differences in men's and women's roles and resources throughout their lives, whereas biomedical researchers emphasize the inherent biological differences between males and females. Although it is difficult to examine a range of social and biological factors within a single study, such interdisciplinary research advances the dialogue across disciplines and can also make valuable contributions to the ways researchers, clinicians, and policymakers approach a wide range of health problems. Although it is no surprise that the social and biological paradigms and related lines of research have developed separately, the persistence of this division now hampers scientific progress in generating much-needed comprehensive explanations of gender differences in health.

Here we offer a variety of suggestions for overcoming barriers to the pursuit of interdisciplinary and transdisciplinary research. Perhaps most obvious is to increase communication across the social and biomedical fields and thereby establish much-needed common terminology and objectives. Over time, collaboration will help narrow the gap between these distinct knowledge fields and the associated frameworks that social and biological scientists draw on for understanding health and illness.

Progress toward this goal could be facilitated by face-to-face interdisciplinary conferences and publication of the ensuing work to promote extended cross-disciplinary discussion. Specifically, to advance work on gender differences in health, we recommend a series of transdisciplinary conferences to accelerate cross-disciplinary dialogue on at least one of the four prevalent conditions reviewed in this book: alcohol and substance abuse, depression, cardiovascular disease, or immune-function disorders. These conditions were selected because of their significant gender differences, as well as the large body of overlapping social and biological research on each. Transdisciplinary conferences would be an efficient way to generate new research questions and hypotheses that would integrate social and biological factors so as to better understand these conditions and improve men's and women's health.

Creating ongoing scientific conversations across disciplines may also require new avenues for publication and dissemination of dialogues and research. Clearly, the National Institutes of Health (NIH) and foundation or other institutional support would be essential to encourage these endeavors. This effort could also serve the needs of government and foundation funding sources by providing a forum for delineating the most promising next steps in terms of basic science and population-based intervention studies. The cross-disciplinary dialogue could reduce health advice confusion by developing expert panels that could organize conflicting findings and make best practices recommendations on the actions that policymakers at different levels might take to reduce gender constraints on choice.

We recognize that some of the barriers to obtaining funding for trans-disciplinary research have diminished since the NIH has undertaken considerable effort to solicit and encourage such proposals. However, the NIH institutes are organized around an organ- and disease-based model that limits opportunities for work examining a broader range of health outcomes. For example, in October 2006 the first National Cancer Institute (NCI) conference devoted to the science of transdisciplinary research and including a discussion about how to advance collaborative work in oncology was held in Washington, D.C. (National Cancer Institute, 2006). This very informative 2-day conference, which one of us attended through the Internet, never considered the issue of gender. Although over the past decade there has been an increase in support for work examining women's health, relatively little attention has been devoted to the need to support research to understand the antecedents of gender differences in health. Advancing research in this area will require a greater institutional commitment from NIH and leading private foundations to fund and promote interdisciplinary research on men's and women's health.

Finally, despite the many strengths and advantages of discipline-based departments within universities, they inadvertently act as knowledge silos that value and encourage disciplinary contributions over interdisciplinary research. Although the current rhetoric encourages interdisciplinary research, universities have only just begun to consider how to promote transdisciplinary work and to remove lingering difficulties with sharing research funds across departments and colleges. Systematic efforts within and across universities will be needed to create equitable systems for evaluating and rewarding both disciplinary and interdisciplinary work.

What Policymakers at Various Levels Can Do

At the National Level. As we documented in Chapters 3 and 6, national policies create very different contexts in which citizens have the opportunity to pursue health. Countries vary greatly in the extent to which they provide protective policies and resources to men and women regardless of their social and economic status. Similarly, national policies also create and maintain the conditions that can lead to differences in quality of life between the most and least advantaged residents, both within and across smaller governing regions such as states or provinces. Citizens of those countries that have enacted protective policies benefit from higher average life expectancy as well as better health on a variety of indicators (see, for example, Banks, Marmot, Oldfield, & Smith, 2006; Lasser, Himmelstein, & Woolhandler, 2006). There is wide variation cross-nationally about who has responsibility for health, whether is it mainly an individual burden or one that is shared between citizens and the state. Those countries that adhere to the latter model specifically move the health agenda forward by establishing universal provisions for child care, education, retirement pensions, and health care, all of which substantially increase the opportunities for individuals and families to create healthy lives. In countries without such provisions, even individuals with substantial means cannot always achieve the same health benefits simply by purchasing child care, education, and health care and saving for retirement.

Countries affect the health and well-being of individuals directly, not only through the provision of health-related resources but also by establishing the degree to which individuals, families, workplaces, and communities are responsible for health. As noted in Chapter 5, in the United States many tasks that affect health are left to individuals and families, including the vast majority of child care, a great deal of elder care, and most provisions for retirement beyond the safety net established by Social Security. This carving-out of responsibilities forces individuals and families to devote considerable time and money to planning for and addressing these needs. These responsibilities consume a significant amount of household resources, and for many, especially those of lesser means or with greater caregiving demands, the responsibilities can present significant or even impassible hurdles to achieving a healthy lifestyle, especially one that minimizes chronic stress and daily hassles and allows for sufficient sleep, appropriate nutrition, and exercise. Unfortunately, gender differences in work, family, and caregiving roles can disproportionately increase responsibilities and exacerbate existing disparities among men and women and place both at a significant disadvantage in developing the capacity to pursue a healthy life.

Some countries have enacted policies for the purpose of bringing about gender equity, particularly to address realms in which women have been disadvantaged, such as employment, retirement benefits, and health care. Policymakers on the national level can look for guidance from those countries that have used gender analysis to identify specific inequities and formulate or modify policies to redress these issues. However, achieving the benefit of this approach for both men and women would require attention to policies and practices that may contribute to men's higher mortality rates compared to women.

We contend that the range of national policies discussed above, some of which were enacted to bring about gender equity, have positively affected women's health as reflected in their higher life expectancy. However, similar efforts have not been made to identify and redress the circumstances of men's lives in order to increase their longevity. Further consideration should be given to whether such an approach could be used, for example, to reduce men's excess alcohol consumption and smoking, both of which contribute directly and indirectly to their premature mortality. Including an examination of health consequences for both men and women would increase the effectiveness of gender analysis when used to formulate national policies that affect the options that families, workplaces, and communities have to create opportunities that increase everyone's capacity to pursue health.

At the Community Level. Recent research findings suggest a whole host of ways in which communities can foster the health of their residents (because both the impediments to health and the level of social and economic capital vary considerably across communities, states also share responsibility for fostering healthy communities for all their citizens). As described in Chapter 4, some of the most interesting work demonstrates the many beneficial effects of land use policies that increase access to green space, walkability, bike paths, and programmed activities at parks and recreation centers. For example, new evidence indicates that proximity to a park is more important in stimulating use than its size (Cohen et al., 2006). Similarly, decision makers at the community level can take health into account when shaping policies that address a wide range of issues, such as the availability of public transportation and the location of housing that can allow people to minimize their commute times, associated expenses, and daily hassles.

Even communities with fewer resources can increase the opportunities for their residents to pursue healthy lives by putting health on the policy agenda. In fact, a recent report from Grantmakers in Health (2006) provides resources for communities and encourages small and larger foundations to make grants for both direct services and policy activities that will inspire collective action and improve health in communities.

In the Workplace. Employers need to learn from their employees what they need in the workplace so they can create favorable conditions that not only improve job performance but also help maintain workers' health. Although some desirable qualities for a healthy work environment are obvious, assessing workers' preferences and options on issues ranging from the number of hours worked and the structure of work shifts to making available nutritious food can help better target workplace policy. With input from employees, organizations can identify multiple intervention points that will allow them to assess which policies best fit with the objectives of their business plan; for example, to reduce turnover or increase productivity.

Because many people spend most of their waking hours in their workplace, employers have a unique opportunity to influence workers' health and to create an environment that supports and encourages a healthy lifestyle. For example, employers have the means to provide a smoke-free workplace and reasonable work schedules for their employees. Just as families face a range of decisions that, though not directly related to health can increase or constrain individuals' choices, decision makers in the workplace can take health consequences for workers into account when making major and everyday business decisions. In many cases (as discussed in Chapter 5) doing so might involve recognizing when business decisions would increase or diminish employees' decision latitude over their work.

What Individuals and Families Can Do

Men and women, as well as policymakers, need to recognize that they have an opportunity (if not a responsibility) to consider potential health implications along with other priorities when making both major and everyday choices. By engaging in this practice routinely, individuals will gain new insights into the ways in which the organization of their everyday lives affects health both directly and indirectly.

Although resources and constraints are not equally distributed across the population in most societies, individual men and women can still benefit from pursuing even limited but frequently unrecognized opportunities to create and maintain a healthy life. It is clearly established that large positive and cumulative effects can be gained from incremental changes in major and everyday choices; for example, by choosing a less stressful job or work environment or making minor modifications in one's routine to reduce daily hassles. Much like saving for retirement, one's goal may be attained most easily by starting early and making many small accommodations, rather than by attempting a drastic mid- or late life-course correction (although taking action at later life-course stages has clear health benefits as well). However, we do not intend to suggest that the benefits are only available to the very young. In fact, many adults only begin to make their health a priority after they or someone close to them experiences a significant illness. In effect, engaging in the practice of taking health into account in various decisions can produce a level of consciousness whereby one habitually considers health when making routine choices, regardless of life-course stage.

Throughout this book, we referred to a vignette of Susan and John to illustrate the constraints faced by a middle-class couple as they attempt to create healthy lives for themselves and their family. They represent a relatively young, healthy, and advantaged household with more resources at their disposal than many members of our society. Moreover, Susan and John are not among those whom we usually consider at high risk of health problems or who experience significant health disparities relative to more advantaged peers. Yet, as we considered the complexities of their lives and the constraints on their choices, we have demonstrated that many potential opportunities to create a healthy life are largely governed by decisions made at other levels. From the vantage point of our model of constrained choice, decision makers at the workplace, community, and national levels can increase or decrease Susan and John's opportunities to create a healthy life. In fact, for those who are less socially and economically advantaged or those who already have health problems or disabilities, decisions taken at these other levels largely determine the extent to which they have any discretion in making health a priority in either major or everyday choices. Thus, the fact that even Susan and John alone cannot create a healthy life demonstrates that responsibility for the health of the population is shared across many levels. Still, there are actions that families and individuals can take to make health a priority.

Families. The goal is to make the health of family members an explicit priority and to create ways to collectively and individually pursue a healthy life. At the family level, perhaps most significant is the need to consider health consequences when making decisions related to the use of time and the acquisition and use of money. Similarly, family members can reexamine the division of paid and unpaid work across members of the household as well as other aspects of household routines with health in mind. By examining the potential health effects of how they have organized everyday life, families can assess whether they need to chart a new course and whether the current arrangements are facilitating every member's opportunities to optimize health. Because family routines change over time as members enter and exit different social roles, the task of evaluating the organization of everyday family life will likely need to be revisited periodically to recognize and take advantage of new opportunities. Taking health into account in examining everyday family decisions and routines may be as valuable as considering health at major decision points, such as whether to move or change jobs.

Individuals. In many areas women appear to be more proactive about their health than men. As noted in Chapter 6, men engage in more risk-taking and other health-damaging behaviors; however, they are typically more physically active than women and less likely to be severely obese. Substantial numbers of men and women and boys and girls are still smoking, drinking to excess, eating high-fat and high-calorie diets, and ignoring the well-established suggestions to exercise routinely. In short, both men and women have ample room for improvement in terms of multiple health-related behaviors as well as stress management and coping. They can also effect change in the number and range of opportunities they have to pursue health by engaging in social and political action to advance health-promoting policies in their workplace, community, state, and country.

In the interim, men and women may make the greatest gains by taking into account potential health implications when considering major life changes, such as in job, residence, or significant social roles and responsibilities, as well as when making everyday choices as to whether to engage in positive or negative health behaviors.

CONCLUDING THOUGHTS

In many countries, health and health behavior figure prominently in national debates on policies and regulations to improve longevity and quality of life. Scientific advances have also created the possibility that people can live longer and healthier lives. At the same time, policymakers and individuals are continually confronted with a confusing but steady stream of somewhat contradictory scientific findings regarding which health behaviors to adopt and which risk behaviors to avoid. Collectively, the dissemination efforts of individual researchers and disease-based advocacy groups inadvertently create a cacophony of sometimes disparate findings, which are selectively echoed and amplified by the media. The disorganized and confusing barrage of information and details typically fails to leave people with a clear and compelling overview of what is known to be effective. In the absence of scientific leadership to provide clear directives for action, individuals and policymakers are all too often left with little opportunity to take advantage of the latest scientific advances and research.

Thus, despite extensive efforts to disseminate health information, individuals, communities, and even governments are uncertain about how to choose and combine strategies for maintaining and restoring health. This lack of clarity provides an opportunity, if not an obligation, for the scientific community to work together to translate the results of research studies across different disciplines into actionable agendas for policymakers and other decision makers, in a form that will help individuals and families decide what works for them.

Partially as a result of this unfettered dissemination of health information, a vast majority of everyday life activities are increasingly viewed through a health lens. From our standpoint in the United States, even leisure time is being medicalized. This recent trend exemplifies both the heightened interest in health and the continuing uncertainty as to how to create a healthy life. For example, many leisure-time pursuits are in part justified now on the basis of their health merits. So shopping is therapy, dancing is exercise, socializing with friends is an important coping tool, and drinking alcohol in moderation provides reported health benefits. Aside from the humor or irony of the tendency to portray one's use of leisure time as an investment in health, this trend represents a response to the continuing and problematic message that health is mainly an individual responsibility. We characterize this trend as problematic because most individuals are unable to replicate or marshal many of the types of health-promoting resources that can be provided by larger decision groups depicted in our model of constrained choice, including countries, communities, workplaces, or even families. To counter this trend, we seek to inspire and foster a new health consciousness at all levels of decision making so that efforts to improve men's and women's health can be effectively coordinated.

With clear directives from the scientific community, policymakers at all levels have new opportunities to take health into account in a much broader range of policies that could help families, workplaces, and individuals be less stressed and more able to pursue health. Countries can take many actions that individuals cannot, such as providing universal day care and long-term care for the elderly, guaranteed access to higher education for everyone, or other programs to address poverty including a strong economic safety net.

Everyone values health, so why not invest in women and men's capacity to pursue health? This investment will be costly initially, but the benefits of prevention are broad and enduring. Ultimately the platform for prevention will be more economical, people will be more productive and happy, and communities will be inviting places to live and work. Moreover, this approach could lessen the disease burden and spiraling costs associated with the large aging population confronting virtually every country.

We contend that the greatest benefit will be achieved by simultaneously increasing efforts to reduce constrained choice and to develop a health consciousness from the national level down to the individual. Although individual men and women still have a large role to play in maintaining their health, society can do far more to promote health by enacting social policies and regulations that limit poor choices and increase opportunities for people to pursue health, rather than relying solely on a platform of individual responsibility.

References

Anderson, R. T., Weisman, C. S., Scholle, S. H., Henderson, J. T., Oldendick, R., & Camacho, R. (2002). Evaluation of the quality of care in the clinical care centers of the National Centers of Excellence in Women's Health. *Women Health Iss, 12*(6), 309–326.

Banks, J., Marmot, M., Oldfield, Z., & Smith, J. P. (2006). Disease and disadvantage in the United States and in England. *JAMA, 295*(17), 2037–2045.

Bird, C. E., Fremont, A. M., Bierman, A. S., Wickstrom, S. L., Shah, M. M., Rector, T., et al. (2007). Does quality of care for cardiovascular disease and diabetes differ by gender for enrollees in managed care plans? *Women Health Iss, 17*(3), 31–38.

Bird, C. E., Fremont, A. M., Wickstrom, S., Bierman, A. S., & McGlynn, E. (2003). Improving women's quality of care for cardiovascular disease and diabetes: The feasibility and desirability of stratified reporting of objective performance measures. *Women Health Iss, 13*, 150–157.

Bird, C. E., & Rieker, P. P. (1999). Gender matters: An integrated model for understanding men's and women's health. *Soc Sci Med, 48*(6), 745–755.

Bird, C. E., & Rieker, P. P. (2002). Integrating social and biological research to improve men's and women's health. *Women Health Iss, 12*(3), 113–115.

Cacioppo, J. T., Berntson, G. G., Taylor, S. E., & Schacter, D. L. (2002). *Foundations in Social Neuroscience*. Cambridge, MA: MIT Press.

Cohen, D. A., Sehgal, A., Williamson, S., Sturm, R., McKenzie, T. L., Lara, R., et al. (2006). *Park Use and Physical Activity in a Sample of Public Parks in the City of Los Angeles* (No. TR-357-HLTH). Santa Monica, CA: RAND Corporation.

Conrad, P. (2004). Medicalization, markets and illness. *J Health Soc Behav, 45*, 158–176.

Conrad, P. (2005). The shifting engines of medicalization. *J Health Soc Behav, 46*, 3–14.

Conrad, P., & Schneider, J. W. (1992). *Deviance and Medicalization: From Badness to Sickness.* Philadelphia: Temple University Press.

Courtenay, W. H. (2000). Behavioral factors associated with disease, injury, and death among men: Evidence and implications for prevention. *J Men's Studies, 9*(1), 81–142.

Eisenman, D. P., Bird, C. E., Collins, R., Golinelli, D., Fremont, A., Beckman, R., et al. (2007). Differential diffusion of new HIV technologies by gender: The case of HAART. *AIDS Patient Care STDs, 21*(6), 390–399.

Epel, E. S., Blackburn, E. H., Lin, J., Dhabhar, F. S., Adler, N. E., Morrow, J. D., et al. (2004). Accelerated telomere shortening in response to life stress. *PNAS, 101*(49), 17312–17315.

Grant, J. E., & Potenza, M. N. (2006). *Textbook of Men's Mental Health.* Arlington, VA: American Psychiatric Publishing.

Grantmakers in Health. (2006, February 23). *From the Ground Up: Improving Community Health, Inspiring Community Action.* Paper presented at the Annual Meeting of Grantmakers in Health, Washington, DC.

Hale, L. (2003). *Healthy Aging: Physiological Correlates of Cumulative Psychosocial Experiences.* Princeton, NJ: Princeton University Press.

Institute of Medicine. (2001a). *Exploring the Biological Contributions to Human Health: Does Sex Matter?* Washington, DC: National Academy Press.

Institute of Medicine. (2001b). *Health and Behavior: The Interplay of Biological, Behavioral and Societal Influences.* Washington, DC: National Academy Press.

Karlamangla, A. S., Singer, B., Greendale, G., & Seeman, T. E. (2005). Increase in urinary epinephrine excretion is associated with cognitive decline in elderly men: MacArthur Studies of Successful Aging. *Psychoneuroendocrinology, 30*, 453–460.

Koivumaa-Honkanen, H., Honkanen, R., Viinamäki, H., Heikkilä, K., Kaprio, J., & Koskenvuo, M. (2000). Self-reported life satisfaction and 20-year mortality in healthy Finnish adults. *Am J Epidemiol, 152*(10), 983–991.

Lasser, K. E., Himmelstein, D. U., & Woolhandler, S. (2006). Access to care, health status, and health disparities in the United States and Canada: Results of a cross-national population-based survey. *Am J Public Health, 96*, 1300–1307.

Loucks, E. B., Berkman, L. F., Gruenewald, T. L., & Seeman, T. E. (2006). Relation of social integration to inflammatory marker concentrations in men and women 70 to 79 years. *Am J Cardiol, 97*(7), 1010–1016.

McEwen, B. S. (1998). Protective and damaging effects of stress mediators. *N Engl J Med, 338*(3), 171–179.

McEwen, B. S., & Stellar, E. (1993). Stress and the individual: Mechanisms leading to disease. *Arch Intern Med, 153*, 2093–2101.

National Cancer Institute. (2006, October 30–31). *The Science of Team Science: Assessing the Value of Transdisciplinary Research,* Bethesda, MD: National Cancer Institute.

Rieker, P. P., & Bird, C. E. (2000). Sociological explanations of gender differences in mental and physical health. In C. E. Bird, P. Conrad, & A. M. Fremont (Eds.),

The Handbook of Medical Sociology (5th ed., pp. 98–113). Englewood Cliffs, NJ: Prentice-Hall.

Rieker, P. P., & Bird, C. E. (2005). Rethinking gender differences in health: What's needed to integrate social and biological perspectives. *J Gerontol: Soc Sci, 60B*, 40–47.

Rieker, P. P., & Bird, C. E. (2006). *Gender, Longevity and Choice: Crafting Another Paradigm to Explain Gender Difference in Health*. Paper presented at the British Sociological Association, Heriot-Watt University, September 14–16, Edinburgh, Scotland.

Scholle, S. H., Weisman, C. S., Anderson, R. T., & Camacho, F. (2003). The development and validation of the Primary Care Satisfaction Survey For Women. *Women Health Iss, 14*, 35–50.

Seeman, T. E., Crimmins, E., Huang, M. H., Singer, B., Bucur, A., Gruenewald, T., et al. (2004). Cumulative biological risk and socio-economic differences in mortality: MacArthur Studies of Successful Aging. *Soc Sci Med, 58*(10), 1985–1997.

Seeman, T. E., McEwen, B. S., Singer, B. H., Albert, M. S., & Rowe, J. W. (1997). Increase in urinary cortisol excretion and memory declines: MacArthur Studies of Successful Aging. *J Clin Endocrinol Metab, 82*(8), 2458–2465.

Seeman, T. E., Singer, B. H., Ryff, C. D., Dienberg Love, G., & Levy-Storms, L. (2002). Social relationships, gender, and allostatic load across two age cohorts. *Psychosom Med, 64*(3), 395–406.

Sherbourne, C. D., Weiss, R., Duan, N., Bird, C. E., & Wells, K. B. (2004). Do the effects of quality improvement for depression care differ for men and women? Results of a group-level randomized controlled trial. *Med Care, 42*, 1186–1193.

Sterling, P., & Eyer, J. (1988). Allostasis: A new paradigm to explain arousal pathology. In S. Fisher & J. Reason (Eds.), *Handbook of Life Stress, Cognition and Health* (pp. 631–651). New York: Wiley.

U.S. Department of Health and Human Services. (2002). *An Evaluation of the National Centers of Excellence in Women's Health. Executive Summary*. Rockville, MD: U.S. DHHS.

U.S. Department of Health and Human Services. (2004). *National Community Centers of Excellence in Women's Health. Program Evaluation Executive Summary*. Rockville, MD: U.S. DHHS.

Weisman, C. S. (1998). *Women's Health Care: Activist Traditions and Institutional Change*. Baltimore: Johns Hopkins University Press.

Weisman, C. S., Curbow, B., & Khoury, A. (1995). The National Survey of Women's Health Centers: Current models of women-centered care. *Women Health Iss, 5*(3), 103–117.

Willett, W., Skerrett, P. J., & Giovannucci, E. L. (2001). *Eat, Drink and Be Healthy: The Harvard Medical School Guide to Healthy Eating*. New York: Simon & Schuster.

Index